PRESIDENT BARACK OBAMA

A MORE PERFECT UNION

JOHN K. WILSON

PARADIGM PUBLISHERS
Boulder & London

Paradigm Publishers is committed to preserving ancient forests and natural resources. We elected to print this title on 30% post consumer recycled paper, processed chlorine free. As a result, for this printing, we have saved:

7 Trees (40' tall and 6-8" diameter)
2,376 Gallons of Wastewater
5 million BTU's of Total Energy
305 Pounds of Solid Waste
572 Pounds of Greenhouse Gases

Paradigm Publishers made this paper choice because our printer, Thomson-Shore, Inc., is a member of Green Press Initiative, a nonprofit program dedicated to supporting authors, publishers, and suppliers in their efforts to reduce their use of fiber obtained from endangered forests.

For more information, visit www.greenpressinitiative.org

Environmental impact estimates were made using the Environmental Defense Paper Calculator. For more information visit: www.papercalculator.org.

Copyright © 2009 Paradigm Publishers

Published in the United States by Paradigm Publishers, 3360 Mitchell Lane Suite E, Boulder, CO 80301 USA.

Paradigm Publishers is the trade name of Birkenkamp & Company, LLC, Dean Birkenkamp, President and Publisher.

Library of Congress Cataloging-in-Publication Data

Wilson, John K., 1969–
    President Barack Obama : a more perfect union / John K. Wilson.
        p. cm.
    Includes bibliographical references and index.
    ISBN-13: 978-1-59451-476-0 (hardcover : alk. paper); 978-1-59451-477-7 (pbk. : alk paper) 1. Obama, Barack. 2. Obama, Barack—Public opinion. 3. African Americans—Public opinion. 4. Racially mixed people—United States—Public opinion. 5. Presidential candidates—United States.
6. Presidents—United States—Election—2008. 7. United States—Politics and goverment—2001–. 8. United States—Race relations—Political aspects. 9. Public opinion—United States. I. Title.
    E901.1.023W56 2008
    328.73092—dc22

                                                                                    2007041090

Printed and bound in the United States of America on acid free paper that meets the standards of the American National Standard for Permanence of Paper for Printed Library Materials.

Designed and Typeset by Straight Creek Bookmakers.

13 12 11 10 09   1 2 3 4 5

Contents

Introduction   *iv*

1 GENERATION OBAMA
The Youth Movement for Barack   1

2 ARE YOU EXPERIENCED?
Obama and the Media   25

3 RACE AND THE PRESIDENT
Is Obama Black Enough?   53

4 THE VAST RIGHT-WING CONSPIRACY
The Conservative Attack on Obama   93

5 WHY LEFTISTS HATE A LIBERAL
The Far Left Attacks on Obama   111

Photo section following page 130

6 "THIS IS MY HOUSE, TOO"
Obama and the Liberal God   131

7 FROM QUEST TO REALITY
Politics and Policy in an Obama Administration   143

8 THE VICTORY
Barack Obama's Improbable Triumph   165

9 THE OBAMA ADMINISTRATION
Turning Hope into Change   193

CONCLUSION
Obama's Hopes and Dreams   205

Notes   *211*
Index   *247*
About the Author   *257*

Introduction

When Barack Obama took the oath of office in front of more than one million people on the Mall in Washington, D.C., on January 20, 2009, with hundreds of millions more watching online and on TV around the world, it marked the dawn of a new era in American politics.

When his predecessor, George W. Bush, had entered office eight years earlier, Obama was an obscure state senator still struggling to pay off his student loans and facing a debt from his failed campaign for Congress in 2000, wondering if he should give up on politics and pursue a more lucrative legal career. But on this day in 2009, Obama stood as the leader of the most powerful country on earth.

Since his speech at the 2004 Democratic National Convention, people who listened to Obama were wondering, "Why can't he be the president?" Obama was asking himself the same question. In January 2007, he answered it by defying conventional wisdom and announcing his campaign for president. Obama's sister, Maya Soetoro-Ng, recalled, "There was always a joke between my mom and Barack that he would be the first black president."[1] Archbishop Desmond Tutu told Obama during his 2006 trip to Africa, "You are going to be a very credible presidential candidate."[2]

But few pundits had much faith in Obama's campaign. Conservative writer William Kristol famously declared, "Barack Obama is not going to beat Hillary Clinton in a single Democratic primary. I'll predict that right now."[3] Like so much else Kristol has written, this prediction was dead wrong.

Yet despite Obama's celebrity status and best-selling books, despite the long campaign and endless reporting, Obama's beliefs and policies are still a mystery to many people. Obama was called the "Rorschach candidate."[4] Of course, as with any other admired politician, people tend to see what they want in Obama. I have written this book as an attempt to understand and explain Obama's approach to politics and why so many people on both the left and the right misunderstand him.

Obama also became the world's biggest celebrity, with magazines and newspapers around the world plastering his face on their covers and front pages. Before he began his presidential race, Obama observed: "I am suspicious of hype. The fact that my 15 minutes of fame has extended a little longer than 15 minutes is somewhat surprising to me and completely baffling to my wife."[5]

This book is not a work of so-called objective journalism. There are, I hope, no "objective" journalists who care so little about the fate of the world that they are utterly indifferent about who is chosen to be the planet's most powerful leader.

I am an admirer of Barack Obama, and I want to make my biases clear, as they were clear a decade ago in my book about Newt Gingrich (whom I do not admire). However, this book is not hagiography. I was not part of Obama's campaign.

Too much of what was written about Obama consisted of horse-race stories about the latest poll numbers and his virile fundraising, paeans to his personal background, or cynical "scandal" stories that attempted to undercut his "clean" image with factually dubious attacks. The substance of Obama's ideas was often ignored by journalists and pundits, who then blamed Obama for lacking substance.

This book also is not a biography of Obama. He has already written two widely praised (and widely sold) books that fully describe his life. Instead, I wanted to write a political analysis of Obama, to understand his values and his plans for the country, and to explain why he represents a new kind of progressive political movement.

The first edition of this book, published in 2007 shortly before the first primaries were held, was subtitled "This Improbable Quest." This was a phrase from Obama's speech in Springfield, Illinois, on February 10, 2007, when he stood in front of 17,000 shivering, cold fans to announce his presidential plans and invite them to join "this improbable quest." It was a highly appropriate description for a campaign that seemed unlikely to win against the powerful Clinton machine and the attacks of the right wing. But what seemed improbable in 2007 has come true.

This paperback edition includes some additional thoughts about the campaign and Obama's presidency, but I have left most of the original book untouched except for some minor corrections. Although Americans know much more about Obama than they did when he first announced his candidacy, the details about his record and his approach to politics still are often little understood or misunderstood. Obama's presidency makes this analysis more important than ever because it provides a guide for how he will act as commander in chief.

I wrote this book not only because I felt it was essential that people understand one of the most important progressive politicians in America but also because I knew Obama long before he was a global celebrity. More than a decade ago, I walked into my class on race, racism, and the law at the University of Chicago Law School and first encountered my teacher. In his early 30s, he looked younger than me. He was thoughtful, soft-spoken, and knowledgeable. He already had a reputation as an up-and-comer, but he was rational and sincere and honest, so I never imagined he could have a successful political career. Like so many other people have done, I underestimated Barack Obama.

Now, facing an economic crisis and the necessity of rebuilding the federal government's competence at home and abroad, Obama must prevail against the partisan and divisive spirit in Washington and bring Americans together to solve some of the worst problems facing a president since the Great Depression.

Generation Obama

The Youth Movement for Barack

Let's bring a new generation of leadership to America, and let's change this country together. —Barack Obama

On December 10, 2006, in his first speech in New Hampshire, Obama said, "America is ready to turn the page. America is ready for a new set of challenges. This is our time. A new generation is prepared to lead."[1]

Obama's announcement of his presidential run on February 10, 2007, in Springfield, Illinois, was filled with appeals to generational change. Obama declared, "Let us be the generation that reshapes our economy to compete in the digital age.... And as our economy changes, let's be the generation that ensures our nation's workers are sharing in our prosperity.... Let's be the generation that ends poverty in America.... Let's be the generation that finally tackles our health care crisis.... Let's be the generation that finally frees America from the tyranny of oil.... Let's be the generation that makes future generations proud of what we did here."

According to fellow Illinois senator Dick Durbin, "I think he represents a generation change in American politics—much like 1960 with John Kennedy. He appeals to younger people and those who want to see real fundamental change in America."[2] Simon Rosenberg, head of the New Democratic Network, said, "Obama has already established himself as the paramount leader of the next generation. There's no one even close."[3]

Obama has said that he looks at "some issues differently as a consequence of being of a slightly different generation."[4] But there is no strong generational identity in the wake of the baby boomers, and what Obama calls for is not so much a repudiation of the 1960s generation as a fulfillment of some of its ideals. Obama suggested that he may have "a particular ability to bring the country together around a pragmatic, commonsense agenda for change that probably has a generational element to it as well."[5] Obama declared in one speech, "America is ready for a new set of challenges. This is our time. A new generation is prepared to lead."[6] He promised a new kind of politics instead of the "24-hour, slash-and-burn, negative-ad bickering, small-minded politics that doesn't move us forward."[7]

As the first major politician of the post–baby boomer era, Barack Obama appeals to a group of "generation Xers" who have always lived in the shadow of the baby boomers and who have faced the generational accusation that those like Obama who grew up in the 1970s and early 1980s were self-centered and indifferent to social causes.

Obama has even more appeal to today's college students, who are the children of baby boomers. For them, Ronald Reagan is a distant memory from the history books. It would be too extreme to suggest that today's students are rebelling against their parents, seeking a unifying figure who can avoid the political and social schisms that have echoed since the 1960s. But Obama does represent a new kind of politics that seems perfectly tailored for this new generation. The Obama generation will be defined by his presidency, earning financial aid for college by working on community service projects and participating in expanded opportunities to get involved in public service.

Some of Obama's approaches are about changing the rhetoric of politics, to bring a more inclusive style to political debate. But his aim is not civility for its own sake; Obama believes a more united politics can be more effective at making progress than the political divisions that have become so common today.

Obama and Community Organizing

The time Obama spent as a community organizer had a profound impact on his approach to politics. Obama was the director of the Developing Communities Project in the mid-1980s, spending four years organizing

African American neighborhoods on the segregated South Side of Chicago. In 1988, Obama wrote about his experience. Obama recalled being told, "I just cannot understand why a bright young man like you would go to college, get that degree and become a community organizer." Obama answered, "It needs to be done, and not enough folks are doing it."[8]

Obama considers his work in Chicago on political empowerment, economic development, and grassroots community organizing to be the "best education" he ever received.[9] Obama noted, "Organizing teaches as nothing else does the beauty and strength of everyday people."[10]

From his organizing work, Obama learned that "oftentimes ordinary citizens are taught that decisions are made based on the public interest or grand principles, when, in fact, what really moves things is money and votes and power."[11] This was Obama's first lesson that fighting against cynicism was a first step in political change.

Obama also learned the concept of "being predisposed to other people's power."[12] It is this idea of seeking to empower others, and not simply accumulating political power for himself, that helped Obama develop a new approach to politics.

In 2004, Obama went back to speak at a convention for the project he once worked on. Obama recalled, "I grew up to be a man, right here, in this area. It's as a consequence of working with this organization and this community that I found my calling. There was something more than making money and getting a fancy degree. The measure of my life would be public service."[13]

But progress wasn't easy. Obama remembered, "Sometimes I called a meeting, and nobody showed up. Sometimes preachers said, 'Why should I listen to you?' Sometimes we tried to hold politicians accountable, and they didn't show up. I couldn't tell whether I got more out of it than this neighborhood."[14]

Loretta Augustine-Herron, a member of the Calumet Community Religious Conference board that hired Obama to run the Developing Communities Project on Chicago's South Side, recalled his approach: "You've got to do it right. Be open with the issues. Include the community instead of going behind the community's back—and he would include people we didn't like sometimes. You've got to bring people together. If you exclude people, you're only weakening yourself. If you meet behind doors and make decisions for them, they'll never take ownership of the issue."[15]

As a candidate and president, Obama still shows his roots—a faith in ordinary citizens, a quest for common ground, and a pragmatic inclination toward defining issues in winnable ways. Reverend Alvin Love, one of the preachers Obama worked with, noted, "Everything I see reflects that community organizing experience. I see the consensus building, his connection to people and listening to their needs and trying to find common ground. I think at his heart Barack is a community organizer. I think what he's doing now is that. It's just a larger community to be organized."[16]

Obama was influenced in his approach to community organizing by the theories of Saul Alinsky. In his book *Rules for Radicals* (1971), Alinsky preached the idea of "agitation," which meant "challenging people to scrape away habit." But unlike Alinsky, who largely abandoned electoral politics in favor of direct community organizing, Obama realized the potential of politics to change people's lives on a mass scale. Obama learned from his four years as an organizer in Chicago about the problems faced by the poor and the difficulty of solving them.

Obama's vision of leadership is a merger between traditional political activism and the community organizing preached by Alinsky, which eschewed electoral politics. One might call it "community politics." This goal of Obama's community politics differs greatly from community service, in which the more privileged members of society volunteer to help the poorer ones. As noble as that may be, it doesn't create the kind of political empowerment sought by Obama. And community politics differs from the older traditions of machine politics because there is no political bribery involved and the goal is certainly not to use voting as a tool to maintain the power of the establishment. Instead, community politics aims to transform politics using the techniques of community organizing. Rather than top-down management where a politician simply presents policies to the public, Obama's community organizing approach is to communicate with voters, listen to their suggestions, and convince them to buy in to a common set of proposals. In 2004, Michelle Obama observed, "Barack is not a politician first and foremost. He's a community activist exploring the viability of politics to make change." Her husband responded, "I take that observation as a compliment."[17]

The question is, can Obama's new approach work? There are reasons for skepticism. No president has ever come from a community-organizing background or tried to bring such activism to an entire nation. The closest anyone has come since the Peace Corps under John F. Kennedy was George H. W.

Bush's lame "thousand points of light" to encourage volunteerism, and Bill Clinton's AmeriCorps program that institutionalized community service within American boundaries. But what Obama is proposing goes far beyond the boundaries of traditional community service volunteers. Obama wants to bring the spirit and tactics of community organizing into the political system, and there is no road map out there for how to do it.

Certainly, Obama has made use of the Internet as a new organizing tool. But the Internet is not a magical electronic solution to our problems. As a community organizer and politician, Obama believes in the hands-on approach to politics. He believes that if you want change to happen, you need to show up. That's why from the start of his campaign, he didn't rely just on traditional campaign appearances or Internet pleas for fundraising. He held a day of neighborhood meetings, organized via his website, to watch one of his town meetings and discuss it. He also held a neighborhood walk day, to encourage people to meet their neighbors to talk about Obama's candidacy. But Obama has also recognized that community politics has to be about more than his campaign. That's one reason why volunteers for Obama went around New Hampshire seeking signatures on a petition for withdrawal from Iraq, rather than making Obama the sole focus of their recruitment efforts.

The first days of the Obama administration provide a glimpse of what community politics will look like under this new president. During the transition, Obama established a website at change.gov where Americans could offer their ideas and personal experiences and apply for jobs in the Obama administration. Press Secretary Robert Gibbs responded to questions from Americans, and Obama's advisors held town meetings on subjects such as health care. The day before his inauguration, Obama led Americans around the country by participating in community service projects to mark Martin Luther King Jr. Day, leading by the example of his paint roller.

The transition included the Citizen's Briefing Book, where thousands of ideas were proposed by citizens and the best suggestions voted upon. Unfortunately, this approach was mocked in the mainstream press because some people proposed ideas such as investigating UFOs, and the Citizen's Briefing Book disappeared from the transition website after it was delivered to Obama. However, Obama can't give up on the idea of public involvement in policy debates even if online voting is not the best way to develop good ideas. He should create a national suggestion box where ideas for government reform and policy innovations can be proposed and receive high-level follow-through. Obama is transforming his campaign structure into Organizing for America to encourage his supporters to help promote his reforms and build a grassroots political movement.

Obama's campaign (like that of every other candidate) was filled with consultants and advisers familiar with the ins and outs of traditional politics, but there were few community organizers helping him to merge politics with organizing. There are so many jobs already attached to the presidency—commander in chief, head diplomat, administrative chief, even national mourner—that the idea of adding organizer to the list is difficult if not impossible. But fixing a broken political system is one of the most important tasks of this president.

Obama and the Baby Boomers

Jonathan Alter observed in *Newsweek,* "The campaign will likely have an intra-boomer subplot. Born in 1961 at the end of the baby boom, Obama and his cohort were shaped by a more ironic and less ideological sensibility than those who came of age in the tumult of the '60s."[19] Obama is a bridge between the baby boomers and this younger generation, as someone who has seen both the virtues and the flaws of the baby boomers and the 1960s era that (rightly or wrongly) has come to define them.

Obama has written, "I've always felt a curious relationship to the sixties."[20] As he noted, "In a sense, I'm a pure product of that era: As the child of a mixed marriage, my life would have been impossible, my opportunities entirely foreclosed, without the social upheavals that were then taking place."[21] In his youth, Obama tried to follow the 1960s generational values: "In my teens, I became fascinated with the Dionysian, up-for-grabs quality of the era, and through books, film and music, I soaked in a vision of the sixties very different from the one my mother talked about: images of Huey Newton, the '68 Democratic National Convention, the Saigon airlift, and the Stones at Altamont. If I had no immediate reasons to pursue revolution, I decided nevertheless that in style and attitude I, too, could be a rebel, unconstrained by the received wisdom of the over-thirty crowd."[22]

Obama realized, "Eventually my rejection of authority spilled into self-indulgence and self-destructiveness, and by the time I enrolled in college, I'd begun to see how any challenge to convention harbored within it the possibility of its own excesses."[23] This reflects Obama's most conservative attitudes, his desire to find a middle ground between conventional thinking and mindless rebellion. Obama's rejection of the 1960s is a product not merely of growing up as part of a later generation, but of personal maturity. Obama's call for a new kind of politics is telling baby boomer politicians to grow up and get beyond petty political bickering.

Baby Boom Politics

A feature in the *Washingtonian* magazine noted, "Obama suddenly has found himself the standard-bearer for a generation."[24] Obama's crusade is not about generational warfare, of the young ganging up to defeat those aging baby boomers who now dominate our society and our politics. Obama is not interested in pitting the young against the old in some kind of "Don't trust anyone over fifty" approach to politics. After all, the earlier variation of that slogan ("Don't trust anyone over thirty") was common in the 1960s when the baby boomers were growing up and generational divisions reached their peak in the climate of antiwar activism and the sexual revolution. As Obama noted, "there are plenty of politically engaged baby boomers who are tired of waiting to see the American Dream realized."[25]

Unlike the baby boomers, younger people today are not generational rebels singing songs "talkin' about my generation." Generations today are much harder to define because they are so diverse. Today's younger generation may not exactly have great respect for their elders, but they also don't have contempt. Perhaps one symbol of cross-generational partnership is the 1960s youth protest group Students for a Democratic Society, which was relaunched in 2006 by a new generation of students working hand in hand with old sixties radicals who have created the associated group Movement for a Democratic Society so that the protest movement doesn't have an age limit.

What Obama represents is indeed a new generation of generational politics, but also a new generation of politics that transcends these artificial divisions. Eric Liu, a former Clinton speechwriter and policy aide, expressed the younger generation's approach to the baby boomers: "Thank you, here's your gold watch, it's time for the personal style and political framework of the 1960s to get out of the way."[26] Obama is not so dismissive about the baby boomers; nor does he neglect the accomplishments of their generation: "The victories that the sixties generation brought about—the admission of minorities and women into full citizenship, the strengthening of individual liberties, and the healthy willingness to question authority—have made America a far better place for all its citizens. But what has been lost in the process, and has yet to be replaced, are those shared assumptions—that quality of trust and fellow feeling—that bring us together as Americans."[27]

Obama has said: "It feels as if many of the battles of the sixties have been refought, over and over again, and the cast of characters who were involved have taken a lot of the frameworks of the sixties—what it means to be a conservative, what it means to be a liberal—and just gone at it. And the country's been very polarized and very divided as a consequence. And you do get a sense that there's this hunger for a different kind of politics, one that I hope, at least, is strongly progressive, and recognizes the need for government to play a role in broadening opportunity for people, but that scrambles some of the old categories, and is less embedded in some of these old battles. And that, I think, is an enormous opportunity. I think that is an enormous opportunity particularly for Democrats."[28]

But Obama rejected the idea that age matters. Obama was interviewed by *New Yorker* writer David Remnick, who asked him if "it's a way of saying that you need somebody younger than a baby boomer." Obama resisted that idea: "No, because it could be attitudinal as well, but the point, though, is that I think the country wants something different."[29] What makes Obama different from other candidates is not so much his age, but his approach to politics. And what he opposes is not an older generation of politicians, but a particular brand of politics based in ideological warfare.

Chris Lehane, a former Clinton White House official, observed that "2008 will represent a hinge moment in generational politics, not just because of the prominence of a post-boomer candidate but because this will be the first cycle when a whole new range of issues as big, if not bigger, than the big issues that defined the boomers will be front and center: Iraq, the war on terror, global warming, energy, technology and globalization."[30]

John Heilemann in *New York Magazine* noted that Obama "promises to deliver us from the tired and tiresome contours—the moralism, narcissism, condescension, and histrionics—of civic discourse as practiced by the baby boom generation. The essence of Obama's pitch is that it's time to move past the old politics and that he's the embodiment of the new. And after the scorched-earth tactics and wretched polarization of the Clinton-Bush years, anyone who dismisses the potency of that message hasn't been paying attention."[31]

In a world no longer defined by the cold war and instead facing new challenges, Obama offers a new generation's approach to these new problems. There is no guarantee that Obama's approach is a better way of solving problems, but it represents a break from the past that offers hope of a more united politics.

The Clinton/Bush Generation

Obama's generational differences have been highlighted because of the particular baby boomers who have prevailed in recent American political fights, such as Bill Clinton, Newt Gingrich, and George W. Bush. Few baby boomers would call these men the best representatives of their generation.

Obama wrote in *The Audacity of Hope*, "In the back and forth between Clinton and Gingrich, and in the elections of 2000 and 2004, I sometimes felt as if I were watching the psychodrama of the baby boom generation—a tale rooted in old grudges and revenge plots hatched on a handful of college campuses long ago—played out on the national stage."[32]

In many ways, Bill Clinton and George W. Bush represent the worst stereotypes of the baby boomer generation. Both Clinton and Bush were among the elite boomers who used their connections to dodge the draft during the Vietnam War. Bush's family name got him special admission to the Texas Air National Guard, where he was virtually guaranteed not to be sent to war, and he even failed to show up for duty while he was serving.

Clinton and Bush also had notorious habits of lying. Both of them concealed their illicit drug use. Clinton reluctantly admitted to trying marijuana but claimed that he "didn't inhale." Bush concealed his drunk driving arrest and refused to answer questions about his use of cocaine and other illegal drugs in his twenties. By contrast, Obama has been open about using cocaine and marijuana during a troubled time in high school and college, but he is forthright about condemning such drugs.

Clinton's deceit reached its high point during the Monica Lewinsky scandal when he angrily insisted, "I did not have sexual relations with that woman" and then attempted to parse the meanings of "what 'is' is" to avoid taking responsibility. Bush, declaring that he would bring back integrity to the White House, instead brought the art of political lying to new heights by using deceit to start a war in Iraq.

Those of us who were too young to be involved in the 1960s protests can sometimes be astonished when we read the history books about what happened then: the protests, the sit-ins, the campus shutdowns, the violent actions on both sides. To people filled with protest nostalgia, the 1960s were an era that can seem glorious in comparison to today's smaller and less controversial campus protests. One hallmark of today's generation of students, even among political activists, is their extraordinary politeness. Little wonder, then, that Obama has gained so much support among youth. He shares their same sense of being earnest and polite, of recognizing that devotion to political change isn't measured by marches and sit-ins, but by taking control of the political system and using it as a force for good. *New York Times* columnist Bob Herbert observed, "When Senator Obama talks about bringing a new kind of politics to the national scene, he's talking about something that would differ radically from the relentlessly vicious, sleazy, mendacious politics that have plagued the country throughout the Bush-Clinton years. Whether he can pull that off is an open question."[33]

Some pundits questioned whether a campaign based on principles of unity could succeed in a political climate fundamentally opposed to that approach, where Obama's version of politics was dismissed as naive or simpleminded. As Obama's chief campaign advisor David Axelrod put it, "Do we have a strategy to tear people down? We don't. And maybe that's incredibly naive, and maybe that is not feasible in modern politics. But we believe it is, and we believe it's important to run a campaign like that."[34]

Obama and the Culture Warriors

Obama also represents a kind of cease-fire in the culture wars. On one hand, he supports traditional liberal (and very popular) positions on abortion rights, freedom from censorship, and equal rights for all. His background includes experience with illegal drugs, like many of those in his generation, but he is unafraid to reveal these personal facts.

On the other hand, Obama evokes religious imagery and ideas in his talks, which is certainly not a traditional liberal stand (beyond purely symbolic invocations). He has expressed personal opposition to gay marriage (although he supports civil unions). There is something affectionately old-fashioned about some of Obama's views, such as when he denounces graduation ceremonies for eighth-graders as a silly attempt at esteem-building or when he worries about the embarrassment of watching TV with his daughters and an erectile dysfunction commercial is shown.

Even conservatives see the power of Obama's generational appeal. John Fund, editor of the *Wall Street Journal*'s right-wing editorial page, observed, "Many voters want to get beyond the stale culture-war issues fought over by rival camps of baby boomers."[35] Michael Barone, a senior writer at *U.S. News and World Report*, observed, "There is clearly a demand in the political marketplace for candidates who can rise above the bitter partisanship that has dominated our politics since Bill Clinton took office in 1993. That partisanship has been bitter in part because Clinton and George W. Bush—both born in the leadoff baby boom year of 1946—happen to have personal characteristics that Americans on opposite sides of the cultural divide absolutely loathe.... Too many people have come to regard the views of the other side as not only wrong, but evil."[36] Barone concluded, "Obama, by emphasizing what Americans of differing views have in common, invites us to an era of less bitter partisanship."[37]

By no means can Obama be called a cultural conservative. But he is someone who understands religious conservatives and often sympathizes with their concerns even while he opposes most of their policies. Obama has learned many lessons from the 1960s, both the social change it inspired and the failures found in some of its excesses. Obama is proposing a paradoxical generational politics that's about transcending generations in the same way that it's about transcending party boundaries.

The New Political Generation

According to PBS commentator Bill Moyers, "Obama represents a generational metaphor. He opens up new gates so that younger people can feel that there's opportunity for them, that they can come in with him and create new possibilities."[38]

Obama inspired a mass movement of young progressives who were truly excited by a candidate for the first time. A March 2007 Harvard Institute of Politics survey found that Obama led all presidential candidates among 18- to 24-year-olds, who supported him at levels 50 percent above the general population in polls. Obama is especially popular among college students.[39] As Reverend Jesse Jackson observed, "This movement with Barack will ensure more people will register to vote and more youth participation."[40]

Obama's vision of politics is reflected in how he decided to run for president. As much as it is possible for any presidential candidate today, Obama was drafted to run. It was the public demand for his books, the public's interest that spurred media profiles, and the various online "Draft Obama" movements that helped persuade Obama to run. Of course, Obama wanted to be president, and the choice was ultimately his. But it was the thirst for a new kind of politics that helped Obama decide that the time was now.

Obama on Drugs

One issue that exposed the disconnect between Obama's appeal and the conventional wisdom of an older generation in Washington is his admitted drug use. A front-page story in the *Washington Post* focused on Obama's use of drugs as a teenager that he reveals in his 1995 book, *Dreams from My Father*: "Pot had helped, and booze; maybe a little blow when you could afford it. Not smack, though."[41] At the time, Obama reflected on the dangers of drug use: "Junkie. Pothead. That's where I'd been headed: the final, fatal role of the young would-be black man."[42]

But Obama's honesty in addressing the drug issue reflects the generational change in politics. Most voters no longer care about youthful drug use; they're much more worried about having an honest person in the White House. Back in 1992, Bill Clinton answered a question about his past drug use by saying that he had tried marijuana, but he "didn't inhale." It was a typical Clintonesque answer that foreshadowed some of his later evasions about "what the meaning of 'is' is." When Obama appeared on the *Tonight Show*, Jay Leno asked, "Remember, senator, you are under oath. Did you inhale?" Obama replied, "That was the point."[43] Some conservatives worried that Obama was making light of illicit drug use; in reality, he was making fun of the old-style politicians who thought they could fool the voters with dishonesty.

The fear that Obama's use of cocaine might make him unelectable reflects an old style of thinking. According to conservative columnist Robert Novak, "When the American people find a presidential candidate who has used cocaine, this is not a good thing. It is a burden to carry."[44] Of course, Obama almost certainly isn't the first person to use cocaine and then run for president. Plenty of presidential candidates would have used the drug when it was legal a century ago and a common medicinal ingredient, even found in Coca-Cola for a time. And George W. Bush probably used cocaine, since he refused to deny doing so before 1974. Bush stopped showing up for his National Guard duty shortly after a new order required random drug tests.[45]

But Obama was the first presidential candidate honest enough to talk in detail about some of the troubles of his youth. This accounted for some of his appeal among younger voters, since he shared his experience rather than trying to cover it up for political advantage. Garth Corriveau, a New Hampshire lawyer, told the *Boston Globe* after an Obama event, "I just turned 30, and the only politics I've known have been divisive. I'm ready for a new kind of politics, and I hope he's the one who can deliver it."[46] One Republican college student drove three hours to hear Obama speak in Iowa, declaring that "Barack's attitude is awesome.... Barack's the only Democrat I'd vote for."[47]

The Myth of Generation I

Like Obama's generation X and the baby boomers before them, the new generation of youth has been smeared with accusations that they are self-centered and spoiled. Brian Williams on the *NBC Nightly News* proclaimed about today's college students, "They're just self-centered enough to be called the Me Generation."[48] His comment was based on a study by Jean Twenge of San Diego State University, who concluded that narcissism among students is a problem proved by increasing scores on the Narcissistic Personality Inventory (NPI). In 2006, two-thirds of college freshman scored above average on the NPI, an increase of 30 percent compared to 1982.[49] Twenge, the author of *Generation Me: Why Today's Young Americans Are More Confident, Assertive, Entitled—and More Miserable than Ever Before*, argues that young people suffer from a sense of entitlement and vanity.[50]

However, the NPI is a deeply flawed survey, and many of the statements in the NPI reflect positive values, not narcissism. "I think I am a special person" is a measure of hope and potential, not necessarily self-centeredness. "I can live my life any way I want to" reflects personal freedom, not narcissism. "I have often met people who were supposed to be experts who were no better than I" reveals a healthy skepticism about authorities.[51] Agreement with the phrase, "If I ruled the world, it would be a better place" is caused by the general belief of most Americans that they could do a better job than George W. Bush did. Do we really want college students who think they're dull and unimportant, who feel compelled to live lives they don't want, who think they're not competent to be leaders? Optimism and confidence aren't dangers to be feared, but goals to be pursued.

The myth of "generation I" is refuted by the skyrocketing levels of community service among young people, despite the growing cost of college that causes many students to work long hours. A study by the Corporation for National and Community Service found that volunteer activities reported by college students increased 20 percent from 2002 to 2005.[52] The Higher Education Research Institute's 2005 survey of college freshmen discovered that feelings of social and civic responsibility were at the highest level in 25 years. Political engagement has also reached unprecedented heights. The Higher Education Research Institute's survey of college students in Fall 2008 found that 35.6 percent of first-year students reported they frequently discuss politics, the highest level ever recorded and more than double the response in 2000.[53] And 85.9 percent of students frequently or occasionally discussed politics, another record.

Twenge cites an example of narcissism: "By its very name, MySpace encourages attention-seeking, as does YouTube."[54] But social networking sites aren't narcissistic; they are a way to reach out to the larger world. However, unlike passively watching the nightly news, social networking requires its users to define themselves and create their own profiles.

It is not surprising that Obama's campaign generated far more interest on social networking sites than has any other politician's. Obama's MySpace page reached 160,000 friends, up until an April 2007 dispute between the Obama campaign and the volunteer who originally started the page.[55] An Obama Facebook page had over 200,000 supporters (along with 60,000 members of Students for Barack Obama) within two weeks of his announcement for president, while his competitors had only a few thousand members.[56] Joe Trippi, Howard Dean's Internet campaign manager in 2004, observed about Obama's Internet presence: "It took our campaign six months to get 139,000 people on an e-mail list. It took one Facebook group, what, barely a month to get 200,000? That's astronomical."[57] Obama drew thousands of people to a George Mason University rally organized online by Students for Barack Obama using Facebook shortly after he announced his plans to run for president.[58] Obama hadn't even met the student organizers until he arrived at the event.[59] By March 1, 2007, just a few weeks after Obama began his campaign, his website My.BarackObama.com attracted 3,306 grassroots volunteer groups, 4,416 personal fundraising pages, 6,706 personal blogs, and 38,799 people with individual profiles building networks to support Obama.[60] Peter Suderman of *National Review* noted, "Obama's social-network campaigning is unmatched."[61]

Even a small dispute over Obama's Myspace page didn't halt Obama's unprecedented rise on the web. A volunteer for Obama had started Obama's MySpace page and later worked with the Obama campaign to get 160,000 friends. However, when the volunteer asked for $50,000 to transfer the webpage and then cut off the Obama campaign's access to it, Obama's workers went to MySpace and took control of the page (as anyone can do when someone else starts up a MySpace page in his or her name).

The Internet helped create the organizing community that Obama envisions. His history as a community organizer in Chicago guided how Obama shaped his campaign. The model for community organizing is to hear from the people affected by the problem and help them to shape a solution. Rather than announcing a detailed health care plan, Obama instead held meetings and webcasts on health care, with an opportunity for people to submit their stories and ideas for changing policy to Obama.

Of course, this new age of decentralized politics takes much of the power out of the hands of political consultants and puts it into the grasp of individuals. One result was the infamous "1984" parody ad, produced by Obama supporter Phil de Vellis, that was viewed by far more than a million people on YouTube. The video took the classic 1984 Apple commercial and put Hillary Clinton in the place of Big Brother, her face on a gigantic screen uttering political platitudes to an obedient audience, before an Obama supporter shatters it with a sledgehammer. This idea of Obama as some kind of rebel force against the dominant political machine was exaggerated, of course. Hillary Clinton wasn't Big Sister. Obama wasn't the leader of a rebel army. He is comfortable working within the political system and being effective at it. But there was a kernel of truth in this video, and Obama's approach to using the technology of the Internet reflected his new approach to politics.

The Voting Generation

One characteristic of this new generation is a commitment to electoral politics. In 2004, 47 percent of 18- to 24-year-old citizens voted, compared to only 36 percent in 2000. This increase of nearly one-third (11 percentage points) was far higher than the overall increase in voting rates from 60 percent to 64 percent. The number of young voters increased from 8.6 million to 11.6 million in just one election, an unprecedented increase that continued in 2008.[62] At colleges around the country, students stood for hours in line to vote at precincts overwhelmed by the demand.

And these young voters are not only voting more, they are voting differently. Unlike the generation who grew up under Ronald Reagan's presidency, who tended to vote Republican more than older voters (even though the younger people were more likely to hold liberal social values), this new generation is the most liberal since the 1960s. According to exit polls in 2006, young people (18 to 29) preferred Democrats 58 percent to 38 percent over Republicans, compared to a gap of only 52 percent to 45 percent for voters of all ages. Among young voters, the gap in party identification was 43 percent Democrat and 31 percent Republican, compared to a 38 percent to 35 percent margin for Democrats among all ages.[63]

Obama had already brought in a new generation of voters. He led a movement in the Chicago area in 1992 that registered 150,000 new voters— mostly African Americans—and helped Carol Moseley Braun narrowly win a primary and general election to become the first black woman elected to the U.S. Senate.[64] Obama's appeal to voters disenchanted with conventional politics brought many new voters into the political process.

The Cynical Generation

Obama is fond of criticizing cynicism. At a Democratic National Committee meeting, Obama proclaimed: "Our rivals won't be one another, and I would assert it won't even be the other party. It's going to be cynicism that we're fighting against. It's the cynicism that's borne from decades of disappointment, amplified by talk radio and 24-hour news cycles, reinforced by the relentless pounding of negative ads that have become the staple of modern politics. It's a cynicism that asks us to believe that our opponents are never just wrong, but they're bad; that our motives in politics can never be pure, that they're only driven by power and by greed; that the challenges that we face today aren't just daunting, but they're impossible."[65]

Obama's perspective proved puzzling to pundits trained for cynicism. Conservative MSNBC host Tucker Carlson complained about Obama's critique of cynicism, "What the hell does that mean? I mean, is it—is it too sort of high flown to be a political message?"[66] Obama argued that if the cynics were right, "politics is not a noble calling, it's a game, it's a blood sport with folks keeping score about who's up and who's down. At best, it's a diversion." According to Obama, "With such cynicism, government doesn't become a force of good, a means of giving people the opportunity to lead better lives; it just becomes an obstacle for people to get rid of. Too often, this cynicism makes us afraid to say what we believe. It makes us fearful. We don't trust the truth."[67]

However, Obama's vision of cynicism is a narrow point of view. Cynicism, strictly speaking, refers to an intelligent skepticism about our political system. Cynicism is a very useful thing. It doesn't create apathy. Instead, it creates an unmet desire for better candidates and better politics. Cynicism is dangerous only if it develops into resignation, into an acceptance of the way things are now in politics, of the corruption and pork in Washington, of the partisan bickering and inability to get things done in government. Obama noted about cynicism, "It's caused our politics to become small and timid, calculating and cautious. We spend all our time thinking about tactics and maneuvers, knowing that if we spoke the truth, we address the issues with boldness, that we might be labeled—it might lead to our defeat."[68] But Obama has it reversed; the truth is that cynicism is created by political corruption, not vice versa. Our politics is small and timid and calculating because it appeases big money interests and political consultants, not because of the cynicism of the public. The public becomes cynical because it sees the small and timid politics that dominate Washington.

Even if Obama is mistaken about the basic causes of our political problems, he understands the consequences clearly. According to Obama, "We internalize those fears. We edit ourselves. We censor our best instincts. It's America that suffers most from this can't-do, won't-do, won't-even-try style of politics. At the very moment when Americans are feeling anxious about the future, uncertain as to whether their children are going to have better lives than they do, we've been asked to narrow our hopes, diminish our dreams."[69]

Obama's way of fighting cynicism is unusual. Most critics of cynicism equate it with political compromise and seek a purer ideological commitment as the solution to cynics. Obama has a very different approach, rejecting the constraints of ideological warfare. For Obama, cynicism is a type of hopelessness, a way of giving up on the political process when it fails to live up to our ideals. To Obama, political compromise is necessary for participation in the democratic system, and so he opposes the cynic who would rather walk away from politics than experience the disappointment of falling short of ideals.[70]

Obama also recognizes the essential difference between having faith in the potential for politics and having blind faith in the current political system. As Obama noted, "We don't want another election where voters are simply holding their noses and feel like they're choosing the lesser of two evils. So we've got to rise up out of the cynicism that's become so pervasive and ask the people all across America to start believing again."[71] Ultimately, Obama is fighting against cynicism because so many people have heard politicians make and break promises about changing politics or leading America in a different direction that few voters believe it anymore.

Cynicism, then, has been a double-edged sword for Obama. As an outsider to conventional politics, he needed to convince the public that something was wrong in Washington. Yet he also needed to persuade people that change was still possible. It's part of the meaning behind the title of Obama's book *The Audacity of Hope*, since it is audacious to hope for political change when so many other politicians have disappointed us. But if people give up all hope, the result will be a kind of cynicism that makes change impossible, and that's what Obama is fighting against.

One of those cynics is Obama's wife. Michelle Obama has admitted, "I'm one of the skeptics that Barack often talks about. Like most people, my view about politics—and it's evolved, but it had been—that politics is for dirty, nasty people who aren't trying to do much in the world." Although she voted regularly, she said, "I think that I had become cynical like many people."[72]

Cynicism and Political Culture

Cynicism is also a part of our larger culture, but the term is often misunderstood. Based on one study linking the *Daily Show* to cynicism, the *Washington Post* reported that Jon Stewart "may be poisoning democracy."[73]

A study by Jody Baumgartner and Jonathan Morris of East Carolina University tested students by showing them 2004 campaign coverage from the *Daily Show* and the CBS *Evening News* and asking them to respond to statements such as "I trust the news media to cover political events fairly and accurately." Perhaps not surprisingly, the *Daily Show* viewers were less likely to trust the media and more likely to have negative views of John Kerry and George W. Bush. The researchers claimed, "Ultimately, negative perceptions of candidates could have participation implications by keeping more youth from the polls."[74]

So why did a generation watching the *Daily Show* vote in such astonishing numbers? The answer is that the researchers' basic premise is wrong. Students had negative perceptions of the candidates, the media, and the political process, but they still voted. The problem is not with the negative perceptions of young people, but with the negative qualities of the candidates. By the reasoning of those academics, Obama's own criticisms of Washington politics might be thought to enhance cynicism. But the opposite is true: Change can only happen when people perceive a problem with existing political institutions.

A different study found that watching the *Daily Show* made people more knowledgeable about politics. The 2004 survey by the Annenberg Public Policy Center found that Americans asked six questions about their political knowledge got an average of 45 percent correct. Viewers of Jay Leno or David Letterman got 49 percent correct, while viewers of the *Daily Show* got 60 percent correct. Young people watching the *Daily Show* were more knowledgeable about basic political questions than those reading a daily newspaper or watching the network news.[75] This knowledge is part of what drives new voters, since the *Daily Show* and similar programs are more popular than the mainstream media among youth. One study indicated that 48 percent of young people watch the *Daily Show*, double the number who follow traditional TV news programs.[76]

The students entering college today have never lived in a world where anyone other than a Clinton or a Bush was president. They have grown up in a country where the president has always been the punch line to a disturbing joke, whether it's about blow jobs in the Oval Office or an incompetent guy too stupid to speak English correctly. Oddly enough, this disturbing view of the most powerful person in the world hasn't led young people into the depths of apathy and cynicism. This seems even stranger for a generation that has grown up watching the *Daily Show* or David Letterman's "Great Moments in Presidential Speeches," who saw a president's administration lie about weapons of mass destruction, where the smoking gun wasn't a mushroom cloud, it was a smokescreen.

How does a generation react when their president is a liar? Certainly, cynicism and apathy are two responses. But political failure also can create an opportunity for change. When President Richard Nixon resigned in disgrace because of his lies and cover-ups, many young people reacted not with despair but with optimism, and a new generation of journalists aspired to match Bob Woodward and Carl Bernstein's work. Of course, blaming the younger generation is a perpetual hobby. Back on March 25, 1971, Nixon met with student body presidents from various colleges and then complained about it afterward to H. R. Haldeman. Nixon was annoyed that "we have to sit and talk to these little jackasses." According to Nixon, "The softness of this younger [generation] is just unbelievable." Nixon and Haldeman agreed that television was to blame and lamented having to do "this therapy meeting with the little assholes."[77]

Unlike Nixon, Barack Obama sees the younger generation as a source of hope rather than annoyance. Obama told thousands of students at George Mason University, "You guys don't have much of a memory of a politics that transcends and brings people together."[78] Obama observed, "I think there is a great hunger for change in the country—and not just policy change. What I also think they are looking for is change in tone and a return to some notion of the common good and some sense of cooperation, of pragmatism over ideology. I'm a stand-in for that right now."[79]

But Obama is not promoting a Pollyanna vision of the world, where all of the problems can be solved by positive feelings or the mere belief that we can fix everything. Obama's idealism is always tempered by realism and a recognition that progress comes in small steps rather than grandiose plans for transforming society. This is what distinguishes him from previous candidates who ran against the Washington establishment.

Obama offered an unusual combination of idealism and pragmatism. He strongly believes in fundamental principles, but he is unafraid of compromising in order to move closer to those ideals. This is unique among politicians seeking the presidency. Some candidates (almost always losers) have been idealists firmly espousing their goals. Others have been pragmatic politicians working the system. What Obama represented is the idea that idealism and pragmatism are not opposites of political life, but positions that can reinforce and support each other. Idealism is more pure when it can be effective. Pragmatism is more effective when it has an ideal pushing behind it.

Obama's 2004 DNC Speech

In his 2004 speech to the Democratic National Convention, Obama asked: "Do we participate in a politics of cynicism or a politics of hope?" Obama is not naive; as he observed, "I'm not talking about blind optimism here—the almost willful ignorance that thinks unemployment will go away if we just don't talk about it, or the health care crisis will solve itself if we just ignore it." Instead, Obama was talking about his optimistic belief that "this country will reclaim its promise, and out of this long political darkness a brighter day will come." Obama called it "the hope of a skinny kid with a funny name who believes that America has a place for him, too."

Obama's new approach to politics turns conventional language on its head. He told the DNC in 2007, "We've been told that consensus on any issue is no longer possible, that we should settle for tinkering around the edges, year after year after year. And along the way we've lost our faith in the political process. We don't really think that we can transform this country." This was a lecture to the Democratic Party about its many, many faults. But it was also an example of Obama reminding himself not to listen too closely to the consultants and the pundits. Obama was talking about himself as much as he was talking about anyone else.

For Obama, consensus is a method for achieving transformational change, and the exact opposite of "tinkering around the edges." This is precisely the opposite of what pundits and politicians typically believe. They see consensus as a method for small, insignificant change. Obama envisions consensus as an opportunity. That's why Obama's 2004 DNC speech rejecting the division of the country into the blue states and the red states was much more than political rhetoric. It's an essential part of his political approach. Obama also refuses to believe that there are blue people and red people. He sees the complexity of individual views, even though they may vote for one party or the other. In 2004, Obama won a substantial number of Republican voters in his Senate race, many of whom were drawn to his inclusive approach. According to the exit polls, Obama won 9 percent of Republican voters in 2008, far above Kerry's 6 percent in 2004.

But the American electorate is characterized by a growing number of independents who refuse party identification because they reject the divisions and partisanship implied by it. And there is also a large number of disillusioned voters who have stopped going to the ballot box because they rarely find anyone worth voting for.

We have long passed the age of the "yellow dog" Democrat, when a voter would support the Democrat even if the candidate was a little yellow dog. But the necessary death of party loyalty hasn't been replaced by any other system, and that's why cynicism often fills the gap. Without party loyalty or a political machine driving them to the election booths, voters must be inspired to vote, and often that inspiration has been absent.

Politics has become a profession roughly equivalent to lawyers or prostitutes in the esteem with which the public views it. But it's more than just the profession. Distrust of politics extends even to a casual commitment to the idealism espoused by Obama. We think it foolish, and naive, for anyone to imagine that politics can be turned to a good purpose. The cynic reigns supreme, and this is a particularly dangerous kind of cynicism. The Bush administration's response to the Katrina disaster only accentuated the cynicism and the public's belief that government is capable of no good. But it also showed the desire for Americans to have leaders who believe that government can serve a larger social purpose.

Can a politician like Obama prevail in a political system built upon opposing values? Obama's advisor David Axelrod noted about Obama, "I think he's going to be the same candidate from start to finish. You know, one of those—that's one of the kind of unfortunate qualities of our politics is that people seem to shift and turn and move according to the political season. It's one of the things that I think contributes to a great deal of cynicism. And so, you know, he I think will be a consistent voice throughout this election."[80]

However, the primary election process, dominated by party activists in early caucuses, tended to discourage Obama's approach to politics, which appealed much more to the independent voters who have been disillusioned by today's political rhetoric. Party activists were more interested in the politics of division, and most conventional politicians running for president are skilled at a certain kind of political mobility, running to the left for the Democratic primaries (or to the far right for the Republican primaries) and then turning on a dime and running toward the center for the general election.

New Generations

At the Selma Voting Rights March commemoration in March 2007, Obama expressed his sense of changing generations in biblical terms: "I thank the Moses generation; but we've got to remember, now, that Joshua still had a job to do. As great as Moses was, despite all that he did, leading a people out of bondage, he didn't cross over the river to see the Promised Land. We're going to leave it to the Joshua generation to make sure it happens. There are still battles that need to be fought; some rivers that need to be crossed."[81]

Obama recognizes the accomplishments of the 1960s generation in the Civil Rights movement. According to Obama, "What really inspired me was the Civil Rights movement."[82] But he also believes that a new generation needs to lead the fight for equality in a time of different battles. As Obama put it, "Moses told the Joshua generation, don't forget where you came from. I worry sometimes, that the Joshua generation in its success forgets where it came from. Thinks it doesn't have to make as many sacrifices. Thinks that the very height of ambition is to make as much money as you can, to drive the biggest car and have the biggest house and wear a Rolex watch and get your own private jet, get some of that Oprah money. And I think that's a good thing. There's nothing wrong with making money, but if you know your history, then you know that there is a certain poverty of ambition involved in simply striving just for money. Materialism alone will not fulfill the possibilities of your existence."[83] *New York Times* columnist Thomas

Friedman wrote about this generation, "So many big problems are going to come due on their watch—from underfunded Social Security to health care to climate change—that the effort needed to fix them will require them to stay involved, redouble their resolve and raise their voices."[84]

Obama noted, "I think that there's the possibility—not the certainty, but the possibility—that I can't just win an election but can also transform the country in the process, that the language and the approach I take to politics is sufficiently different that I could bring diverse parts of this country together in a way that hasn't been done in some time, and that bridging those divisions is a critical element in solving problems like health care or energy or education."[85]

There are reasons to be optimistic. Stephen Trachtenberg, president of George Washington University, said, "I've been a college president for thirty years, and these kids are more optimistic about the future than any I have seen—maybe more than they have reason to be."[86] Obama noted, "People are very hungry for something new. I think to some degree I'm a stand-in for that desire."[87] There is a danger that Obama can become a hope receptacle where everyone tosses their idealism and dreams for changing society, imagining that Obama can simply dump all of these ideas into policy reforms that would transform the country. Nothing like that is possible. But if this new generation of voters becomes an Obama generation of activists, it would be a radical shift. Obama's story can inspire a new group of people to work on behalf of social change.

There have been many comparisons of Obama with earlier, inspirational politicians such as John F. Kennedy or Robert Kennedy (not to mention the people comparing him to Elvis and Jesus).[88] Bill Moyers observed, "When I look at Barack Obama, I think about John F. Kennedy, who leaped over Hubert Humphrey's generation to bring in fresh voices and fresh ideas."[89] In an age of cynicism, perhaps it is not possible for politicians like Obama to inspire a new generation to bring political change. But the response to Obama's rhetoric of inclusion reflects some hope for a new kind of politics. As Obama applied his community organizing to a presidential campaign, he encountered the usual skepticism of pundits and political consultants. Mark McKinnon, a former Bush media strategist, declared about Obama, "He's a walking, talking hope machine."[90] But hope alone is never enough. Obama's dream of social change is possible only if he can convince Americans to look past all the cynicism and embrace a new approach to politics.

CHAPTER TWO

Are You Experienced?

Obama and the Media

If somebody attacks you, you hit back swiftly, you hit back decisively, and you hit back truthfully. —Barack Obama

The greatest barrier to Barack Obama's presidential campaign has been the attacks on his qualifications by the press. Over and over again, the media damned Obama as inexperienced. *Washington Post* media critic Howard Kurtz claimed that the "walk on water coverage" of Obama "ranges from glowing to gushing," and asked, "Will journalists continue to swoon over Barack Obama or finally ask some hard questions about his record and lack of experience?"[1] But far from critiquing the mainstream press about Obama, Kurtz was simply repeating the attacks on his experience that were almost universal.

Throughout the media coverage of Obama, his name became synonymous with "inexperienced." Lynn Sweet in the *Chicago Sun-Times* cited "the weakness on his resume—his lack of experience."[2] Larry Sabato of the University of Virginia declared, "The number one weak spot for Barack Obama is inexperience. He is young, the youngest in the field. He is very inexperienced compared to other candidates in his party and in the Republican Party."[3] Sometimes the media devalued Obama's experience in trivial ways, such as *USA Today, Christian Science Monitor,* and many other media outlets incorrectly claiming that Obama served for seven years in the state senate, when in fact it was eight years.[4]

Even liberals and leftists attacked Obama's alleged inexperience. On the website *Huffington Post,* Brent Budowsky, a former Democratic legislative staffer, denounced Obama's experience in harsh terms: "Senator Obama has close to zero national security experience, close to zero national defense and foreign policy experience, close to zero national political experience, close to zero national legislative experience and close to zero experience being tested in the crucible of brutal national politics."[5] Jonathan Zimmerman of New York University wrote in the *Chicago Tribune,* "My fellow liberals, we cannot have it both ways. If George W. Bush was unqualified to be our president, Barack Obama is even more so."[6] Author Earl Ofari Hutchinson criticized "his political inexperience, and a skimpy Senate track record."[7]

Conservatives joined the attacks on Obama's experience. Columnist John Fund of the *Wall Street Journal,* when asked the question, "Is he qualified?" answered "Not by conventional standards."[8] The *New York Post* reported that Obama needs "to puff up his slim résumé."[9] The *New York Daily News* noted, "Obama's biggest problem may not be that he's black but that he's green."[10] But it was the mainstream press that pushed the myth of Obama's inexperience. The *Christian Science Monitor* editorialized about Obama, "He's too inexperienced to have a long political track record."[11] ABC reporter Jake Tapper on *Nightline* declared that Obama's opponents' "experience outmatches his."[12]

In order to be a card-carrying member of the establishment media, it seemed, you had to find something negative about Obama. And his "experience" quickly became the easiest story to tell. The key advantage of calling Obama inexperienced was that it required no actual knowledge about him or his record. In fact, knowing nothing about Obama's political experience greatly aided any pundit desiring to dismiss him as "inexperienced." Much like the earlier media tropes about Al Gore (lied about inventing the Internet) or John Kerry (coward and traitor), the idea of Obama as inexperienced was not merely unproven but the opposite of the truth.

The attacks on Obama are nothing personal. In fact, Obama is probably well liked by most journalists. But the marketplace demanded that the media cover a popular figure, and because the details of Obama's life had already been extensively covered in his own books, journalists had little new to do except try to find holes in Obama's story or the differing accounts that are inevitable in any account of the distant past.

The Substance and the Style

One Associated Press article began, "The voices are growing louder asking the question: Is Barack Obama all style and little substance?"[13] It was nearly impossible to find the "substance" of any other presidential candidates questioned. The Associated Press declared that other candidates "don't have such a barrier to prove they are qualified to be president."[14] But this barrier was one invented by the media.

The Associated Press proclaimed that Obama "began his campaign facing the perception that he lacks the experience to be president especially compared to rivals with decades of work on foreign and domestic policy. So far, he's done little to challenge it. He's delivered no policy speeches and provided few details about how he would lead the country."[15] In reality, Obama had talked about his policies in many speeches, and his website was full of detailed proposals. As Obama noted, "The truth of the matter is I probably have a more detailed and specific record of what I think and where I stand than any candidate in this race. I've written two very detailed books that give people a pretty good window into my heart and soul. I've given policy speeches on just about every important issue that we face."[16] Yet Tim Russert on *Meet the Press* wondered, "Is there now a second phase of the coverage of Barack Obama where reporters and voters will start demanding from him real specifics on the real challenges confronting our country and world?"[17] MSNBC anchor Peter Alexander claimed that "the conventional wisdom on Barack Obama is that he's a great speaker, a terrific orator, but hasn't really been all that specific about policy."[18]

It was the media that didn't want to talk about policies, not Obama. Noam Chomsky noted about the media coverage of Barack Obama, "They didn't say a word about his policies on anything."[19] In the media spotlight, the horse race and the celebrity approach always prevail over policy debates, but it was particularly strange for the press to attack Obama for not having policy proposals he did, in fact, have, when the media wouldn't talk about them. Of course, Obama could hardly be expected to match in a few months the candidates who had been planning for years to run for president, but his policy details often exceeded what other candidates offered. Arianna Huffington, the founder of *Huffington Post*, observed, "Just two days into Obama's official campaign—a full year and nine months before the election—we know quite a bit about where Obama stands."[20]

New York Times columnist David Brooks noted, "Obama's inexperience is his most obvious shortcoming. Over the next four years, the world could face a genocidal civil war in Iraq, a wave of nuclear proliferation, more Islamic extremism and a demagogues' revolt against globalization. Do we really want a forty-something in the White House?"[21] An article coauthored by former Bill Clinton advisor Dick Morris (infamous for talking to the president while engaged with a prostitute) wondered about Obama "whether he is another cynical politician or just a helplessly naïve neophyte." According to Morris, "Obama is a political infant, a babe in the woods."[22] Obama was a 45-year-old man who had been a legislator for the past decade, not a child. Yet the pundits treated Obama like he was some little sibling annoying his baby boomer brothers by wanting to play with their toys. According to Morris, "One thing is sure—in the age of terrorism, we don't need a president who can't find the men's room."[23] Actually, in an age of terrorism, what we don't need is another president who likes to piss on other countries, even if he can find the men's room. Obama is older than Teddy Roosevelt, John F. Kennedy, and Bill Clinton were when they ran for president, and none of them was deemed too immature for the presidency.

Clinton versus Obama

The treatment of Obama's experience by the press stands in sharp contrast to how Hillary Clinton was regarded. The Associated Press even devoted an entire story to Obama "tackling questions about his experience." According to this story, "With just over two years in the U.S. Senate, Obama has faced questions over whether he has sufficient experience to be president." By contrast, the story observed that "Hillary Rodham Clinton stresses her long career in public life and often warns voters that the next president will need to 'hit the ground running.'"[24]

John Fortier, a research fellow at the American Enterprise Institute, declared that the question is, "Do Democratic voters prefer the establishment candidate Clinton or will they take a bit of a gamble on an exciting but inexperienced candidate?"[25] Fox News accused Obama of "relative inexperience against Hillary Clinton and others."[26] New York representative Charles Rangel, a Clinton supporter, said about Obama: "In terms of qualification and background, I don't think anyone says he has it now."[27] David Brooks of the *New York Times* commented, "People look at Washington, and they think, I want something new. Obama's something new. Then they look at the world, and they say, I want somebody seasoned. Hillary is actually seasoned."[28]

But as MSNBC's Tucker Carlson noted, "I think he has more experience than Hillary Clinton.... He was actually in the rough and tumble of the state legislature. I mean, no, this guy's got a lot more experience than her [*sic*]."[29] Carlson's view was a distinctly minority position. Virtually every media outlet described Obama as inexperienced. Yet it would be almost impossible to find anyone in the media in the 2008 campaign that even raised the question of whether Hillary Clinton or John Edwards had enough experience. It is equally difficult to find any journalists who asked what prominent legislation Hillary Clinton or John Edwards got passed while they were in the Senate. Yet the same question was routinely asked about Obama.

An Associated Press article erroneously referred to John Edwards as "the only other candidate to serve less time in elective office than Obama," ignoring the fact that Obama spent more time as an elected official than all but one (John McCain) of the seven leading candidates for president.[30] Obama's twelve years of legislative experience (eight years in the Illinois Senate and four years in the U.S. Senate by 2008) was unmatched by Hillary Clinton (eight years in the U.S. Senate by 2008), John Edwards (six years in the U.S. Senate), Rudy Giuliani (eight years as mayor of New York City), Mitt Romney (four years as governor of Massachusetts), and Fred Thompson (eight years in the U.S. Senate). Yet only Obama's experience was ever questioned by the media. Even Rush Limbaugh was puzzled at why Obama alone was being attacked for inexperience: "You know, the question could be asked of Mrs. Bill Clinton."[31]

Obama had far more years as an elected official and experience with international politics than George W. Bush did in 2000 or Ronald Reagan did in 1980. Even Newt Gingrich said, "Abraham Lincoln served two years in the U.S. House, and seemed to do all right." Gingrich noted about Obama, "He's talking to Americans. He's finding a way to come together."[32] PBS commentator Bill Moyers made a similar point: "People say, 'Obama is so inexperienced.' No, he's as experienced as Lincoln was when Lincoln went into the White House. Lincoln had two years in Congress and eight years in the state legislature."[33]

The media's focus on Obama's experience was particularly odd because voters don't care about how long candidates have been floating around in the cesspool called D.C. politics, and if anything they prefer a fresh face that hasn't been corrupted in Congress yet. In the 2008 Democratic primary race, the most experienced candidates—Joe Biden, Chris Dodd, Dennis Kucinich—have all languished in the race, while the least experienced people—Obama, John Edwards, Hillary Clinton—were the frontrunners. Obama observed, "If the criterion is how long you've been in Washington, then we should just go ahead and assign Joe Biden or Chris Dodd the nomination. What people are looking for is judgment."[34]

The lack of significance of experience in Democratic politics was also reflected in the success of John F. Kennedy, Jimmy Carter, and Bill Clinton, who defeated far more experienced opponents in the primaries as well as the general election. Democrats with an enormous amount of experience who managed to win a primary usually lost the general election: George McGovern, Walter Mondale, Al Gore, and John Kerry.

Lack of experience also worked for the Republicans in recent years, where Ronald Reagan and George W. Bush prevailed over more experienced opponents and won the presidency, while the heavily experienced Gerald Ford and Bob Dole both lost the general election.

In fact, it's difficult to make any convincing argument that politicians with national experience are more likely to get elected president. The evidence from the past three decades is so contrary to this assertion that it's hard to imagine why any politician would want to be known as the "experienced" candidate. Vice President Dick Cheney expressed doubt that Obama could be president: "I think people might want a little more experience than that, given the nature of the times we live in."[35] As Obama has noted, "Dick Cheney and Donald Rumsfeld had an awful lot of experience, but displayed poor judgment in this Iraq war in my mind."[36] Americans want someone who's right rather than a politician with a lot of experience at being wrong.

The experience issue clearly worked against Obama. On July 29, 2007, *Fox News Sunday*'s Brit Hume called the battle between Clinton and Obama "the contest between experience and change." An April 2007 Pew Research Center survey found that 39 percent of Democratic voters considered Hillary Clinton to have the "best experience" to be president, compared to only 5 percent for Obama.[37] Obama was the only candidate in either party regularly questioned about experience, as when George Stephanopoulos asked the Democratic candidates in their August 19, 2007, debate, "is Barack Obama experienced enough to be president?" Former Republican Congressmember J. C. Watts observed, "What experience does Hillary Clinton have? I don't think that being the wife of a president any more qualifies you to be an expert on foreign policy than my playing football in the Canadian league."[38]

All of these media attacks on Obama's alleged lack of experience had a powerful impact on the public. As the Gallup News Service put it in a headline, "Experience a Major Reason Clinton Has Edge over Obama." The May 2007 Gallup poll found that "among those who prefer Clinton over Obama, the most common reason given for their choice is that 'Clinton is more experienced than Obama.'"[39]

Media Distortions of Obama: The Appearance of Corruption

The media complained about the positive coverage Obama sometimes received. Slate.com's Timothy Noah started a feature titled "The Obama Messiah Watch."[40] Columnist John Kass of the *Chicago Tribune* criticized "the relentless media fawning and hype."[41] Jim Warren, an editor at the *Chicago Tribune*, dismissed Obama as "the prom king of American politics" and added, "At some point, the bubble is, obviously, going to burst."[42]

Obama's political future, like that of any politician, depends upon the media. The establishment press determines whether a candidate is "mainstream" and "electable" or "too radical" for the public, and the media love to attack the ethics of a politician who aggressively pursues ethics reform.

When Obama bought a new house and then purchased a small part of the next door lot from a contributor named Tony Rezko in 2006, he was caught up in the backlash a few months later when Rezko was indicted on corruption charges.

Katie Couric reported, "As Barack Obama runs for the presidency, he's being dogged by questions about his personal business dealings."[43] At the first Democratic debate in 2007, Brian Williams of NBC asked Obama about his connections to Rezko. The same thing happened on ABC's *This*

Week with George Stephanopoulos. As Obama explained, "I didn't see the appearance of impropriety because I paid full price for the land."[44] But this fact didn't stop the media from implying impropriety on Obama's part.

After Obama graduated from Harvard Law School, Rezko had offered Obama a real estate job (which he refused), and when Obama began his first run for public office in 1995, Rezko was among his first contributors.[45] After Obama began looking for a new home in Hyde Park in 2005, it's not surprising that he asked for advice from Rezko, who was familiar with the neighborhood. Rezko discovered that the lot next door to the house Obama was eyeing was for sale by the same owner, and he bought it the same day the Obamas closed on their home.

As a result, John Kass, a conservative *Chicago Tribune* columnist, declared, "Obama's appraiser told him the fair market value of that slice was $40,500. Since that's one-sixth of the Rezko side, it means Rezko paid $625,000 for property that was actually worth $243,000. That would make Rezko a complete fool. But he's no fool."[46] The appraiser's estimate was clearly wrong. Fox News Channel incorrectly reported that Rezko "sold half that lot to Obama for one-third its original value" when he actually sold one-sixth of the lot for one-sixth of its value ($104,500).[47]

A year after the 10-foot-wide strip of land was sold to Obama, a Rezko business associate bought the rest of the lot for $575,000, resulting in a profit for the Rezkos of $54,000 from the two land sales.[48] This sale proved that Obama paid fair market value for his portion of the land.

After it was proven that Kass was wrong, he wrote another column hinting at a different theory about Rezko and Obama: "Rezko paid more than the asking price for the side lot, and Obama paid less than the asking price for the big house. It's the Chicago way."[49] This wasn't true, either. Rezko had paid the list price, not an excessive amount.

Tom Fitton, president of Judicial Watch, made a similar accusation: "Obama approached Rezko with the idea to simultaneously purchase adjoining lots in Southside Chicago. Rezko obliged. Obama obtained his lot for a reduced price. Rezko later sold a portion of his property to Obama."[50] None of this was true, but the mainstream press picked up the story. Ben Wallace-Wells wrote in *Rolling Stone,* "In a complicated but legal deal with Rezko, who bought a vacant lot next door to Obama's in Chicago, the senator was able to secure his own house at $300,000 below the asking price."[51] However, it's not unusual at all in the real estate business to see a

15 percent price cut on an expensive house that's been on the market for four months. Nor is it unusual that a vacant lot next door would sell to a condo developer without such a discount. A "deal" between Obama and Rezko never happened, but the misinformation continued. Jim Pinkerton of *Newsday* declared about Obama on the Fox News Channel, "All of the sudden he miraculously ends up with a fancy house."[52] There was no miracle involved in Obama's home purchase. He signed a three-book deal for $1.9 million and used the advance money to buy his $1.65 million house, which had originally been priced at $1.95 million.

The Rezko Connection

Tony Rezko's behavior certainly raises questions. For example, Rezko donated money to every major Democratic politician in Illinois, then helped organize a $3.5 million fundraiser for President George W. Bush in 2003.[53] After giving large campaign donations to then-Illinois governor Rod Blagojevich, Rezko arranged to have his buddies appointed by Blagojevich to state boards such as the Teachers' Retirement System Board and the Illinois Health Facilities Planning Board. With his friend Stuart Levine, who was on the pension board, Rezko threatened to hold up a $220 million deal to invest teachers' pension fund money unless $2 million was paid to Levine or $1.5 million was donated to Blagojevich's campaign.[54] Rezko and Levine also demanded a $1 million cut from a developer to build a hospital.[55] Rezko was indicted for pretending to sell his Papa John's pizza restaurants while secretly maintaining control of them, then fraudulently using the transaction to get $10 million in loans.[56]

However, at the time Obama bought his house, there was no public indication of Rezko's problems. When Obama bought a small strip of Rezko's land in 2006, rumors were swirling around Chicago that the federal government was investigating Rezko, but he wasn't indicted until October 2006.

Rezko's eye for scouting political talent was amazing, but he did not capitalize on Obama's influence. Obama said he had known Rezko for twenty years and "he had never asked me for anything. I've never done any favors for him."[57] In fact, Rezko already had a far more powerful politician as his buddy: then-governor Rod Blagojevich. The reality is that all politicians have connections to people like Rezko. What matters is whether they acqui-esce to the demands of such donors or serve the public good.

Obama declared, "I am the first one to acknowledge that it was a bone-headed move for me to purchase this 10-foot strip from Rezko, given that he was already under a cloud of concern. I will also acknowledge that from his perspective, he no doubt believed that by buying the piece of property next to me that he would, if not be doing me a favor, it would help strengthen our relationship."[58]

The *Chicago Sun-Times* accused Obama of downplaying the $50,000–$60,000 in donations he received from Rezko (Rezko, before his legal troubles started, had cohosted a fundraiser for Obama). The newspaper claimed the actual amount was $168,000, but came up with that figure by counting every donation to Obama from anyone ever associated with Rezko, even if there was no evidence Rezko prompted the donation.[59]

The *Chicago Sun-Times* also revealed that in 1998, Obama wrote a let-ter endorsing a low-income housing development for which Rezko was a codeveloper. As the *Sun-Times* put it, "NOT A FAVOR? As a state senator, he went to bat for now-indicted developer's deal."[60] *Chicago Tribune* colum-nist John Kass wrote, "No favors? When you transcend politics and walk on water, I guess it all depends on what your definition of favor is."[61] The common definition of a favor in this context is a political action done in exchange for donations. Rezko's lawyer reported that Rezko had not asked Obama to write the letter. Instead, Obama (along with a local state repre-sentative and an alderman) endorsed the project because it had widespread community support.[62] It's difficult to imagine any politician on the south side of Chicago who wouldn't endorse government funding for affordable housing and social services for low-income senior citizens in that area.

The *Chicago Sun-Times* reported that, in 1997, Rezko's company failed to turn the heat back on in one of his buildings, while giving $1,000 to Obama's campaign fund.[63] However, there's no evidence that Obama knew about problems with Rezko's buildings. A state senator doesn't deal with tenant complaints, and the Chicago newspapers (which benefit from real estate developers because of the advertisements they buy) never reported on Rezko's dealings as a landlord until after he was indicted.[64]

In an attempt to continue the Rezko "scandal," the *Chicago Tribune* reported that Rezko had written a letter of recommendation for the son of a business associate who received 1 of 99 internships in Obama's office in 2005, working a total of five weeks for the grand sum of $804.[65]

Despite all of these rumors about Obama and Rezko, none of the evidence indicated any wrongdoing. Conservative Republican Tom Bevan called the evidence against Obama "pretty darn weak."[66] Conor Clarke of the *New Republic* reported that Obama's real estate deal with Rezko was a "nonscandal." According to Clarke, "Journalists have followed the smoke and haven't found the fire. At that point, accusing someone of something that looks wrong stops making sense."[67] The mistake Obama made was to have any dealings at all that would give the appearance of impropriety.

Obama's Investments

Another exaggerated but damaging media story about Obama was published on the front page of the *New York Times* after Obama decided to invest $100,000 in high-risk stocks and a UBS financial advisor recommended by his friend George Haywood bought shares of AVI BioPharma and Skyterra on Obama's behalf. According to the *New York Times*, "The stock purchases raise questions about how he could unwittingly come to invest in two relatively obscure companies whose backers happen to include generous contributors to his political committees."[68] The explanation was simple: It was a blind trust fund. It was lousy financial advice (Obama lost $13,000 on the stocks), but there was nothing sinister or unethical about it.

The *New York Times* reported, "One of the companies was a biotech concern that was starting to develop a drug to treat avian flu. In March 2005, two weeks after buying about $5,000 of its shares, Mr. Obama took the lead in a legislative push for more federal spending to battle the disease."[69] But for anyone to imagine that a senator who had just signed a $1.9 million book contract would propose a bill in order to boost a $5,000 investment in a company working on an unrelated clinical treatment for avian flu is stretching indeed.

Obama noted, "At no point did I know what stocks were held. And at no point did I direct how those stocks were invested." Obama only found out about the specific investments when one of the companies mistakenly sent shareholder information to his home; then Obama promptly sold the stocks.[70]

Fox News Channel host Alan Colmes noted about the story, "It's very clear that this is not a conflict of interest." Right-wing talk show host Neal Boortz agreed, "I don't see the huge story here, either."[71]

In order to have an appearance of impropriety, there actually has to be an impropriety. It simply never happened in Obama's relationship with Rezko or in any of the other so-called scandals. Buying land at a fair market price from a real estate developer who was later indicted isn't a crime. Neither is buying stocks with a blind trust. Turning ethics into a game of six degrees of separation from misconduct makes the whole notion of a scandal meaningless and ignores the real scandals in politics where money routinely is used to buy access and power.

Media Deceptions

False cries of corruption were not the only lies spread in the media about Obama. In his book *Dreams from My Father,* Obama mentioned the experience of reading a *Life* magazine article about 25 years earlier when he was nine in Indonesia about a black man trying to lighten his skin with chemicals.[72] The *Chicago Tribune* investigated Obama's memoir and discovered that no such article was ever published by *Life* (but Obama may have been recalling a 1968 article in *Esquire* about bleaching called "A Whiter Shade of Pale" or any number of similar articles in other magazines).[73] Because of Obama's faulty recollection of the *Life* story, Richard Cohen proclaimed in the *Washington Post*, "This tendency to manipulate facts may bear watching in Obama."[74] Faux conservative talk show host Stephen Colbert had the best response to Obama's magazine memory "scandal": "If we can't trust you to remember which magazine you read in Indonesia when you were nine, how can we possibly ever trust you to protect our country?" Colbert concluded, "The whole inspiring story of your childhood is falling apart, Barack."[75]

Mike Allen of the *Politico* declared on the day of Obama's presidential campaign announcement that "Barack Obama's free ride is ending," and hard questions were asked of him such as "Why has he sometimes said his name was Arabic and other times Swahili?"[76] Colbert answered this media attack, "Just because, in fact, it is both? Oh, the truth is so convenient." As Colbert concluded (summarizing the media coverage of Obama's life), "Obama's a liar, pass it on."[77]

Obama complained about superficial and inaccurate media coverage: "The problem is not that the information's not out there, the problem is that's not what you guys have been reporting on. You've been reporting on how I look in a swimsuit."[78] This prompted more attacks from the media. Morton Kondrake complained on Fox News Channel, "Obama just went off on the press sort of gratuitously, saying 'you're not paying enough attention to what I'm saying.'"[79]

Defending Obama

However, other analysts rejected the attacks on Obama's experience. Glenn Greenwald on the website *Salon* criticized "the media-concocted uproar over Barack Obama's 'lack of substance.'"[80]

New Yorker editor Hendrik Hertzberg observed, "It would be a horrible irony if he were to be edged out on the basis of experience because it is precisely his experience that makes him such a formidable character. It's just a different kind of experience. It's not a machine-graded resume, where computer programmers would say he doesn't have A, B and C. But he has categories of experience that other people don't have."[81] *New York Times* columnist Nicholas Kristof wrote, "The conventional wisdom about Barack Obama is that he's smart and charismatic but so inexperienced that we should feel jittery about him in the Oval Office."[82] But Kristof rejected that idea: "In some respects, Mr. Obama is far more experienced than other presidential candidates."[83] Kristof noted, "His experience as an antipoverty organizer in Chicago, for example, gives him a deep grasp of a crucial twenty-first-century challenge—poverty in America—that almost all politicians lack."[84] *Chicago Tribune* columnist Eric Zorn attributed the attacks on Obama's experience to "resentment that he's not playing by the old rules—that he hasn't acquired his political capital by spending years swapping favors and grandstanding in lesser offices or by climbing the coattails of his politically powerful father."[85] By failing to follow the media's preferred path to power, Obama was establishing himself as an outsider who provoked a media backlash similar to what brought down Howard Dean in 2004.

Writer Rosa Brooks noted, "He actually has a lot more experience than people give him credit for. I think there's an overwhelming media trope that says, oh, we've got the experienced person, Hillary, on the Democratic side. And then we've got this new guy who has no experience.... He's got plenty of experience at the state legislative level; he's got plenty of experience as an organizer."[86] But the media seemed unable to see beyond the conventional definitions of political "experience."

As Kristof observed, "What sets Mr. Obama apart is the way his training has been at the grassroots rather than in the treetops. And that may be the richest kind of background of all, yielding not just experience, but also wisdom."[87]

Obama's Foreign Experience

Obama's foreign policy experience came under particular attack. Chris Matthews, the host of *Hardball* on MSNBC, proclaimed about Obama, "His lack of any foreign policy experience, national security experience could be a big minus."[88] Conservative commentator George Will declared, "He seems to me, obviously a brittle candidate. He's hostage to events because his national security experience is minimal, so it's a risk they might be willing to take."[89] But as Kristof observed, "In foreign policy as well, Mr. Obama would bring to the White House an important experience that most other candidates lack: he has actually lived abroad. He spent four years as a child in Indonesia and attended schools in the Indonesian language, which he still speaks."[90]

University of Chicago professor Richard Stern argued that "Barack Obama's boyhood years in an Indonesian school might be the equivalent of years of anthropological or ambassadorial presence in Jakarta, that his years at the racially mixed private school in Hawaii count for understanding of racial peace and strife as much or more than five years' work at the NAACP, that his years of community work on Chicago's South Side, his subsequent terms in the Illinois and United States Senate, his lecturing at the University of Chicago Law School close to such men as Cass Sunstein, Richard Posner, Douglas Baird, and Richard Epstein have taught him more about dealing with varieties of intellect than a dozen years of diplomatic intercourse in the capitals of Europe, Asia, and Africa."[91] Obama himself noted, "My experience growing up in Indonesia or having family in small villages in Africa—I think it makes me much more mindful of the importance of issues like personal security or freedom from corruption. I've witnessed it in much more direct ways than I think the average American has witnessed it."[92]

The media have denounced Obama for his alleged lack of international experience, even though his global knowledge is one of his strongest attributes. Editor in chief Mortimer Zuckerman of *U.S. News and World Report* declared Obama "virtually a freshman" in foreign affairs: "His political rivals have decades of experience with personalities and interests abroad."[93] Morton Kondracke, executive editor of *Roll Call*, attacked Obama's "inexperience with national and international affairs. A businessman from Chicago told me recently, 'Obama's a fine young man, but the presidency is not an entry-level job.'"[94] A *CBS Evening News* profile accused Obama of being "without any serious national security credentials."[95] But Obama has the best national security credential of anybody running for president: He opposed the war in Iraq from the beginning. And it means that the rest of world, disgusted at Bush's approach to national security, will have an American president who can gain respect and admiration.

Even the conservative magazine the *Economist* agreed, "Mr. Obama has already shown that he possesses something more important than expertise—judgment. His prediction about the Iraq war back in 2002 has proved strikingly prescient."[96] In 2002 Obama said, "I know that even a successful war against Iraq will require a U.S. occupation of undetermined length, at undetermined cost, with undetermined consequences. I know that an invasion of Iraq without a clear rationale and without strong international support will only fan the flames of the Middle East, and encourage the worst, rather than best, impulses of the Arab world, and strengthen the recruitment arm of al-Qaeda."[97] Everything Obama said five years ago has come true. As columnist Margaret Carlson noted about the war on Iraq, Obama "was dead-on correct about the seminal issue of our time."[98]

Obama could become the most popular U.S. president around the world in American history, especially because of his early opposition to the war with Iraq. He has a diplomat's skills at dealing with opposing forces, much more so than anyone in either party who ran for president. As senator and a member of the Senate Foreign Relations Committee, Obama made trips to Russia, Ukraine, Azerbaijan, Iraq, Kuwait, Israel, Jordan, Palestine, South Africa, Kenya, Djibouti, Ethiopia, France, Germany, England, Afghanistan, and Chad. Anyone who doubts Obama's talents at international politics need only look at his 2006 trip to Africa. Obama was greeted like a conquering hero. But he did much more than just soak up the applause. Obama probably did more than any Congressmember ever has to help fight the spread of AIDS by the simple act of publicly taking an HIV test. Nor did Obama hold his tongue about corruption in Africa, prompting an angry rebuke from the government of Kenya. Obama's trip brought extraordinary attention to Africa in the American media and created positive views of the United States from Africans.

Obama has already proven his diplomatic talents in dealing with international issues. As Kristof pointed out, "Obama's visit to Africa last year hit just the right diplomatic notes. In Kenya, he warmly greeted the president—but denounced corruption and went out of his way to visit a bold newspaper that government agents had ransacked. In South Africa, he respectfully but firmly criticized the government's unscientific bungling of the AIDS epidemic. In Chad, he visited Darfur refugees."[99]

Revenge and the Democratic Debate

Perhaps the best example of the media's bias against Obama (and rational foreign policy) came at the first Democratic debate on April 26, 2007. The debate's moderator, Brian Williams of NBC, asked, "If, God forbid, a thousand times, while we were gathered here tonight, we learned that two American cities had been hit simultaneously by terrorists, and we further learned beyond the shadow of a doubt it had been the work of al-Qaeda, how would you change the U.S. military stance overseas as a result?"

The elite media clearly wanted a militaristic reply, preferably one quoting dialogue from some action movie where the hero avenges his murdered child/girlfriend/buddy by launching a ruthless barrage upon the enemy, interspersed with witty remarks, while magically managing not to hurt any innocent bystanders. Instead, Obama responded, "Well, first thing we'd have to do is make sure that we've got an effective emergency response, something that this administration failed to do when we had a hurricane in New Orleans. And I think that we have to review how we operate in the event of not only a natural disaster, but also a terrorist attack." Obama added, "The second thing is to make sure that we've got good intelligence, A, to find out that we don't have other threats and attacks potentially out there; and B, to find out do we have any intelligence on who might have carried it out so that we can take potentially some action to dismantle that network." Obama then explained, "But what we can't do is then alienate the world community based on faulty intelligence, based on bluster and bombast." He said, "instead, the next thing we would have to do, in addition to talking to the American people, is making sure that we are talking to the international community. Because as has already been stated, we're not going to defeat terrorists on our own. We've got to strengthen our intelligence relationships with them, and they've got to feel a stake in our security by recognizing that we have mutual security interests at stake."

Later in the debate, after other candidates had given some conventional responses about killing people, Obama added: "We have genuine enemies out there that have to be hunted down; networks have to be dismantled. There is no contradiction between us intelligently using our military and, in some cases, lethal force to take out terrorists and, at the same time, building the sort of alliances and trust around the world that has been so lacking over the last six years."

Obama's response was exactly correct. If America was attacked, then any president's first response must be to help the victims and make sure that other attacks are not imminent, not to bomb somebody as quickly as possible for revenge. Even George W. Bush, after 9/11, responded in this same way. Imagine if Bush had decided after 9/11 to respond by bombing Saudi Arabia, the home of many of the hijackers as well as part of al-Qaeda's financial backing.

Syndicated conservative columnist Robert Novak summarized the establishment media's attack on "Obama's mediocre performance."[100] According to Novak, "Obama's unsatisfactory answer generated criticism in Democratic circles that he is too inexperienced and that his managers are relying on his personality and biography rather than taking vigorous positions."[101] In the mainstream media, of course, "vigorous" refers to a politician's willingness to blithely invade other countries and kill people around the world in order to appear tough.

Chicago Sun-Times reporter Lynn Sweet wrote, "Obama failed to cast himself as a forceful commander in chief."[102] MSNBC military analyst Jack Jacobs called Obama's response "pusillanimous" because "Obama responded with the usual platitudes but did not say specifically that he would retaliate against the terrorists." According to Jacobs, "While Clinton has at least a modicum of experience, one gets the impression that Obama doesn't have much to say about the national security of the Republic, at least partially because he hasn't thought very much about it."[103]

George Stephanopoulos on ABC's *This Week* on May 13, 2007, repeated the conventional wisdom about Obama's reply, "It shows that his instincts are soft." But Obama refused to back down. He repeated his answer and said, "That is what I think every American should want their president to respond." But for Stephanopoulos, the question literally was, "Can you be ruthless?" Obama politely answered, "I have the capacity, I think, to make strong decisions" and noted his opposition to the Iraq war. Obama certainly is not perfect, and his sound bites sometimes fail to express his ideas, but in this debate Obama was condemned for getting an answer exactly right by pundits who seemingly (once again) never considered the possibility that they might be wrong.

The media's influence in shaping the public perception of Obama was enhanced by the fact that so few people actually watched the debate for themselves, and thus had to rely on the mainstream media's distorted frame. What is most offensive about the media's response to Obama is the fact that America continues to suffer through a war in which the media's failure to challenge the conventional militaristic wisdom has been widely excoriated. Being in the midst of a war caused by the misdirected desire for vengeance against al-Qaeda, one might think that the media had learned to distrust the use of simplistic solutions to global problems.

Obama and the War in Iraq

Back in October 2002, Obama spoke out publicly against war with Iraq and personally challenged George W. Bush's desire to start a war: "You want a fight, President Bush? Let's fight to make sure our so-called allies in the Middle East, the Saudis and the Egyptians, stop oppressing their own people, and suppressing dissent, and tolerating corruption and inequality, and mismanaging their economies so that their youth grow up without education, without prospects, without hope, the ready recruits of terrorist cells. You want a fight, President Bush? Let's fight to wean ourselves off Middle East oil through an energy policy that doesn't simply serve the interests of Exxon and Mobil. Those are the battles that we need to fight.

Those are the battles that we willingly join. The battles against ignorance and intolerance. Corruption and greed. Poverty and despair."[104]

Despite being humiliated by their role as cheerleaders for war in Iraq, the mainstream press condemned Obama for failing to promise another hastily conceived attack based on unquestioned intelligence. In gauging the war on Iraq, the mainstream media were almost universally wrong and Obama was right on target, yet the press seemed to learn nothing from their mistakes about the importance of America being careful before leaping into battle.

The Experience of War

On October 26, 2002, an obscure Illinois state senator took time away from his reelection campaign to speak at an antiwar rally at Federal Plaza in downtown Chicago. The rally received little attention in the media and the senator's words even less coverage, but what Barack Obama said then will be remembered as one of the most powerful and prescient statements about the Bush administration and its crusade to attack Iraq: "I don't oppose all wars. What I am opposed to is a dumb war. What I am opposed to is a rash war. What I am opposed to is the cynical attempt by Richard Perle and Paul Wolfowitz and other armchair, weekend warriors in this administration to shove their own ideological agendas down our throats, irrespective of the costs in lives lost and in hardships borne. What I am opposed to is the attempt by political hacks like Karl Rove to distract us from a rise in the uninsured, a rise in the poverty rate, a drop in the median income, to distract us from corporate scandals and a stock market that has just gone through the worst month since the Great Depression. That's what I'm opposed to. A dumb war. A rash war. A war based not on reason but on passion, not on principle but on politics."[105]

In October 2002, when Obama firmly opposed a war with Iraq, he was going against public opinion. Polls showed George W. Bush with a 68 percent approval rating, and 58 percent favored a war in Iraq to dethrone Saddam Hussein. In the poll, 84 percent believed that an attack was justified if Iraq repeatedly blocked inspectors from suspected weapons sites.[106] When Obama spoke out against the Iraq war in 2002, he had every reason to believe that the war would get even more popular once it began. In January

1991, when Congress voted narrowly to authorize the Gulf War against Iraq, fewer than half of Americans favored immediate military action. But once the war began, immediately more than three-fourths of Americans expressed support for it, and George Herbert Walker Bush reached the highest approval ratings of any president in the history of polling.[107]

Obama had every reason in 2002 to believe that his opposition to the war in Iraq might cost him any hope at national office. As he later observed, "The conventional wisdom—not just in Washington, but all across the country—was that it was political suicide to get out front and oppose this thing."[108] That's why Hillary Clinton, John Edwards, and so many other Democrats voted to give George W. Bush the authorization to invade Iraq, even though they had many private doubts. Democratic consultant Robert Shrum wrote in his book, *No Excuses: Concessions of a Serial Campaigner* (2007), that he advised John Edwards to support the authorization for war in Iraq even though Edwards was "skeptical, even exercised" about supporting the war. According to Shrum, Edwards's advisers believed that he had to support the war in order to have credibility on national security issues.[109] Shrum wrote, "Every national security expert in the Democratic Party was for the war."[110]

Obama knew when he made this speech that he would be running for the U.S. Senate in 2004, and he knew that this stand might cost him an election. And for a time, it seemed that might happen. Obama recalled, "It certainly didn't look like a cost-free decision when Saddam Hussein's statue was being pulled down in Baghdad. I was in a hotel room in the middle of my Senate campaign, watching that happen, and President Bush's job approval rating was at 60 percent. Those who voted for the authorization felt pretty good."[111] But Obama never wavered from his opposition to the war.

No other major Democratic candidate for president opposed the war with Iraq before it happened. As Obama pointed out, when he spoke out against the impending war in 2002, "I was putting my viability as a U.S. Senate candidate at risk."[112] Everyone, including Hillary Clinton and John Edwards, thought they had to support the war for their political careers. In 2004 Democratic primary voters made the mistake of picking a candidate who supported the war because they thought an antiwar candidate couldn't win. The 2006 elections showed that consistently opposing the war in Iraq is by far the most beneficial political stand. Against a popular prowar Republican candidate such as John McCain in 2008, the Democrats needed a consistently antiwar contender, not someone who could have been targeted as a "flip-flopper" like Kerry was in 2004.

Unlike other Democrats such as John Edwards or Hillary Clinton, who were stuck with some variation of a John Kerryesque "I opposed the war after I supported it," Obama had a consistent position on the Iraq war. *New York Times* columnist David Brooks indicated that John McCain's stern prowar position could not be effectively challenged by Hillary Clinton: "She was there with him."[113]

But Obama's opposition to the war, although it brought him millions of votes in 2008, has a greater significance than winning the election. It indicates that he has the intelligence not to be fooled by false evidence and media manipulation, along with the independence to reject a Washington consensus. It also indicates that he has the strength of character not to sacrifice his principles for political expediency. As fellow Democratic senator Russ Feingold put it, "Those who were there and came to the judgment the Iraq war was a good idea have to answer for some concerns I have about their judgment. That was a really bad judgment. I'm prepared to support a Democrat who voted for that war, but I think the American people would prefer a president who had the judgment to see it was not a good idea."[114] Feingold indicated that he would like to see as a candidate "somebody who at least said it was a bad idea.... I would be happy if Obama or Gore ran."[115]

Bill Clinton, trying to defend his wife's (and his own) support for the war in Iraq, pointed to a *New York Times* article from July 26, 2004, in which Obama declared, "But I'm not privy to Senate intelligence reports. What would I have done? I don't know. What I know is that from my vantage point the case was not made."[116]

The week of the 2004 Democratic National Convention, Obama appeared on NBC's *Meet the Press* and was asked by Tim Russert: "How could they have been so wrong and you so right as a state legislator in Illinois and they're on the Foreign Relations and Intelligence Committees in Washington?" Obama replied, "Well, I think they have access to information that I did not have." Obama, naturally, was trying to explain the prowar votes of his party's candidates, John Edwards and John Kerry, not suggesting that they were right. As Obama noted to Russert, "I would have voted not to authorize the president, given the facts as I saw them at that time."[117] In reality, as Senator Dick Durbin later revealed, there was nothing in the secret intelligence available only to senators that would have justified war. In fact, Durbin said that senators had more skeptical information than the deceptions being fed to the American public: "The information we had in the Intelligence Committee was not the same information being given to the American people. I couldn't believe it."[118] So senators should have been more willing to oppose the war than the public, which was being deceived by the Bush administration.

Saddam and Weapons of Mass Destruction

Obama knew that Saddam Hussein was an evil man, but also understood that he posed no threat to the United States. Obama declared in his October 26, 2002, speech in Chicago, "I suffer no illusions about Saddam Hussein. He is a brutal man. A ruthless man. A man who butchers his own people to secure his own power.... The world, and the Iraqi people, would be better off without him. But I also know that Saddam poses no imminent and direct threat to the United States."[119]

Some critics of Obama might wonder, how could he possibly know that Saddam did not possess weapons of mass destruction? In fact, it's notable that Obama does not invoke the distorted propaganda term "weapons of mass destruction" in his speech. We all know that reports of weapons of mass destruction in Iraq were a lie. That's the lie about the Iraq war that we know about, the lie we saw revealed by the press after it was too late.

But the bigger lie was the use of the phrase "weapons of mass destruction" itself. "Weapons of mass destruction" is not an objective term created by journalists to describe a set of weapons. Rather, it is a brilliant propaganda term created by the military to propagate a lie. "Weapons of mass destruction" is a phrase that says nuclear, biological, and chemical weapons are going to kill enormous numbers of people; hence, mass destruction. There's only one problem: Most biological and chemical weapons are not capable of mass destruction. They may be weapons of terror, or weapons killing a few people, or weapons inconveniencing soldiers, but they can't inflict any more mass destruction than a conventional explosive, and often less.

This leads to a curious fact. In Iraq, we used some of the largest conventional weapons ever made on the planet, weapons that inflict mass destruction but are not called "weapons of mass destruction," to attack a country falsely accused of having weapons that were never capable of mass destruction but were called weapons of mass destruction. The Bush administration was using our quite rational fear of nuclear weapons, which *are* weapons of mass destruction, to justify attacking an enemy that, at most, had some old, almost useless chemical weapons that were never capable of mass destruction. The standard used to define "weapons of mass destruction" is so vague and broad that any decent college campus has a chemistry lab capable of creating such weapons.

As Obama realized back in his 2002 Chicago speech against war, Iraq was not the real danger facing the United States: "You want a fight, President Bush? Let's fight to make sure that … we vigorously enforce a nonproliferation treaty, and that former enemies and current allies like Russia safeguard and ultimately eliminate their stores of nuclear material, and that nations like Pakistan and India never use the terrible weapons already in their possession, and that the arms merchants in our own country stop feeding the countless wars that rage across the globe."

Obama's legislative work shows his understanding of the fact that conventional weapons can often be more dangerous than so-called weapons of mass destruction. The Lugar-Obama Act, passed by the Senate and signed into law in 2006, moved to help secure the hundreds of thousands of anti-aircraft missiles and similar conventional weapons that can be used to shoot down civilian airplanes and for other terrorist activities.[120] These weapons are far easier and more effective for terrorists to obtain and use than chemical gas weapons, yet the Bush administration has done next to nothing to restrict the trade in such dangerous weapons.

Ending the War in Iraq

Antiwar critics were disappointed by Obama's failure to lead a crusade against the war in Iraq once he was elected to national office. However, quixotic stands are not Obama's political specialty. He is far more interested in finding pragmatic solutions, not public grandstanding.

Obama observed, "Back in 2002, as the president was launching this war and as Congress was forced to vote on it, I was very clear in opposition precisely because I felt that once we got in, it would be very hard to extricate ourselves. That, unfortunately, has proven to be true."[121] According to

Obama in 2007, "We have a vital interest there that has to be served. And we don't want a complete collapse of Iraq. But we also have to recognize that the president's general approach and philosophy has ended up strengthening some of our most powerful enemies there."[122]

Obama could have taken a politically popular stand for immediate withdrawal from Iraq. But as in 2002, when he recognized the flaws of the war and resisted popular support for it, in 2007 he recognized the potential dangers of an immediate American withdrawal in the middle of a Iraqi civil war and expressed caution, despite the public's desire to get out completely. As Obama noted, "I think we have an obligation to be responsible about how we approach this. Nobody that I know has talked about a precipitous withdrawal."[123]

However, Obama stepped up the pressure to end the war in Iraq as the political movement against war grew. Proposing the Iraq War De-escalation Act of 2007, Obama wrote, "This plan would not only place a cap on the number of troops in Iraq and stop the escalation, it would begin a phased redeployment of U.S. forces with the goal of removing all U.S. combat forces from Iraq by March 31st, 2008."[124] Obama said, "We need to look at what options we have available to constrain the president, to hopefully right the course that we are on right now, but to do so in a way that makes sure that the troops that are on the ground have all the equipment and the resources they need to fulfill their mission and come home safely."[125]

As a practical matter, it made little difference which Democratic candidate got picked in 2008, since all of them promised to end the war in Iraq rapidly. The disaster in Iraq revealed an individual's political character. Obama's initial stand on the war in Iraq mattered because it reflected his judgment. Obama understands why wars without allies are dangerous in the long term for the United States: "The war in Iraq has been—was flawed not just in execution but in conception, and has done enormous damage to our standing around the world. I think it has weakened us in our capacity to deal with terrorism."[126]

The D.C. Experience Factor

Why do the media think that experiences only matter if you're working in Washington, D.C.? Why doesn't serving in state politics count as an experience? Why is selling out to corporate interests in D.C. considered more valuable experience than helping people as a community organizer in Chicago? Given George W. Bush's shaky understanding of the Bill of Rights, we should regard editing the *Harvard Law Review* and teaching constitutional law at the University of Chicago as the best possible experience for a presidential candidate.

The media seem to imagine that experience is like a tree falling in the woods: If the press didn't report on it, it must not have happened. Likewise, the media ignored Obama's experiences before he came to the U.S. Senate and treated him like some kind of magical creature who didn't exist before the media shined a spotlight on him.

The Bush administration has given us a kakistocracy (government by the worst people possible). The lesson to be learned from George W. Bush is that competence, not experience, matters most. The one area where George W. Bush had experience was as an executive. He had been governor of Texas and a businessman. Yet Bush turned out to be a terrible executive, hiring incompetent cronies ("heckuva job, Brownie") and failing to manage anyone properly.

It's true that Obama, like most of the candidates for president, didn't have any executive experience as a governor. But Obama's experience as a community organizer may be even better. After all, getting people to work for you when you're paying them is easy. Convincing people to organize when you can't pay them is a much harder job, and that's what Obama did on the streets of Chicago.

Although Obama lacks formal executive experience as a state governor, he has been a leader of several organizations. He ran a community organizing drive where he had to depend upon his power to inspire volunteers rather than using high-priced consultants. He ran the *Harvard Law Review,* the largest and most prestigious and perhaps most divisive law journal in the country. And he quickly established the most powerful political campaign for president in American history. After announcing his plans to seek the presidency in January 2007, Obama had to create a national campaign immediately and go up against candidates who had been planning and building their presidential campaign for years. Yet in the first quarter, despite banning contributions from lobbyists and political action committees, despite having an active campaign for only part of the period, Obama raised more money for the primary campaign from more donors than any candidate from either party had ever done. The years Obama spent in community organizing and teaching constitutional law and writing are far more valuable to becoming a great president than decades of being absorbed into the Washington establishment spent by professional politicians.

As Michelle Obama said about her husband, "We are all too familiar with those baseless claims. We've heard this spewed from the lips of rivals ... every phase of our journey, he is not experienced enough, he should wait his turn. He is too young, he is not black enough, he is not white enough ... he is too articulate. He can't raise the money. Don't be fooled by these claims because they are mere distractions. Distractions to keep us focused once again on what is not possible. Distractions that keep us mired in fear so that we are unable to focus on the real issues that are dragging us down as a nation. What we need right now is a leader. And a leader is more than a set of finite experiences."[127]

Race, Experience, and Affirmative Action

There's a veiled racism in some of the claims that Obama isn't "qualified" to be president. It's something African Americans are accustomed to hearing from less-qualified whites who think the black guy is getting the attention and the applause only because of his race.

Matt Taibbi of *Rolling Stone* observed, "There is something subtly racist (in Biden's case, not so subtle) in the way these more entrenched Democrats are riding Obama's lack of credentials and acting like the 2008 nomination is their birthright, like he hasn't 'waited his turn' or something, paid his dues."[128]

The "liberal" racist doesn't dismiss black people because they're black; he dismisses black people because they are "unqualified" or "lack credentials" or "don't have experience." In a common white "liberal" racist motif, blacks are seen as receiving undue credit or recognition because of their race, while whites merely receive what is due to them.

So, does that mean that the attacks on Obama's experience were racist? Not necessarily. The media love to attack someone new, as Howard Dean showed in 2004. And the media devour their victims in packs, preferring the safety of repeating what other pundits are saying. And, of course, the media elites certainly can't imagine that anyone could have a meaningful experience in the Midwest, since the only important work in the universe takes place in Washington, D.C.

Jake Tapper of *ABC News* reported, "Obama has few legislative accomplishments. But he's aggressively trying to turn his inexperience into an asset by arguing those with the most experience created an ugly partisan atmosphere and led the nation into the war in Iraq."[129] David Greenberg wrote in a *New York Times* blog about Obama, "There is nothing he can do to address his major shortcoming: the absence on his résumé of the kind of major achievement that qualifies a person for the White House."[130] Of course, Obama has many achievements, and it is hard to find a "major achievement" of most senators running for president. What exactly was the major achievement of Hillary Clinton, or John Edwards, or Fred Thompson? But this question was mainly asked in the establishment press about Obama, not his opponents.

There's more to experience than a certain number of years sitting around Washington. Electing a president isn't based on seniority. As Obama noted, "I think that experience question would be answered during the course of the campaign. Either at the end of that campaign, people would say, 'He looked good on paper but the guy was kind of way too green' or at the end of the campaign they say, 'He's run a really strong campaign and we think he's got something to say and we think he could lead us.'"[131]

Obama's experiences, like his approach to politics, challenge the conventional wisdom of the Washington political and media establishment. But although Obama ran as an outsider seeking to change Washington's culture of corruption, Obama is a different kind of outsider than other presidents who made similar promises, such as Bill Clinton, Jimmy Carter, and George W. Bush. He is an outsider accustomed to working with legislators from the other party, and an outsider committed to pragmatic solutions. Obama's wide range of experiences, from community organizer to lawyer to professor to politician, all indicated a president who could overcome the limitations of our political system revealed by the media attacks on his experience.

—❦—

Race and the President

Is Obama Black Enough?

I'm comfortable in my own skin.

—Barack Obama

Barack Obama has been black for a long time. Since he was born, in fact. So it must have surprised him when other African Americans, during his earlier political campaigns, began whispering about him behind his back, saying that he wasn't black enough. After Obama announced his campaign to be president, the whispers turned into op-ed columns and blogs openly declaring that Obama was too white or too African or too privileged to be considered black, while white pundits engaged in a comical attempt to define blackness.

On *60 Minutes,* Steve Kroft told Obama, "There are African Americans who don't think that you're black enough, who don't think that you have had the required experience." Obama replied, "When I'm walking down the South Side of Chicago and visiting my barbershop and playing basketball in some of these neighborhoods, those aren't questions I get asked. I also notice when I'm catching a cab. Nobody's confused about that either." Kroft even asked Obama how he "decided" to be black (certainly, no one is asking Mitt Romney how he decided to be white). Obama replied, "If you look African American in this society, you're treated as an African American, and when you're a child, in particular, that is how you begin to identify yourself. It's interesting though, that now I feel very comfortable and confident in terms of who I am and where

I stake my ground. But I notice that ... I've become a focal point for a racial debate."[1] No racist ever inquires about his target's family tree. No racist decides that a white relative or an immigrant background changes his feelings about a black person.

At the same time that his blackness was being questioned by white reporters, Obama faced the age-old question about racism in America: Can a black person be elected president of the United States? Obama might not be black enough for a few radicals, but pundits feared that he was far too black for the American public. He was caught in the racial catch-22 of American politics, where a black candidate can be simultaneously too black and too white.

The pundits weren't alone. The group most skeptical of the possibility of a black president was African Americans. And that distrust sparked much of the doubt about Barack Obama's candidacy. The concerns about Obama reached the point that civil rights veteran Roger Wilkins introduced Obama at one speech by declaring, "I want to tell you a secret from me to you. This man is black enough. I guarantee you."[2]

The Whiteness of Barack Obama

The issue of Barack Obama's blackness, in a political sense, has been questioned for many years. Salim Muwakkil noted in the *Progressive*, "Early in his political career, Obama faced considerable opposition from Chicago's substantial black nationalist community. For some, his Harvard pedigree and verbal eloquence cast suspicion on his degree of 'blackness.' Members of this community wondered if Obama felt as connected to the folks in the 'hood' as he did to the educated elite with whom he spent so much of his time."[3]

In 2000, when Obama ran for Congress against incumbent Bobby Rush, a former Black Panther, the *Chicago Reader* reported about Obama, "His enemies also say he's too white and too bright." One black leader, Lu Palmer, declared about Obama in 2000, "If you so impress white folks at these elite institutions, and if they name you head of these elite institutions, the *Harvard Law Review,* that makes one suspect."[4] The *Chicago Reader* even reported, "There are whispers that Obama is being funded by a 'Hyde Park mafia,' a cabal of University of Chicago types, and that there's an 'Obama Project' masterminded by whites who want to push him up the political ladder."[5]

Obama learned the danger of being unable to win black votes in that campaign. As Obama said about the race against Rush, "He didn't just defeat me, he spanked me."[6] Rush explained his victory over Obama this way: "I'm a race politician, and he's not."[7] Rush held some resentment against Obama and endorsed one of his white opponents in the 2004 Democratic Senate primary. But Rush endorsed Obama for president, and Rush noted, "Look, man, Moses was able to defeat the pharaoh because Moses knew the castle."[8] Rush doesn't see Obama as a "race politician," but as something potentially more powerful: an African American who can work within the white establishment.

In 2004, black Republican Alan Keyes was even more explicit in playing the blackness card when he accused Obama of "wrongly claiming an African American heritage." Keyes declared, "My ancestors toiled in slavery in this country." He added, "My consciousness, who I am as a person, has been shaped by my struggle, deeply emotional and deeply painful, with the reality of that heritage."[9] Obama rejected this idea, declaring that he didn't have "a lot of patience with identity politics, whether it's coming from the right or the left." He denounced "those self-appointed arbiters of African American culture who declare who is and isn't 'black enough.'"[10]

By the time Obama ran for the U.S. Senate, Muwakkil reported, "Obama now enjoys widespread support among Chicago's black nationalists. And he didn't do it by pandering to their particular issues or by warping his platform to fit their concerns. He did it by persuading them of his integrity."[11]

But it was when Obama announced his plans to run for president that the doubts about his race became a major media story. And it was the press that fueled this debate about Obama's race. On *NBC Nightly News,* reporter Rob Allen proclaimed, "Obama's rise to stardom inspires tremendous pride, but the mainstream's embrace and Obama's ties to mostly white institutions like Harvard raise questions."[12]

The Blackness Police

In this battle of who is "black" and who gets to have quotation marks around their blackness, the issues of racial purity are particularly strange.

For African Americans, who come from so many different backgrounds, the notion of a singular experience defining "blackness" seems bizarre. As Obama noted, "My view has always been that I'm African American. African Americans by definition, we're a hybrid people. One of the things I loved about my mother was not only did she not feel rejected by me defining myself as an African American, but she recognized that I was a black man in the United States and my experiences were going to be different than hers."[13] For Obama, race is not an exclusionary choice, but a way to embrace a tradition without forsaking other traditions and experiences. All definitions of race will seem irrational at some level, because race is a fundamentally irrational idea. Race is an imaginary concept with very real consequences.

Obama has gone from accusations of "not black enough" to "not black at all." Debra Dickerson, the author of *The End of Blackness,* wrote in a *Salon* column, "Barack Obama would be the great black hope in the next presidential race, if he were actually black."[14] According to Dickerson, "'Black,' in our political and social reality, means those descended from West African slaves. Voluntary immigrants of African descent (even those descended from West Indian slaves) are just that, voluntary immigrants of African descent with markedly different outlooks on the role of race in their lives and in politics."[15] Dickerson says Obama should be called "African-American," not black.

But it's absurd to imagine that the child of millionaires living in a lavish house is "black" because of his slave ancestry, while the identical-looking impoverished child of an African immigrant is not black, despite suffering racism, due to the lack of this background. In this twisted analysis, a guy who looks black, who grew up black in predominantly white schools, who has a black wife and a black family, who attends a black church and lives in a substantially black neighborhood, who was a politician representing a black district, and who worked as a community organizer in black areas of Chicago, isn't really black.

Dickerson appeared on the *Colbert Report* to explain her theory about Obama to Stephen Colbert, who seemed equally befuddled by the theory as both himself and the conservative character he plays. Colbert asked, "If he's not black, why doesn't he just run as a white guy? Because we know black people will vote for white people and white people will vote for white people. But we're not sure white people will vote for black people." Colbert declared, "I am disappointed in this. Because I was really looking forward to voting for a black guy—I was really hoping to leave the voting booth and say, hey I voted for a black guy." As Colbert put it, "If you hadn't told me he wasn't black, I would have thought that I was supporting a black person. And then, I would have been supporting all black people." Colbert concluded, "So it sounds to me like you are judging blackness not on the color of someone's skin but on the content of their character, which I think realized Dr. King's dream in a very special way." Colbert suggested that Obama could get some black "street cred" by experiencing slavery as "Al Sharpton's slave."[16]

It's tempting to dismiss Dickerson as another pseudointellectual playing a dispiriting game of "blacker than thou." But she had a point when she observed, "The swooning from white people is a paroxysm of self-congratulation."[17] However, Dickerson noted, "I've got nothing but love for the brother, but we don't have anything in common."[18] Dickerson generously declared, "I'm willing to adopt him. He married black. He acts black. But there's a lot of distance between black Africans and African Americans."[19] There are differences between black people of various backgrounds. But it's the similarity of treatment under racism that defines them.

The Black Critics of Obama

Writer Stanley Crouch argued in a column titled "What Obama Isn't: Black Like Me" that Obama is not really black because of his ancestry: "Obama did not—does not—share a heritage with the majority of black Americans, who are descendants of plantation slaves."[20] To claim that blackness depends on a slave history is like saying whites can't be racist unless they have a family history of owning slaves.

According to Crouch, "While he has experienced some light versions of typical racial stereotypes, he cannot claim those problems as his own—nor has he lived the life of a black American."[21] Crouch seems to think there is only one stereotypical life of a black American. Certainly, Obama believes himself to be a black American. The idea that black people who have a white parent are not "real" black people seems strange.

According to NPR's Juan Williams, "There are widespread questions about whether this son of a white American mother and a black Kenyan father really understands the black American experience."[22] Pollster Gerald Goldhaber noted, "Some blacks are saying, 'This guy is not one of us,' that he has not experienced discrimination or poverty."[23] This notion is particularly strange because Obama has written an entire book detailing his struggles with race. Obama noted, "I can recite the usual litany of petty slights" caused by racism, such as "white couples who toss me their car keys as I stand outside a restaurant waiting for the valet."[24] He wrote, "I know what it's like to have people tell me I can't do something because of my color, and I know the bitter swill of swallowed-back anger."[25]

The idea that Obama never experienced poverty is also odd considering that Obama wrote about the extreme poverty he saw as a child in Indonesia, where his family didn't have a refrigerator but he was considered well-off because he had shoes. Then Obama chose to work with the most powerless people in Chicago and struggled to survive on a community organizer's salary despite large student loan debts.

The Black President and the Black Critics

Not all of the black critics of Obama were worried about his racial background. Al Sharpton warned, "Just because you are our color doesn't make you our kind."[26] According to Sharpton, "It's not about his genealogy, it's about his policies.... What is it that you're going to represent?"[27] According to Bruce Dixon of *Black Agenda Report,* "To hear the mainstream media, black dissatisfaction with Senator Obama is all about his black African father, his white American mother, his light complexion and his Columbia and Harvard Law degrees." Dixon claimed, "This is a racist calumny and slur of the first magnitude against all of black America. Our people have never rejected leading figures because of light complexions, immigrant parents or advanced degrees."[28] For Dixon, the real problem with Obama was his politics, not his parentage: "In many quarters of black America there are sane, solid and sensible reasons for black voters to question whether Barack Obama will represent them at all. Many remember that his first act as a U.S. Senator was to refuse to stand with the Congressional Black Caucus and California Senator Barbara Boxer in opposition to Ohio's nullification of hundreds of thousands of black votes."[29] Dixon recalled that at Obama's 2004 victory party for winning the Democratic primary, "The white and black people there that night imagined that they had elected another Paul Wellstone or a Harold Washington, a senator who would bring their concerns to the halls of power, whether the powerful were ready to hear them or not. One wonders what they think today."[30]

But Dixon misunderstands Obama's approach to politics. Obama has never been the traditional black politician who stands in front of a camera and tries to generate media attention to social problems to shame politicians into acting. He has always been a pragmatic progressive. Although Obama has worked to ensure voting rights, he didn't challenge George W. Bush's 2004 election because he knew it would be a futile, purely symbolic cause with no chance of success, a move that would alienate his colleagues without actually accomplishing anything.

Princeton professor Cornel West, one of the leading African American public intellectuals, denounced Obama for announcing his presidential plans on February 10, 2007, before a mostly white crowd in Springfield, Illinois, thereby missing Tavis Smiley's "State of the Black Union" conference. West claimed that this showed how Obama "speaks to white folks and holds us at arm's length."[31] Harry Belafonte declared, "Careful about Barack Obama, because we don't know what he's truly about."[32]

Obama and Poverty

The rhetoric included suggestions that other candidates were "blacker" than Obama because of their attention to poverty. PBS talk show host Tavis Smiley declared, "The black vote is not as monolithic as it used to be."[33] He added, "Barack Obama will not get my vote just because he's black" and noted that "John Edwards has been the most courageous person so far in talking about poverty."[34] Dixon wrote that Representative Dennis Kucinich (D-Ohio) was the "blackest candidate in the ring" because of his voting record.[35]

Eddie Read, chair of the Black Independent Political Organization in Chicago, declared, "I would not embrace Obama because I know that nothing's going to happen out of it. He doesn't belong to us."[36] According to Read, "He would not be the black president. He would be the multicultural president. A black president would fight for black economic and political power."[37]

Like most African Americans (and most whites, for that matter), Obama doesn't come from a wealthy and politically influential family. Illinois state senate president Emil Jones observed, "He doesn't share the same kind of background as most African Americans, but he's addressed those issues that related to underprivileged communities throughout Illinois."[38] Vanderbilt professor Carol Swain noted, "He has a track record for being concerned about people who are poor, and it seems to be genuine."[39]

When Obama graduated from Harvard Law School, he could have easily gotten a Supreme Court clerkship or taken one of the hundreds of offers from corporate law firms and become incredibly rich, ignoring the problems of less affluent African Americans. Instead, he returned to Chicago and joined Miner Barnhill & Galland, a civil rights firm. Obama filed suits on behalf of victims of discrimination, helped community organizers, worked for whistleblowers exposing corruption, and aided black voters seeking better political representation. Obama helped the Association of Community Organizations for Reform Now (ACORN) sue the state of Illinois to make sure that it implemented a federal law to help the poor register to vote.[40]

As columnist Mary Mitchell wrote, "If working as an organizer in a place like Altgeld Garden to empower residents to fight against environmental pollution and lead poisoning, moving on to the Illinois General Assembly and supporting legislation that targeted racial profiling and wrongful convictions, and pushing for the earned income credit wasn't enough to prove his commitment to African Americans, platitudes meant to assuage those voters won't be enough to win this race."[41] Obama could have abandoned his "blackness." Of course, at some level Obama could never escape the fact that he has black skin. But he could have chosen to avoid African Americans, to never visit Africa, to have a white family, to never work on helping African Americans in Chicago, to be a black politician who appeals to white voters. Barack Obama could have been a star in the Republican Party. Obama's blackness, like his religion, is all the more remarkable because it is something he chose to embrace.

The problem Obama faces in reaching African American voters is similar to what he encounters with progressive voters: high expectations. Michael Fauntroy, who wrote *Republicans and the Black Vote*, noted, "Many times, black Americans hold other blacks to a litmus test that's much higher than they would anyone else."[42] If Obama were a white candidate with such a strong record as a civil rights lawyer and legislator serving

African Americans, he would get very strong support. But the fact that he's black raises the bar for him among some African American pundits and voters.

Obama's Supporters

Debating Obama's blackness became a popular media sport. Filmmaker John Ridley observed "the bizarre spectacle of left-leaning blacks cannibalizing Barack Obama."[43] But it wasn't just the left wing going after Obama's moderate views. A much broader section of the black community expressed doubts about Obama, often based on the misinformed rumors or media reports about race.

As Cliff Kelly, the host of a talk show on a black radio station in Chicago, observed, "Some of my callers are suggesting that maybe he's not black enough. My comment is 'Well, who is?'"[44] But much of the controversy over Obama's race seemed to be more media invention than a serious discussion. Speaking with people at historically black Claflin University, *Washington Post* writer Eugene Robinson reported, "I wasn't able to find anyone willing to qualify Obama's blackness with an asterisk."[45]

Chicago journalist Laura Washington noted, "Some of the black nationalists are whispering that 'Barack is not black enough.' He's of mixed race, he hangs out in Hyde Park, and is a darling of white progressives."[46] But *In These Times* senior editor Salim Muwakkil noted that "it's perverse for black nationalists to reject the son of a Kenyan for not being black enough."[47] Law professor and *Nation* columnist Patricia Williams observed, "It is surely ironic that Obama—one of the very few Americans of any stripe who has actual first-degree relatives in Africa—is being figured in some quarters as an imposter of African American-ness."[48] The debate over Obama's "blackness" represented an odd kind of American nationalism in sharp contrast to the 1960s-style black nationalism that regarded African roots as something to celebrate.

Obama had many supporters who rejected the racial politics wielded against him. Carol Swain, a political scientist at Vanderbilt University, noted, "Barack Obama says he's black. He's married to a black woman and he has black children. That makes him black enough for me and, I believe, most of the people."[49] As Michael Eric Dyson, author of *Debating Race*, put it: "He's got a black wife, black family, he goes to a black church, he's lived in the black community on the South Side, he's pretty black to me."[50] Kimberly Jade Norwood, a professor of law and African and African American Studies at Washington University, wrote sarcastically about Obama's critics, "It doesn't matter to these writers that Senator Obama actually has black African blood running through his veins. It does not matter that he identifies with being black. It doesn't matter that he is married to a black woman. It does not matter that he attends a black church. It does not matter that he lives a culturally black experience. It does not matter that he can't catch a cab in New York City to save his black ass. It does not matter that he is a proud and vocal champion for change in policies and practices that negatively impact black America. None of that matters! Apparently the test for blackness now is being a descendant of West African slaves and only West African slaves."[51]

Other critics questioned whether the media concerns about Obama's blackness were real at all. Eugene Robinson of the *Washington Post* noted that after Obama spoke to an overwhelmingly black crowd in Orangeburg, South Carolina, "When I talked to people about the so-called issue, I heard bemusement, I did not hear anybody thinking that somehow he was not authentically black. And they wondered what everybody was talking about." According to Robinson, "The experience of life as a black man in America is one that he has had.... I don't think this is an issue for him, really, in the black community."[52] Melinda Chateauvert, an assistant professor of African American studies at the University of Maryland, noted, "A lot of my students are multicultural and don't have the problem with Barack Obama that you hear on the other levels, in the barbershop discussions."[53] University of Illinois professor Sundiata Cha-Jua said, "To talk about Obama as being somehow not African American is an attempt to foment a divisive conversation in the African American community.... It's completely bogus."[54]

Some commentators expressed anger at black leaders who failed to embrace the Obama candidacy. Princeton professor Melissa Harris-Lacewell wrote, "It is time for black political leadership to throw their full support behind Barack Obama. No more public questioning of his racial identity. No more accusations that he is disingenuous."[55] Roland Martin, editor of the black newspaper the *Chicago Defender,* said, "We have folks playing coy, whispering behind the scenes, questioning his blackness, and in some cases, complete silence. This is nothing more than black-on-black hate at its best."[56]

Michelle Obama and Blackness

Michelle Obama responded to the question of whether her husband was "black enough" this way: "I grew up on the South Side of Chicago. I'm black. My parents are black, went to public schools. There will be people who will say that about me, that I'm not black enough.... It has nothing to do with Barack. It has everything to do with the challenges of what race means in this country. I've suffered with the whole anti-intellectual thing. There might be some people who would say, 'You went to Princeton and Harvard. You speak properly.' I heard that growing up, 'You talk like a white girl.' There isn't one black person who doesn't understand that dynamic. But I've grown up to know that it doesn't have anything to do with me." According to her, "The one thing I do know is that that question isn't seeping into the core of the black community."[57]

Michelle Obama has been thinking about the meaning of race and success in a white-dominated world for a long time. Her 1985 undergraduate thesis, "Princeton-Educated Blacks and the Black Community," revealed a sense of racial alienation and searching similar to what Barack Obama wrote about in *Dreams from My Father*. In her thesis, Obama (then Michelle LaVaughn Robinson) wrote: "My experiences at Princeton have made me far more aware of my 'Blackness' than ever before. I have found that at Princeton no matter how liberal and open-minded some of my White professors and classmates try to be toward me, I sometimes feel like a visitor on campus; as if I really don't belong."[58] She felt that "Regardless of the circumstances under which I interact with whites at Princeton, it often seems as if, to them, I will always be black first and a student second."[59] In her thesis, Michelle Obama surveyed black Princeton alumni. She wrote, "I wondered whether or not my education at Princeton would affect my identification with the black community. I hoped that these findings would help me conclude that despite the high degree of identification with whites as a result of the educational and occupational path that black Princeton alumni follow, the alumni would still maintain a certain level of identification with the black community. However, these findings do not support this possibility."[60]

Michelle Obama wrote that she began attending Princeton determined to "utilize all of my present and future resources to benefit" the black community "first and foremost."[61] But she worried about "further integration and/or assimilation into a white cultural and social structure that will only allow me to remain on the periphery of society; never becoming a full participant."[62] She felt that Princeton "has instilled within me certain conservative values," to seek "a prestigious graduate or professional school or a high-paying position in a successful corporation."[63]

Michelle Obama seemed headed down that path. She attended Harvard Law School and then joined a law firm in Chicago. But then, leaving behind corporate law firms, she took a job as an assistant in Mayor Richard Daley's office. In 1993, she became the founding executive director of the Chicago office of Public Allies, part of the AmeriCorps project started by Bill Clinton. In 1996, she took a job as director of the University of Chicago's Community Service Center.[64]

When I interviewed Michelle Obama a decade ago in that post, she seemed cautious about her role with this overwhelmingly white university. After all, the University of Chicago was an institution that in the 1940s and 1950s had enforced racial covenants, secretly supported segregationist neighborhood groups, and even contemplated moving the entire university to California in order to escape the black people moving into Hyde Park. But although Michelle Obama knew about the deep alienation between the University of Chicago and the black community on Chicago's South Side, she saw it as an institution that could be changed for the better, and her job was to bridge the two communities.

In 2002, Michelle Obama became the executive director of community affairs for the University of Chicago Hospitals, a position that in 2005 was elevated to a vice presidential post supervising 17 staffers and 1,000 volunteers.[65] Although all of these jobs involved working for predominantly white organizations (after all, that's where the jobs are), Michelle Obama always took positions that involved helping the black community in Chicago benefit from these wealthy white institutions.

Barack Obama had a similar experience of alienation and fear of betraying the black community. In *Dreams from My Father,* he revealed that as a student at Occidental College he worried about "being mistaken for a sellout." According to Obama, "It remained necessary to prove which side you were on, to show your loyalty to the black masses."[66]

The question of race has been central to the Obamas' relationship. Their first date was to see Spike Lee's movie *Do the Right Thing*.[67] Michelle reported that one of the things that attracted her to Barack was his commitment to the black community. According to University of Pennsylvania professor Michael Eric Dyson, Michelle "brings a sturdy insistence on not forgetting the difficulties of struggling black people" and serves as Barack's "built-in keep-it-real factor" and his "traveling authenticity."[68]

But if Michelle Obama helps bring "authenticity" to her husband, she is also trying to question the stereotypes of black authenticity. As she noted, "One of the things I hope happens through our involvement in this campaign is that this country and this world sees yet another image of what it means to be black. And it's not an unusual image. It's just not the one you see all the time. Everybody in the black community knows that Barack and I are more closely aligned with what and who the black community is."[69]

Obama on Affirmative Action

Traditional support for affirmative action has promoted a stereotype of black oppression and suggested that all African Americans come from a background of deprivation and discrimination that must be compensated for in college admissions.

On average, this is true: The average African American is forced to attend inferior public schools under much more difficult conditions than the average white person, and as a result affirmative action is justified. But by relying on stereotypes rather than individual realities, colleges distort the purpose of affirmative action. Instead of taking a chance on students who have had to struggle the most to achieve, colleges prefer to admit the most privileged African Americans from wealthy suburbs who are the most likely to succeed and the most acclimated to a predominantly white environment.

Obama was viewed with suspicion by some supporters of affirmative action because he suggested that his daughters should not benefit from affirmative action due to the fact that they have had a privileged upbringing. Obama declared his daughters "should probably be treated by any admissions officer as folks who are pretty advantaged."[70] Obama noted, "I think that we should take into account white kids who have been disadvantaged and have grown up in poverty and shown themselves to have what it takes to succeed."

Jonathan Chait of the *New Republic* praised Obama for "transforming affirmative action into a program of race-blind economic uplift."[71] But Obama is not race blind, and neither is his ideal of affirmative action, which would combine both race-based and class-based preferences. Obama declared, "I don't think those concepts are mutually exclusive. I think what we can say is that in our society race and class still intersect, that there are a lot of African American kids who are still struggling, that even those who are in the middle class may be first generation as opposed to fifth or sixth generation college attendees, and that we all have an interest in bringing as many people together to help build this country."[72]

Race-based affirmative action needs to continue because racial oppression still exists, but Obama sees class-based affirmative action as a way to make the system more just and more politically viable. Obama noted, "I would like to think that if we make good decisions and we invest in early childhood education, improved K through 12, if we have done what needs to be done to ensure that kids who are qualified to go to college can afford it, that affirmative action becomes a diminishing tool for us to achieve racial equality in this society."[73] The key word in what Obama said is "if." If children of all races are given the tools to achieve, if they are provided with an opportunity to afford college, then affirmative action ceases to be necessary. This is not a repudiation of affirmative action, but a recognition that it has always been conditional. Obama does not see affirmative action as some kind of racial spoils system that must be permanently defended; instead, it is a small Band-Aid for ills of a society filled with racial inequality. Obama has rejected the idea of "color-blindness as a means to deny the structural inequalities" in society.[74]

Obama's daughters are certain to be beneficiaries of affirmative action in college admissions, but not because of their race. Instead, Obama's kids (as the children of Columbia, Princeton, and Harvard alums) will receive the "legacy preference" given to the most privileged children of Ivy League graduates.[75] The Obama girls will also receive the kind of privilege given to children of celebrity politicians, the same preference that enabled an underqualified George W. Bush to enter Yale and Harvard. Obama's children shouldn't receive a special advantage in college admissions, not because affirmative action is wrong, but because it is right.

Poverty and Debt

Obama does not come from a background of money and privilege. In Indonesia, Obama saw the "desperation" of poor families during floods who "scrambled to rescue their goats and their hens even as chunks of their huts washed away."[76] Obama attended public school because his parents couldn't afford the private schools. Obama was better dressed than the other kids, because he had shoes and socks, which were considered luxuries for many children.[77]

Obama's background stands in sharp contrast to that of George W. Bush, who was born into a life of advantage in a political family, and who never had to worry about getting into college, because his entrance into Yale was assured by the "legacy" preference for the son of a alumnus. He never had to worry about paying off college loans, because his family was rich. He never had to worry about being drafted to fight in Vietnam. He never had to worry about getting a job, because family connections brought him endless opportunities. He never had to worry about working his way up through the political system by laboring in the state legislature, because his name gave him a free ride. Yet despite all of his privileges, Bush never gave back to the community. Bush's father was famous for calling upon Americans to volunteer and be part of a "thousand points of light," but George W. Bush was never even a dim bulb.

Barack Obama's reaction was the opposite. His family was not famous, and yet when he did get some advantages, receiving a scholarship to a private school in Hawaii and then admission to Columbia University as a transfer student, Obama reacted with a sense of obligation to others. Obama could have become a corporate lawyer or a personal injury lawyer. Instead, Obama chose the low-paying area of public interest law. As Obama noted, "At every juncture of my life, I could have taken the path of least resistance but much higher pay. Being the president of the *Harvard Law Review* is a big deal. The typical path for someone like myself is to clerk for the Supreme Court, and then basically you have your pick of any law firm in the country."[78]

Obama's career choice was a major financial sacrifice. As Obama noted, "For the first ten years after my wife and I graduated from law school, our debt from tuition was bigger than our mortgage. It was extraordinarily difficult to climb out from under that."[79] After Obama's failed 2000 race for Congress, his campaign was $20,000 in debt, and it took him two years to scramble out of these debts.[80] This level of debt almost caused Obama to give up on politics in order to make more money as a full-time lawyer. As Michelle Obama said, "No one could have predicted that the next United States senator from the state of Illinois would have been a skinny guy with no money and a funny name."[81] Of course, Obama is not poor; no poor person wins a U.S. Senate seat. But unlike most of his colleagues in the Senate, he has experienced poverty and debt, and consequently he has spent much of his working life helping the impoverished and disadvantaged.

The African American Immigrant

Some of the black community's failure to embrace Obama stems from ignorance. A barber told the *New York Times,* "When you think of a president, you think of an American. We've been taught that a president should come from right here, born, raised, bred, fed in America. To go outside and bring somebody in from another nationality, now that doesn't feel right to some people."[82]

UCLA professor Peter Hammond noted, "They may feel it's as if he's taking advantage of being black without paying his dues. Black folks might be saying, 'Here's this guy who is presenting himself as a brother, but he was raised in Indonesia.'"[83] Ronald Walters, head of the African American Leadership Institute at the University of Maryland, said about Obama: "He's going to have to win over some African Americans. They have a right to be somewhat suspicious of people who come into the country and don't share their experience."[84] According to Walters, when African Americans hear about Obama, "they hear Indonesia, Kenya, Hawaii—everything but Alabama."[85]

Of course, Obama was born in this country, and he shares the experience of being treated as an African American throughout his life. University of Illinois professor Sundiata Cha-Jua observed, "His parentage is not unusual in the African American community." (About 10 percent of the U.S. black population is immigrants or the children of immigrants from Africa or the West Indies.)[86] Melissa Harris-Lacewell of Princeton University noted, "An awful lot of black Americans are actually recent immigrants from Africa, recent immigrants from the West Indies or are people of multiracial heritage like Barack Obama."[87] Gwen Ifill, host of the PBS show *Washington Week in Review*, observed, "People seem to set up this really interesting test for Barack Obama of blackness, which I have found absent in any other dialogue involving people who clearly appear to identify and work in the black community, and I'm not quite certain where it comes from." As the daughter of West Indian immigrants, Ifill explained that she didn't understand how "that makes me less black."[88]

Black anti-immigrant bigotry is just as wrong as white anti-immigrant bigotry. It's absurd to claim that black immigrants don't face any discrimination today because they don't have a history of slavery. Since when do racist whites ask for a family tree before they discriminate? How many Ku Klux Klan members say to themselves, "I was going to hate that black guy, but then I found out he was from Africa"?

There is not one single black experience from which all other African Americans must be denigrated as deviations. The particular combination of Obama's life may be relatively unusual—an African parent, a multiracial family background, brought up by his extended family during multiple divorces, growing up overseas and in Hawaii, feeling isolated as a black minority—but many of these elements of Obama's life are fairly common among African Americans (and people of all races).

New York Times editorial writer Brent Staples declared, "At bottom, the hue and cry over Barack Obama's identity stems from a failure by black traditionalists to recognize multiracial versions of themselves. Soon enough, perhaps by year's end, however, the Obama story, which seems so exotic to so many people now, will have found its place among all the other stories of the sprawling black diaspora."[89] By challenging the singular story of blackness, Obama is enabling the media and many black pundits to recognize the diversity within the black community. When Obama appeals to racial and political unity rather than division, it is because he recognizes from personal experience that the diversity within different races can exceed the differences between them.

Obama and the Civil Rights Movement

Obama's background also proved controversial because he is part of a younger generation of black activists and politicians. Tucker Carlson noted,

"One of the reasons I like Barack Obama is I think his election, or at least nomination as the candidate, would effect a transformation in black politics, which really is, in my view, caught in 1968, in the Black Power movement, in the Civil Rights movement.... Barack Obama is not a product of the Civil Rights movement. He's a product of a much broader experience than that. Black politics will never be the same after his running for president."[90]

Obama is not a "post–Civil Rights" politician; he is a "because of Civil Rights" politician. As Donna Brazile observed, "Now we have a politician that's coming to us not from the Civil Rights chapter but the chapter that Martin Luther King wanted us to get to."[91] Obama was far too young to ever march in the Civil Rights movement of the 1960s, but he has been directly involved in civil rights ever since then. He was a community organizer helping black folks on the South Side of Chicago fight for their civil rights. After finishing law school, Obama became a civil rights lawyer and taught civil rights law at the University of Chicago. As a state legislator, Obama led efforts to pass legislation to stop racial profiling by police and similar civil rights legislation. Obama could have pursued a lucrative law practice and then used his fortune to gain a political seat. Instead, Obama chose to return to Chicago and serve the people he had helped before. He joined a small civil rights law firm in Chicago rather than pursue the hundreds of opportunities to get rich.

Michael Fauntroy, author of *Republicans and the Black Vote*, argued, "Obama's candidacy, for all its promise, will prove to be an uncomfortable test for African Americans because it will force blacks to accept someone who is so different from the Civil Rights–based black politics to which they are so accustomed."[92] DePaul professor and *Chicago Sun-Times* columnist Laura Washington argued, "The black political establishment will see Obama as one thing only—a threat. A threat that undermines and erodes their political clout."[93]

Obama was attacked when he said, "Don't tell me I don't have a claim on Selma" because his biracial parents had met before the pivotal March 7, 1965, march. But Obama was calling attention to his claim on the whole Civil Rights movement and to how powerfully it had influenced his beliefs even though he was too young to witness it personally.

Obama's idea of civil rights isn't showing up to the controversy du jour and making sure there's a camera on him. Obama's fight for civil rights involves organizing black communities and passing legislation and enforcing the law to ensure equal rights. As Princeton professor Melissa Harris-Lacewell noted, "Barack helped us to remember that the Civil Rights struggle was not and is not a parochial, domestic effort. It was a broad, international human rights struggle."[94]

Just as Obama represents a new generation of progressive politicians who aim to bridge political divisions and pursue progressive causes by consensus, Obama also represents a new kind of black politician who seeks to unite people of all races in the pursuit of human rights. Obama has noted, "This is something the outside world imposes on our community, this notion that there is one black leader. My whole thing is, we have got a collective leadership.... That comforts me because that tells me that I don't have to carry this all on my shoulders."[95]

The Conservative Race

Some of the strangest ideas about Obama and race came from right-wingers. Steve Sailer, founder of the Human Biodiversity Institute (a far-right group that promotes the idea of genetic racial differences in intelligence), proclaimed, "Obama is a 'wigger.' He's a remarkably exotic variety of the faux African American, but a wigger nonetheless."[96] According to Sailer, Obama is too genetically different to be called African American: "Even genetically, Obama, whose East African descent is apparent in his unusual features, has only a distant relationship to the West Africans who are the ancestors of almost all African Americans."[97] Sailer concluded, "The roots of racial differences in America stretch far back into the history and prehistory of other continents."[98]

For Sailer, race is an eternal genetic difference that can never disappear.[99] But there is another kind of racism that prevails when color-blindness is simply another kind of blindness. This is the kind of racism that says there is no racism, that any problems in the black community are the product of its own failings (or government aid), and that everything would be fine if only we stopped talking about racism. Seeing racism is the first step to ending racism, and it is the only first step possible. Racism does not disappear when it is denied; it simply becomes more entrenched.

Ironically, conservatives like Sailer see liberals like Obama as racist against whites. According to Sailer, "He tries to turn himself into an authentic angry black man … nursing a pervasive sense of grievance and animosity against his mother's race." Sailer wondered, "Why was Obama so insistent upon rejecting the white race?"[100]

For some on the right, Obama's perceived "whiteness" is what is valued about him. Conservative *Washington Times* columnist Suzanne Fields declared, "He's no Charlie Rangel or Jesse Jackson; it's easy to listen to him and never think of his color. He may suffer from lack of experience, but not his race."[101]

For conservatives, Obama's race has become a convenient excuse for dismissing his ideas and treating him as some kind of affirmative action baby. John McWhorter of the Manhattan Institute claimed that "the reason that he's considered such a big deal is simply because he's black."[102] As Steve Sailer put it, "White people love highly accomplished blacks who speak with white accents. He wouldn't be a serious candidate for president at age 45 if he weren't part black."[103] Edward Blum of the American Enterprise Institute claimed, "One of the reasons Americans are enthralled with him is precisely because he is black and for the unique American melting pot story of his heritage. Without a doubt, most Americans would love to see a black win the presidency, thus concluding the long and difficult struggle of blacks to achieve political representation and power. For white Americans, such an outcome would have the tacit effect of exonerating them of the country's historical racial failures."[104]

Racism is still a powerful part of the Republican Party. At the most important national conference of conservatives in 2007, Ann Coulter declared that Bill Clinton deserved to be called the first black president because he is "half-white and half-trash."[105] Her bigoted comment linking black people with "trash" was greeted with cheers and laughter by 6,000 top advocates in the conservative movement.

Racial insults are commonplace on the right. Rush Limbaugh and conservative talk show hosts on KSFO called Obama a "Halfrican."[106] Limbaugh declared, "You are not African American, Mr. Obama. You do not share the heritage of this country that African American implies."[107] Rush Limbaugh further proclaimed, "So are we to conclude here that he didn't define himself as black, that the way he looks does? Well, if you didn't decide it, then how did it happen? … Well, renounce it, then! If it's not something you want to be, if you didn't decide it, renounce it, become white! … If you don't like it, you can switch. Well, that's the way I see it.

He's got 50-50 in there. Say, 'No, I'm white.'"[108] Limbaugh also repeatedly played a parody song called "Barack the Magic Negro" (to the tune of "Puff the Magic Dragon"), featuring a bad Al Sharpton imitator singing about Obama as a "magic Negro" (a term used by a *Los Angeles Times* op-ed writer) and declaring, "He's black, but not authentically."[109]

Glenn Beck, a conservative talk show host hired away from *CNN Headline News* to work on the Fox News Channel, declared on his February 12, 2007, radio show about Obama: "He's very white." According to Beck, "For whites, I think he's colorless. You don't notice that he is black. So he might as well be white."[110] According to this perspective, if Obama is smart and thoughtful and appealing, he "might as well be white."

The conservative attack on Obama's race even inspired a cartoon for the *Onion* parody newspaper in which a Democratic donkey is calling to ask, "Obama? Some conservatives say you're not really black ... but you are, right?" Obama is shown on the other end of the line, wearing a "Surrender in Iraq!" T-shirt and applying "vote-getting makeup" called "politically correct 'African American' face."[111]

Obama's Black Church

In 1988, when Barack Obama walked down the aisle of the Trinity United Church of Christ and committed himself to Christianity, he wasn't thinking about how it would play politically two decades later.

There is no doubt Obama's church has influenced his views. The title of Obama's book *The Audacity of Hope* is taken from a sermon by Obama's pastor, Jeremiah Wright. However, Obama has never embraced the allegedly "Afrocentric" viewpoint of his church highlighted by his critics.

Trinity United is an enormous congregation of 8,000 people on 95th Street in Chicago, with members ranging from the poorest to the professional elite of African Americans. Trinity's motto reads, "Unashamedly Black and Unapologetically Christian." The church's "black value system" includes a call for members to become "soldiers for black freedom."[112] According to the church's mission statement, "Trinity United Church of Christ has been called by God to be a congregation that is not ashamed of the gospel of Jesus Christ and that does not apologize for its African roots!" However, very little of the mission focuses on race, instead emphasizing class: "Our congregation is a combination of the haves and the have-nots; the economically disadvantaged, the underclass, the unemployed and the employable."

But conservative critics took sharp aim at the church's mention of race. Tucker Carlson claimed that the church "sounds separatist to me" and "contradicts the basic tenets of Christianity."[113] Conservative columnist Erik Rush, based on reading the church's website, called it a "coven" and "more like a cult or an Aryan Brethren Church." He wondered, "Do they consider themselves Americans? Do they consider themselves Christians? Are they worshiping Christ, are they worshiping African things?"[114] Right-winger Catherine Moy declared that the information about Obama's church "is going to make people's eyeballs pop clean out of their heads."[115]

Of course, it is hard to imagine any other presidential candidate being scrutinized for anything ever said in church and held personally responsible for every word. Obama himself declared, "Commitment to God, black community, commitment to the black family, the black work ethic, self-discipline and self-respect. Those are values that the conservative movement in particular has suggested are necessary for black advancement. So I would be puzzled that they would object or quibble with the bulk of a document that basically espouses profoundly conservative values of self-reliance and self-help."[116] Obama went on to say, "My church believes in the African American community strengthening families or adhering to the black work ethic or being committed to self-discipline and self-respect and not forgetting where you came from, I don't think that's something anybody would object to. I think I'd get a few amens."[117]

The last great institutional segregation in America is the church. Every Sunday around the country, blacks and whites worship largely in separate churches. Trinity United Church of Christ isn't racist for focusing on the black community. It is a black community of believers precisely because of the long tradition of Sunday segregation in America. It's not racist for a black church in a black community to talk about helping black people. Theologian Martin Marty noted, "For Trinity, being unashamedly black does not mean being antiwhite."[118]

There should be no obligation for a black church to engage in faux color blindness, to pretend that there is no racial segregation in the world when it's immediately visible to everyone around Chicago. The former pastor of Trinity, Jeremiah Wright, created the biggest crisis in Obama's campaign when tapes of his controversial sermons surfaced. The most frequently recycled clip showed Wright saying, "God damn America." Yet the view that God dislikes certain policies of the U.S. government and might punish the country for them is commonly expressed at thousands of white churches every Sunday, where legal abortion (rather than Wright's critique of foreign policy) is the topic. Although Obama had not been in attendance during Wright's most outrageous statements, he was considered "guilty by association."

For Obama, joining a church wasn't an expression of fervent belief in every doctrine espoused by that church. It was an opportunity for him to hear another point of view. It was also a way for Obama to hear from his primarily African American constituents. Ben Wallace-Wells reported in *Rolling Stone*, "This is as openly radical a background as any significant American political figure has ever emerged from; as much Malcolm X as Martin Luther King."[119]

However, African American scholars and journalists rejected the characterization of Obama's church as radical. According to Laura Washington of the *Chicago Sun-Times*, "Chicago's Trinity United Church of Christ is a very mainstream, middle-class congregation."[120] Melissa Harris-Lacewell, a Princeton professor who attended Trinity, dismissed criticism of the church, arguing that it indicates how "most white Americans, most of the time, can be utterly ignorant of how black people worship on Sunday."[121]

Guilt in Black and White

America's long racial divide has had deep political consequences. This made Barack Obama more than just another candidate for president. Instead, he became a symbol, perhaps unwillingly, for how Americans view race and for the racial divide in those perceptions.

Philip Kasinitz, a sociology professor at the City University of New York Graduate Center, noted about Obama: "He's a black politician for whom whites don't have to feel guilty."[122] But this presumes that white people feel guilty about anything. *Hardball* host Chris Matthews declared, "I don't think you can find a better opening gate, starting gate personality than Obama as a black candidate. I can't think of a better one. No history of Jim Crow, no history of anger, no history of slavery. All the bad stuff in our history ain't there with this guy."[123] Salim Muwakkil, senior editor at the left-wing magazine *In These Times*, wrote, "Many blacks wonder if mainstream whites love Obama because of his lack of history as a slave, which elicits no feelings of historical guilt.... They love Obama because he doesn't hate them, as they suspect blacks should."[124]

But no living American has a "history as a slave," and Muwakkil presumes that white people have feelings of guilt for slavery—and they don't. White guilt is one of the weakest forces in the universe. People have been appealing to white guilt for years, to urge concerted effort against the problems afflicting black neighborhoods with inferior schools, lack of public investment, crime, poverty, racial profiling, and a whole host of social ills. But all of that white guilt has resulted in almost zero social change. The truth is that the vast majority of white people don't feel the slightest bit guilty about anything ever done to an African American, even if they did it. Slavery is the distant past, and Jim Crow a story from the history books. Considering the skill with which whites denied guilt for these evils while they were happening, why should we expect today's generation of whites to assume some responsibility for them? So whites don't see Obama as the salve for their racist scars, because they don't see the scars of racism to begin with. As Obama wrote in *The Audacity of Hope*, "Rightly or wrongly, white guilt has largely exhausted itself in America; even the most fair-minded whites ... tend to push back against suggestions of racial victimization—or race-specific claims based on the history of race discrimination in this country."[125] In *Black Agenda Report*, Paul Street called this line "soothing to the master race."[126]

David Bositis of the Joint Center for Economic and Political Studies noted, "I see a new generation of younger black politicians who are eager to go to the top. Their aim for the top is not going to be achieved by appealing to the crimes of white people against African Americans in the past or to appeals to their guilt. It's going to be achieved by appealing to a common American experience."[127] Commentator Juan Williams made a similar argument: "This generation[al] shift from racial debates tied to guilt and anger over slavery opens the door to a new kind of black politics that is personified by Senator Obama."[128] The notion is that Obama's African ancestry removes any discussion of American slavery, a place where the white guilt trip can become a lovely African vacation.

Black critics attacked Obama for giving whites an easy way out of analyzing racism. According to Glen Ford on the left-wing website *Counterpunch*,

"By assisting white Americans to believe that painless absolution of collective responsibility for the past and current national sins can be achieved by looking kindly on an ingratiating black man's presidential candidacy, Obama has become an active participant in the Great Diversion."[129]

Much has been made of Obama's famous comments in his 2004 speech at the Democratic National Convention: "There is not a black America and a white America and a Latino America and Asian America—there's a United States of America." In *The Audacity of Hope,* Obama wrote, "When I hear commentators interpreting my speech to mean that we have arrived at a 'postracial politics' or that we already live in a color-blind society, I have to offer a word of caution. To say that we are one people is not to suggest that race no longer matters—that the fight for equality has been won, or that the problems minorities face in this country today are largely self-inflicted."[130]

Los Angeles Times columnist Gregory Rodriguez noted, "Barack Obama does not remind Americans of the racial divide or of the chains that first created it. Instead, he points to an alternative history that Americans have never been able to achieve."[131] However, what Obama points to is not an alternative past free from racism, but an alternative future that has the potential to break free from this history.

The Articulate and the Angry

Immediately after announcing his campaign for president, Senator Joseph Biden managed to shove his entire political foot into his mouth while trying to tiptoe through the minefield of race in America by saying about Obama: "I mean, you got the first sort of mainstream African American who's articulate and bright and clean and a nice-looking guy. I mean, that's a storybook, man."[132] The stereotypical term "articulate" used to describe Obama (as George W. Bush has also done) is offensive because it suggests that a black person who can speak intelligently must be unusual.

Journalism professor Curtis Lawrence wrote in the *Chicago Sun-Times,* "I think Obama's appeal to some white people is his perceived calmness—that he's not stuck on the Civil Rights movement, that he can shrug off a Biden comment and do the good ol' boy thing with Senator John McCain."[133] The question of race raised a new point on ABC's *This Week,* when George

Stephanopoulos asked Obama, "You have a very cool style when you're doing those town meetings where you're out on the campaign trail, and I wonder, how much of that is tied to your race?" Stephanopoulos explained, "One of your friends told the *New Yorker* magazine that the mainstream is just not ready for a fire-breathing black man, so do you turn down the temperature on purpose?"[134] Obama denied that it had anything to do with race. In fact, Obama's conversational style in town meetings is little different from that of other politicians. Stephanopoulos's question about race reflects what Syracuse University professor Elisabeth Lasch-Quinn has called the "myth about what blackness is." According to Lasch-Quinn, "I'm talking about the idea that there's one black response to things ... the idea that it is basically rage. Part of the question about whether Obama is black enough seems to be asking, 'Is he angry enough? Is he devoted to the idea that black people are separate enough?' It's a notion of uniformity—that there's only one black identity, and it's one of rage."[135]

The Whiteness of Guilt

Stephen Steinberg, a sociologist at Queens College, called "the magic of Obama" his appeal to white voters as "an act of exorcism from the sin of racism—pull the lever and, poof, it's gone."[136] One of Obama's white friends reportedly said, "White people like dealing with him because he doesn't make them feel guilty. I don't think he goes out of his way to do that, but the fact that he does helps a lot."[137]

One particularly embarrassing example of this attitude was *New Republic* writer Leon Wieseltier, who declared, "I plan to be moved to tears on the day that I vote for a black man for the presidency of this stained and stirring country."[138] This is a vision of Obama as a kind of amnesiac soap that washes away all of America's racial sins and enables us to forget about that ugly history of racism. Obama helps white America feel good about overcoming racism without all of the inconvenient details, such as actually working to overcome racism.

The notion that one black president can overturn all racism in American history is not sensible. White America doesn't need Barack Obama in order to embrace its longtime habit of racial forgetting. This conservative view helps the right wing explain the popularity of Obama despite his liberal viewpoints. By claiming that white people love Obama because he cures them of racial guilt, right-wingers could explain and dismiss Obama as merely an affirmative action presidential candidate whose race alone explained his popularity. The idea was that racist whites could vote for Obama and say to themselves, "Some of my best presidential candidates are black." The master of this move was faux conservative talk show host Stephen Colbert of Comedy Central, whose approach to race included finding a "black friend" to take a picture with him, as well as frequently declaring that he "can't see race" and doesn't even know what race he is. Colbert's mockery of "color blindness" was meant to reveal the continuing importance of race.

Although Obama does not emphasize racial divisions, he does remind us of them on occasion. Obama noted in a Selma, Alabama, speech, "It reminds us that we've still got a lot of work to do, and that the basic enforcement of antidiscrimination laws, the injustice that still exists within our criminal justice system, the disparity in terms of how people are treated in this country continues. It has gotten better. And we should never deny that it's gotten better. But we shouldn't forget that better is not good enough."[139] Obama has also been concerned that his background makes it easy for whites to favor him. Obama wrote in *Dreams from My Father,* "I ceased to advertise my mother's race at the age of twelve or thirteen, when I began to suspect that by doing so I was ingratiating myself to whites."[140]

Does Obama appeal to certain positive stereotypes about African Americans held by whites? It's a common stereotype in white America that black people are more hip than white folks. It's the African American stars that set the coolness agenda, from sports to music to movies. You can look at the NBA or the Grammys and see a proliferation of black stars. Obama's celebrity status, in this sense, is not fundamentally different from that of Oprah or Kanye West or Will Smith.

Of course, a positive stereotype is still a racial stereotype, and one that can have destructive consequences. Typically, white Americans have embraced African Americans as their entertainers, but never trusted them with political power. It never strained the white psyche too much to admire an individual black singer's musical skills while ruthlessly denying all other black people equality. This was the fear of some African American critics, the idea that Barack Obama was a pop star whom whites would applaud but would never give any real power.

Obama's race even became fodder for popular culture. William Shatner's character on *Boston Legal* declared about Obama, "He speaks perfect white, as well as black."[141] Tina Fey's character on *30 Rock* commented on "my white guilt, which is supposed to be used only for good, like overtipping and supporting Barack Obama."[142]

Is it white guilt that inspires much of the support for Obama? To be sure, there is a feel-good element for whites. What better proof to yourself that you cannot be a racist than supporting a black man for president? We can dream of the day when being a black candidate for national office is considered a positive factor for getting white votes rather than a negative, but that day has not yet come.

Would Barack Obama have been so appealing to some voters if he were white? No, because Barack Obama wouldn't be who he is if he were white. He wouldn't have developed his sensitivity to religious believers if not for his attachment to the black church and its links, past and present, to the Civil Rights movement. He wouldn't have developed his tremendous and unique public speaking talent (which he largely lacked when I first met him) without the models of African American preachers and politicians he learned from. He wouldn't have developed his understanding of the globe without his personal attachment to Africa, the land where his father came from. And Obama wouldn't have developed his ability to bridge racial divides if he had been a white politician who could take black Democratic votes for granted rather than a black politician who had to work hard in order to overcome the suspicions of white voters and media toward black politicians. If Barack Obama were white, he would be just an unusually smart and charismatic progressive. It is not Obama's race that matters, but how Obama's race taught him so much about American values.

The Blackness of Bill Clinton

Perhaps the most puzzling part of Barack Obama's candidacy was the initial lack of support given to him by black voters. As *Chicago Tribune* columnist Clarence Page noted, "For Obama, the emerging question has been whether he can attract black voters."[143] A *Washington Post/ABC News* poll before Obama announced his campaign for president found that 60 percent of black voters supported Hillary Clinton compared with only 20 percent for Obama.[144] A February 2007 poll by the *Washington Post* showed some dramatic changes, as 44 percent of black Democrats supported Obama compared to only 33 percent for Clinton.[145] But an April 5–9, 2007, *Los Angeles Times*/Bloomberg Poll found 41 percent of black voters nationwide backing Clinton, with only 34 percent supporting Obama.[146]

According to George Washington University law professor Paul Butler, "The African American reaction to Barack Obama's candidacy has to be one of the more stunning displays of color blindness I've seen in politics."[147] But why were African Americans so willing at first to embrace Hillary Clinton over an African American candidate?

Right-wing talk show host Sean Hannity was baffled by it: "For whatever reason, the Clintons, and especially Bill Clinton, has this impression of being very friendly to the African American community. He didn't appoint people to the highest positions of government the way George W. Bush did. Why is that perception there?"[148] Former lieutenant governor of Maryland Michael Steele, a Republican, answered him, "Many African Americans identified, quite frankly and quite honestly, with Bill Clinton's situation when he was going through the whole Monica Lewinsky thing. There was such a drum beat. There was such a drumming against him in so many ways that there was an identification that began to connect between many African Americans who understood what it's like to kind of not be believed or have people relentlessly come after you. So I think there was sort of a symbiotic relationship that was developed there. I mean, particularly when you consider the number of African Americans who were incarcerated during those eight years are [sic] the highest ever."[149]

Alan Colmes tried to defend Clinton's record: "Bill Clinton—his policies were friendly to African Americans. He brought up the African American job rate, certainly for teens and for African American males. He had a surgeon general who was black."[150] Of course, Clinton fired that surgeon general, Joycelyn Elders, after she failed to condemn masturbation. As for the low unemployment rate during the Clinton administration, the biggest reason for a declining black unemployment rate was the enormous increase in black imprisonment, which he did nothing to stop.

Yet Bill Clinton's almost mythic status among African Americans remains strong. Perhaps the most extreme expression of African American admiration for Bill Clinton came from Nobel Prize–winning author Toni Morrison in 1998 during the impeachment crisis, when she called Bill

Clinton "the first black president." According to Morrison, "Clinton displays almost every trope of blackness: single-parent household, born poor, working-class, saxophone-playing, McDonald's-and-junk-food-loving boy from Arkansas," and compared Clinton's scrutinized sex life to the stereotyping and double standards that blacks typically endure. According to Morrison, "African American men seemed to understand it right away" and "when the president's body, his privacy, his unpoliced sexuality became the focus of the persecution, when he was metaphorically seized and body-searched, who could gainsay these black men who knew whereof they spoke?"[151]

Morrison argued, "The message was clear: 'No matter how smart you are, how hard you work, how much coin you earn for us, we will put you in your place or put you out of the place you have somehow, albeit with our permission, achieved. You will be fired from your job, sent away in disgrace, and—who knows?—maybe sentenced and jailed to boot. In short, unless you do as we say (i.e., assimilate at once), your expletives belong to us.'" Morrison contended that Clinton moved "from target sighted to attack, to criminalization, to lynching, and now, in some quarters, to crucifixion" and "the always and already guilty 'perp.'" Morrison declared that Bill Clinton was "blacker than any actual black person who could ever be elected in our children's lifetime." (Ironically, Obama has reported being inspired by Morrison's novels, although probably not her cynicism about the chances of seeing a real black president.)[152] But Bill Clinton was, of course, guilty of cheating on his wife and lying under oath about it. The slap on Clinton's wrist wasn't a lynching, let alone a crucifixion. For Morrison to imply that Bill Clinton should be called "black" because of his sexual misadventures and lies seems like the worst kind of racial insult imaginable.

Saturday Night Live mocked the debate over Obama's blackness with a "Blackness Scale" with characters imitating Al Sharpton and Reverend Jesse Jackson, who noted, "There is only so much blackness the American voter can take." The skit put Obama in the middle of the blackness scale, "above Will Smith and just below Bill Clinton."[153] Howard Fineman of *Newsweek* even mockingly called Obama "the white Bill Clinton."[154]

The idea that Bill Clinton should be called the "first black president" is absurd. Morrison noted how "virtually all the African American Clinton appointees began, one by one, to disappear," but neglected to mention how Clinton himself was responsible for failing to defend them. Clinton withdrew the nomination of Lani Guinier as assistant attorney general for civil rights in 1993 because her advocacy of voting rights for African Americans caused critics to label her a "quota queen."

In 1992, Clinton had consciously appealed to racist whites by denouncing the controversial statements of rapper Sister Souljah (and Reverend Jesse Jackson for allowing her to speak on a panel). As Debra Dickerson observed, Clinton's Sister Souljah moment was a calculated effort at "reassuring whites that he knew how to keep blacks in line."[155]

Sister Souljah, Lani Guinier, Joycelyn Elders—exactly how many African American women did Bill Clinton need to denounce or abandon before the myth of Clinton's "blackness" could be abandoned as the joke it is?

Leftist African Americans have also questioned Clinton's status. University of Illinois professor Sundiata Cha-Jua has argued, "Clinton was horrible for black people."[156] Columnist Earl Ofari Hutchinson, fearing that Obama will fail to talk about issues affecting minorities such as affirmative action, racial profiling, and the death penalty, also noted that "Clinton wrote this original flawed script for Democratic presidential contenders when he virtually excised all talk of racial issues from his election campaigns in 1992 and 1996. But Clinton also hinted that a big part of his winning strategy was to shake the Democrats loose from the grip of Jesse Jackson and the Civil Rights leaders."[157]

According to a CNN report, "[Hillary] Clinton and her husband, former president Bill Clinton, have deep roots in the black community."[158] *Ebony* magazine noted "the tremendous popularity the Clintons enjoy among African Americans."[159] South Carolina state senator Robert Ford declared, "I am sure there will be some young blacks who will be behind Obama, but elderly blacks are going with Hillary because they love Bill and they love Hillary for standing behind him for eight years."[160]

Ultimately, Bill Clinton's current popularity with all Americans, especially liberal-leaning African Americans, has more to do with the obvious failures of George W. Bush than any particular virtues of the Clinton administration. Of course, there is no reason Hillary Clinton should be burdened with the sins of her husband. But there's also no reason Hillary Clinton should be the beneficiary of this mysterious admiration of Bill Clinton by African Americans.

Obama is accustomed to the reluctance of African American voters to embrace him before they understand who he is. *Ebony* magazine explained,

"Most Black Americans simply did not know Obama."[161] In 2004, one *Chicago Tribune* columnist repeated the question being commonly asked, "Was Obama 'black enough' for black voters?" A poll the month before the primary election showed him getting only 38 percent of black voters in Illinois, although three weeks later that number had grown to 62 percent.[162] Despite the early polls in 2004 indicating skepticism by black voters, Obama ended up getting the overwhelming number of African American votes in both the primary and general elections for the U.S. Senate.

Barack Obama noted, "It would be presumptuous of me to expect that people would vote for me because of my race."[163] Actually, it's not presumptuous at all to assume that African Americans voters will support African American candidates because they think they will better understand and represent their interests. Knowing that African Americans face special barriers to success in politics (ranging from racism to lack of money), African Americans had every reason to support Barack Obama.

For a few black leaders, it was all about the money. South Carolina state senator Darrell Jackson endorsed Senator Hillary Clinton, declaring: "I strongly feel as if she is the best-qualified candidate to lead on day one."[164] However, his strong feelings for Hillary Clinton might have been influenced by the $10,000-a-month contract his political consulting firm had just signed with her campaign after rejecting an offer from Obama's campaign.[165] Jackson apparently rejected the contract from (and endorsement of) the Obama campaign because it paid less.[166]

However, the caution of black leaders, and even more so of African American voters, may have had little to do with any fondness for the Clinton family or its political machine.

Pessimistic African American Voters

The key reason so many black voters were skeptical of Obama was because blacks (unlike most white Americans) didn't believe white people would ever elect a black president. A September 2006 Gallup poll asked, "Do you think Americans are ready to elect a black president?" Sixty-four percent of whites agreed, but only 43 percent of nonwhites.[167]

Black voters were leery of supporting Obama because they didn't trust white voters, not because they didn't trust Obama. David Bositis, political analyst for the Joint Center for Political and Economic Studies, observed: "There are places in the South where people don't think anybody black can be elected to anything."[168] Diane Sawyer declared on *Good Morning America*, "Senator Barack Obama is watching black political leaders throw support to Hillary Clinton. And why? They have said publicly they don't think America is ready to elect a black candidate."[169]

South Carolina state senator Robert Ford embraced Hillary Clinton because he feared what would happen to the Democratic Party if an African American was nominated for president in a racist society. Ford said in apocalyptic terms, "It's a slim possibility for him to get the nomination, but then everybody else is doomed. Every Democrat running on that ticket next year would lose—because he's black and he's top of the ticket. We'd lose the House and the Senate and the governors and everything. I'm a gambling man. I love Obama. But I'm not going to kill myself."[170]

Obama responded to Ford at a speech in South Carolina before nearly 3,000 people: "I've been reading the papers in South Carolina," Obama said, before using a preacher's cadence to paraphrase Ford's remarks. "Can't have a black man at the top of the ticket. But I know this—that when folks were saying, we're going to march for our freedom, they said, you can't do that. When somebody said, you can't sit at the lunch counter. ... You can't do that. We did. And when somebody said, women belong in the kitchen not in the boardroom. You can't do that. Yes we can. I don't believe in this can't do, won't do, won't even try style of leadership. Don't believe in that. Yes, we can." The frenzied crowd was chanting, "Yes, we can" in one of Obama's more dramatic moments on the campaign trail. Summing up the message of his campaign, Obama declared: "At every turn in our history, there's been somebody who said we can't. I'm here to tell you, Yes we can."[171]

The Polling of Pessimism

An early CBS poll in 2007 showed Obama losing by 14 points among whites but by 24 points among blacks.[172] One key racial difference found in polls was the pessimism of African Americans who believed that Americans would not elect a black president. Ultimately, Obama won overwhelming black support in the primaries and because he proved his ability to win over white voters in Iowa.[173]

University of Illinois professor Sundiata Cha-Jua noted that while whites will claim that they are willing to vote for blacks, "when the vote actually occurs, that's not what actually happens." According to Cha-Jua, "To expect a smart, savvy black person to win in the United States at this moment, I'm not crazy."[174] *Chicago Sun-Times* columnist Laura Washington wrote, "Two hundred years of 'Living in America' have made us cynical about racial progress. The possibility that a 45-year-old black man could come out of nowhere to be elected president of the United States—that doesn't jibe with our well-worn skepticism."[175]

Black pessimism is a powerful phenomenon. George Wilson, host of XM radio's *G.W. on the Hill,* noted, "Is America ready for a black president? And the overall consensus, at least of my callers, is that America is not ready for an African American president.... When white America has embraced a candidate, as they have Barack Obama, there's a certain amount of distrust that goes with this among a number of African Americans."[176] While 58 percent of white voters thought that a white man would get the Democratic nomination for president in 2008, 81 percent of black voters believed this.[177] These numbers were all the more remarkable because the two leading Democratic candidates were not white men.

As Earl Ofari Hutchinson observed on *Huffington Post,* "It's not fashionable to come off to pollsters sounding like a bigot. But when the contest is between a white and black candidate, many whites suffer acute election conversion when they get in the privacy of the voting booth."[178] National Public Radio interviewed one man on the street who declared: "A black president? No. Are you crazy? Come on. Who we kidding? We are a country founded in racism and equity fits nowhere in that." Another man said, "There's a lot of inborn hatred in a lot of American people and I think that they haven't gotten over some of the past misunderstandings about blacks in general to be able to allow them to lead the country."[179] Carolyn Christiel, a teacher, told the *Chicago Tribune,* "Society is so tainted. What makes me think they are going to let this black man win?"[180] Alondra Jones, a student at Howard University, said, "In 2007 we are far more progressive on race than we were in 1967. But we are not at the point now where the whole of America will allow a black man to win the presidency. Maybe in another 25 or 26 years. I'm hopeful."[181]

Even white writers such as Andrew Greeley doubted that Obama could be elected in a racist society: "It is foolish happy talk to say the United States is ready for an African American (or perhaps Kenyan American) president. Racism is alive and well in the United States and still is as American as cherry pie."[182] Jeremy Levitt, a law professor at Florida International University, wrote, "The hard reality is that whether Democrat or Republican, white voters generally do not support black candidates. Whether this is because of overt racial bias or other prejudice is uncertain; however, the outcome remains the same: White men rule."[183]

But the myth of the unelectable African American was really just a myth. Civil rights leader Representative John Lewis (D-Ga.) declared, "In the depth of my heart, I believe it is possible for Senator Obama to become president of the United States. I think the American people are prepared to take that great leap. They're prepared to lay down the burden of race."[184]

Certainly, there were optimists. Secretary of State Condoleezza Rice declared: "I think we've overcome. Americans, a great majority of Americans, have overcome that.... Yes, I think a black person can be elected president."[185] Former Virginia governor Doug Wilder declared about Obama's candidacy, "I think absolutely that the nation is ready."[186]

In a May 2007 poll, 46 percent of whites but only 8 percent of blacks said they would not vote for Obama.[187] Although that primarily reflects the racial distribution of Republicans and Democrats, Obama has convinced skeptical African Americans in the past to support his campaigns. Obama's top consultant, David Axelrod, noted, "When he started his race for the Senate here in Illinois, he was polling at about 31 percent of the African American vote and he ended up with 95 percent at the end of the race."[188]

Some of the most skeptical commentators about Obama were African American progressives who doubted that America was ready for a black president. Earl Ofari Hutchinson, author of *The Emerging Black GOP Majority,* wrote on Alternet.org, "He is too new on the political scene, too untested, too politically nice, too liberal, and most of all he's an African American."[189] When Obama was featured by the centrist Democratic Leadership Council (DLC) as one of the hundred Democratic leaders to watch, Bruce Dixon of the *Black Commentator* worried that Obama was "in the process of becoming 'ideologically freed' from the opinions of the African American and other Democrats whose votes he needs to win" (in response, Obama asked to have his name removed from the DLC list).[190]

Black progressives also worried that Obama might be trying to distance himself from the black community. *Chicago Sun-Times* columnist

Mary Mitchell noted, "It is understandable that Obama doesn't want to be pigeonholed as the so-called black candidate, but he can't be so afraid of that label that he alienates the very base that could lift him in the primary election. Frankly, his universalist strategy might work for white voters, but black voters have been take for granted long enough."[191] Obama contended that he could be a universalist candidate and a black candidate, too.

The Civil Rights movement succeeded because it appealed to universal values and forced white people to see the injustice of racism. The black separatists who denounced Martin Luther King Jr. for working within the white-dominated political system were proven wrong, and the separatists who criticized Obama's universal rhetoric were wrong, too.

Cathy Hughes, the developer of Radio One, attacked Obama as an illusion: "I called it a dazzling deception. And black folks have historically gone for dazzling deception. African Americans, if it looks good to us, we're like, OK, well, let's give it a try. I'm not going for this dazzling deception because I think this election is too critical to the future of America, not just African Americans but all Americans. I want someone in there who knows what they're doing, who's qualified for the position and who has done more than taken photos, waved at the crowd and kissed babies."[192]

The Bradley Effect

Obama has argued, "I think that the country has matured. Are there individuals who might not vote for me because of race? I'm sure there are, but, frankly, I think it's a small minority of the country."[193] But analysts were skeptical whether people were telling the truth when they said they would support a black candidate.

It's called the "Bradley effect": It occurs when racist whites vote against black candidates even though they tell pollsters the opposite. The term "Bradley effect" comes from the 1982 election, when Los Angeles mayor Tom Bradley, an African American, narrowly lost his race for governor despite polls that showed a lead of 9–22 percentage points. Of course, racism has always existed in American politics; what changed in the 1980s was that racism became less prevalent, enabling black candidates to run credibly for city and then statewide offices. In

Chicago, African American Harold Washington became mayor in 1983, but he won by 3.4 percentage points despite having a double-digit lead in the polls. In 1989, David Dinkins beat Rudy Giuliani for mayor of New York City by 2 percentage points despite a double-digit lead. Also in 1989, Douglas Wilder won the governor's race in Virginia by less than 1 percentage point despite a lead of 4–11 points in various polls. In 1990, Harvey Gantt lost a racially charged race against Senator Jesse Helms by 6 points, despite some polls that showed him leading.[194] Ron Walters, director of the African American Leadership Institute at the University of Maryland at College Park, noted "the lingering fictitiousness of public opinion polls when it comes to assessing white support for black candidates."[195]

But was the Bradley effect real? Certainly, polls have been wrong before. When Carol Moseley Braun ran for the U.S. Senate in Illinois in 1992, polls within a week of the election predicted her defeat in the Democratic primary by up to 19 points. Instead, she won by 3 points. The best evidence for the Bradley effect was the 1989 Wilder election, when a face-to-face exit poll that was accurate for other races showed Wilder winning by 10 percentage points.

Is the Bradley effect history? All of the examples given for it are from 1980–1990, and nearly two decades have passed since then. A 1958 poll found that 53 percent of Americans admitted that they would not vote for a black presidential candidate. By 1984, 16 percent of people declared they would not vote for a black president. However, in 2003, 92 percent of Americans said they would vote for a black president, while only 6 percent would not. A 2006 *Newsweek* poll found that only 3 percent said they would not.[196]

The people who voted against Bradley, Wilder, and Dinkins despite telling pollsters the opposite were those who, in the abstract, were racist toward black candidates. No one knows whether they intentionally lied to pollsters or simply let their racist feelings sway an undecided choice. But in generational terms, many openly racist voters have died off.

Recent races suggest that the Bradley effect may be gone. Republican Michael Steele lost his 2006 Senate race in Maryland by 10 points, but the polls predicted such a large loss. In Massachusetts, Deval Patrick won the 2006 governor's race 56 percent to 35 percent despite what one observer called "a series of race-baiting television ads that could have been authored by Jesse Helms."[197]

Tennessee Democratic Senate candidate Harold Ford Jr. lost his 2006 Senate race in Tennessee, but polls indicated he might have lost by an even larger margin. Vanderbilt political scientist Carol Swain argued, "What is remarkable is that Ford lost his bid by a mere 3 points in a Republican-leaning state. Despite the subtle injection of race into some of the campaign advertisements, Ford did well despite his youth and his singleness."[198] The Republican National Committee launched a TV ad against Ford, showing a white woman pretending to have met Ford at a Playboy party and telling him, "Harold, call me."[199] According to Swain, "The closeness of the Ford/Corker race called into question whether the so-called Bradley effect, in which white voters overstate their support for black candidates in biracial contests, was operative in the Tennessee race."[200] Obama saw the significance of this: "I thought that the Harold Ford election showed enormous progress. Something that hasn't been noted is the fact that Harold Ford did better among white voters than the polls would have indicated."[201] According to Obama, "I don't know that a white Democrat would have done any better, and maybe even worse."[202]

If the Bradley effect seemed to disappear even in a contest where race became a leading controversy, it suggests that black candidates may not necessarily face an impossible uphill struggle. This doesn't mean that racism has been eliminated from American politics. There are still plenty of places, from the good old white boy network to the lobbyists to the media to the money, where race clearly matters, and African Americans in particular face a disadvantage. But the idea that a majority of whites are outright racists who would never support a black candidate is history. As Swain argued, "The hard-core racist element that would oppose a black man because he is a black man is not sufficiently large enough to deny the nomination or election of the right person."[203]

One danger is the power of racism to become a self-fulfilling prophecy based on mistaken perceptions. Even if there were no racists left in America, if a sufficient number of nonracists believed that these racists existed and would oppose Obama, then they might make a logical conclusion that they should oppose Obama in the primary in order to avoid losing the general election. This kind of rational (or irrational) racism helps explain why racism is so powerful and able to resist extermination in a liberal society.

Racial Polling

However, the Bradley effect only identifies concealed racism. But there was also the problem of openly expressed bigotry. A December 2006 *Newsweek* poll found that 7 percent of respondents said they would not vote for a "qualified" black presidential candidate (or were unsure), compared to 14 percent who would not vote for a "qualified" woman. However, the public was much more suspicious of the motives of fellow Americans, with 35 percent saying that America was not ready for a female president and 30 percent believing the country was not ready for a black president.[204]

Other polls showed even less evidence of widespread racism. A February 2007 Gallup poll found that only 5 percent of respondents said that they would not vote for a black presidential candidate. Far more people objected to a Jewish (7 percent), female (11 percent), Hispanic (12 percent), or Mormon (24 percent) candidate.[205]

An ABC poll found that 69 percent of Americans said it wouldn't matter if a presidential candidate was a woman and 17 percent said they would be more likely to vote for a woman. Likewise, 84 percent said it wouldn't matter if a candidate was black, and 9 percent said they would be more likely to vote for a black candidate.[206] If this poll was accurate, then the "affirmative action" voters who were more likely to support blacks or women actually exceed the "bigot" voters who opposed them.

Jake Tapper of *ABC News* noted, "Eighty-four percent of Americans say a candidate being black would not affect their vote one way or the other. But the dirty little secret, what some experts call the 15 percent lie, [is] the 15 percent of white voters who tell pollsters they'd be willing to vote for a black candidate. But in the privacy of the polling place, [they] never ever actually would."[207] In the end, it was open racism, not hidden racism, that hurt Obama the most. These early polls turned out to be inaccurate: Race-based voting against Obama in the primaries and the general election was much higher than the earlier polling about race had indicated. Whereas Hillary Clinton benefitted from gender-based voting, Obama lost more votes than he gained from Democrats who considered race in their voting. In the general election, far more people voted against Obama and said race was a factor than the earlier polls had indicated. Obama's victory proved that racism can be overcome by a popular candidate, but the exit polls proved that racism remains a powerful force even within the

Democratic Party. Even more disturbing is the unknown number of voters who were influenced by race but didn't admit it in the exit polls. The dirty little secret of American racism was exposed by the Obama candidacy, but many commentators still refuse to see it.

The Continuing Significance of Race

Certainly, racism is still an effective tool in American politics. One of the worst racist attacks in recent memory was led by George W. Bush's campaign. In 2000, Bush's smear experts called up voters in South Carolina before the Republican primary, asking them what they would think about John McCain if they knew he had fathered an illegitimate child who was black. In reality, McCain's daughter was adopted from Bangladesh.[208] Bush demolished McCain in South Carolina and ensured himself an easy path to the Republican nomination. The Bush campaign's racist attacks were highly effective—so effective, in fact, that McCain hired Bush's strategists to run his 2008 campaign.[209]

As Larry Wilmore, the so-called senior black correspondent for Comedy Central's *Daily Show,* observed: "The last thing a black candidate wants is to be seen as the black candidate." According to Wilmore, "For every three black votes you get, you scare away five white votes."[210] Comedy aside, this "three-fifths" rule for black votes isn't quite so funny because it's historically true.

Barack Obama's presidency will not end racism or radically transform our entire political system. One person, one campaign, does not wipe away centuries of racism. But it is more than a just a symbol of change. The Obama presidency, and the fact that he was not dismissed by politicians and media as earlier black candidates like Shirley Chisholm and Jesse Jackson were, indicates that real change is happening.

CHAPTER FOUR

The Vast Right-Wing Conspiracy
The Conservative Attack on Obama

There is not a liberal America and a conservative America—there is the United States of America. —Barack Obama

To the right-wing movement in America, Barack Obama is an enigma. His speeches espousing bipartisanship have baffled them, and the Far Right's attacks on Obama have centered around his name and bizarre rumors that he is a Muslim Manchurian candidate secretly programmed as a child to hate America.

Even before Obama began running for president, the mainstream press and right-wing pundits began to focus on his middle name, Hussein. On November 7, 2006, Chris Matthews on MSNBC noted Obama's middle name would "be interesting down the road." A few weeks later, Republican strategist Ed Rogers appeared on Matthews's show and explicitly referred to "Barack Hussein Obama." Obama's middle name became fodder for MSNBC, Fox News, and CNN correspondents to casually mention as if it were a serious political issue. CNN's *The Situation Room* on December 11, 2006, featured correspondent Jeanne Moos noting, "Only one little consonant differentiates" *Obama* and *Osama* and adding, "as if that similarity weren't enough. How about sharing the name of a former dictator? You know his middle name, Hussein." On the same show, CNN senior political analyst Jeff Greenfield criticized Obama for not wearing a tie, claiming that this linked him, fashionwise, to Iranian President Mahmoud Ahmadinejad.[1]

After Obama's candidacy was announced in 2007, right-wing talk radio hosts began to focus on him, often using cheap insults or racial remarks. MSNBC and syndicated radio host Don Imus proclaimed, "Obama's a creep," and declared, "First of all, he's not qualified to be president, that's one, and two, he's a flip-flopping weasel."[2] Imus didn't explain what he was talking about but seemed to reflexively attack Obama as "flip-flopping" because the right wing had denounced John Kerry in 2004 as a "flip flopper" on the war in Iraq and the strategy proved highly successful. Imus's executive producer, Bernard McGuirk, said on the air that Obama has "a Jew-hating name."[3] Perhaps not surprisingly, Obama was the first presidential candidate to support firing Imus and McGuirk after their infamous remarks calling the Rutgers women's basketball team "nappy-headed hos."

Rush Limbaugh, the leading conservative talk radio host, also relied on name-calling to attack Obama. Before Obama announced his candidacy, Limbaugh gave Obama the name "Barack Hussein Odumbo" (in reference to Obama's "big ears").[4] Limbaugh also routinely referred to him as "Osama Obama," based on a slip of the tongue by Senator Edward Kennedy. Obama had experienced this before; he noted that during his 2004 Senate campaign, a Republican operative created a website with "an image of me superimposed over a picture of bin Laden. I think people like to play with my name."[5]

As Obama formed an exploratory committee for a presidential campaign and began rising in the polls, Limbaugh started to make racial insults, calling Obama "a half minority."[6] Limbaugh also repeatedly played a parody song, "Barack the Magic Negro" (sung by a bad Al Sharpton impersonator to the tune of "Puff the Magic Dragon").

Unable to find anything accurate to attack Obama with, many on the right simply denounced Obama as insubstantial. Mary Matalin, a former assistant to George W. Bush and Dick Cheney, declared, "He's a nothing, based on nothing. He's an empty vessel. He's not running on anything. He's running on no agenda."[7] Conservative commentator John Podhoretz called Obama the "Rorschach candidate."[8] Republican strategist Ed Rogers declared on *Hardball*, "Help me, somebody, who underestimates Barack Hussein Obama. This man is a blank canvas, where people project their desires and their ideal candidate, because nobody knows anything about him."[9] In the eyes of the Far Right, the absence of any basis to smear a candidate becomes the smear in itself, since anyone without negatives is a "blank slate" or "empty vessel."

Reagan speechwriter Peggy Noonan in the *Wall Street Journal* called Obama "the man from nowhere, of whom little is known."[10] Dick Armey, the former Republican House majority leader, declared, "I'm fascinated by Obama. Here is a man who has been in town, Washington, for two years, as near as I can tell hasn't done a thing. Apparently, there is no performance criteria in the process of selecting somebody to be president. Nobody asks the question, what has he, in fact, ever done?"[11] None of these conservatives applied the same logic to George W. Bush, who came to Washington, D.C., with far less experience and far fewer qualifications than Obama. Former Bill Clinton adviser Dick Morris proclaimed, "Obama can be whatever he wants, because he's a kid."[12] John Hood, president of the John Locke Foundation, noted on a *National Review* blog, "Barack Obama is the candidate of the moment—and I don't mean that in a good way. He's the candidate of the trendy, the easy answer, the NPR-segment-at-22-past-the-hour. He's pretty and fluffy, like a cloud. Clouds blow away."[13]

The Muslim and the Madrassa

One shocking story hit the news after Barack Obama began exploring the possibility of running for president. *Insight* magazine reported it on January 17, 2007: "Are the American people ready for an elected president who was educated in a madrassa as a young boy and has not been forthcoming about his Muslim heritage?" *Insight* claimed that Obama "spent at least four years in a so-called madrassa, or Muslim seminary, in Indonesia."[14]

Quickly, a wave of outrage and fear about Obama hit the conservative blogosphere and flowed across the columns of right-wing columnists and the "news" programs of the Fox News Channel.

There was only one problem with this spectacular story: It came from false sources and evidence. The twists and turns of this story reveal a great deal about the Far Right's attack tactics against Obama. How questionable information on Obama's religious background emerged can be seen in how it played out in several media sources. A brief outline of these media reports follows. *Insight* was part of the far-right *Washington Times* company, but after years of bleeding Moonie money for the conservative cause, it had been converted into a cheap little webzine that did no reporting of its own. Instead, *Insight* published rumors. It had stopped using bylines so that it could pay unnamed reporters (alleged to be mainstream journalists) to reveal the unverified lies that spread around the swamp of Washington politics. The right-wing website claimed, "*Insight* cited reports from its very credible sources that the opposition research is seeking hard evidence that Mr. Obama is still a Muslim or has ties to Islam."[15] As Howard Kurtz of the *Washington Post* observed, these were "allegations lacking a single named source."[16]

Insight decided to report the story as a campaign tactics story under the headline, "Hillary's Team Has Questions about Obama's Muslim Background." *Insight* later declared, "If read carefully, one can see that *Insight*'s story simply reported on a potential attack strategy on Obama by his Democratic Party opponents."[17] This was the ultimate in smear tactics: Declare that one candidate is tied to evil, and then blame another candidate for leaking the false story. Normally, a journalistic entity might care if it was being used to spread an obvious lie. But *Insight* was undeterred. The website declared, "*Insight* stands by its story. Having laid the ground, we now leave it to the mainstream print and broadcast news organizations to ferret out more facts and make judgment calls on relevance."[18] As the *Washington Post* editorialized, "*Insight* didn't even have the decency to slink away."[19]

Immediately, conservative talk radio began repeating the story, as did the Fox News Channel and the right-wing columnists who dominate much of the op-ed space in American newspapers. Syndicated columnist Mark Steyn wrote in the *Chicago Sun-Times* that Obama "graduated from the Sword of the Infidel Slayer grade school in Jakarta."[20]

On the Fox News Channel morning show *Fox and Friends*, cohost Steve Doocy said: "Why didn't anybody ever mention that that man [Obama] right there was raised—spent the first decade of his life, raised by his Muslim father—as a Muslim and was educated in a madrassa? We should also point out that Barack Obama's father is the one who gave him the middle name of Hussein. And the thing about the madrassa, and you know, let's just be honest about this, in the last number of years, madrassas have been, we've learned a lot about them, financed by Saudis, they teach this Wahhabism which pretty much hates us."[21]

Juan Williams declared on *Fox News Sunday*, "He comes from a father who was a Muslim and all that. I mean, I think that, given that we're at war with Muslim extremists, that presents a problem."[22] Fox News Channel host John Gibson called it "the madrassa bomb dropped on Barack Obama." According to Gibson, "Clinton has reportedly outed Obama's Muslim past."[23]

Comedy Central's faux news anchor Stephen Colbert praised Gibson, noting that the story was "too important to corroborate" before reporting it.[24] Colbert lamented the fact that CNN "debunked a perfectly good made-up story."[25] A further clue to the *Insight* story came from this sentence: "The sources said the young Obama was given the name Hussein by his Muslim father, which the Illinois Democrat rarely uses in public."[26] No one needed a "source" to tell them that. Obama's name is Barack Hussein Obama Jr. because he has the same name as his father, who was an atheist, not a Muslim. Obama's father was given the name by Obama's Muslim grandfather, whom Obama never met. The information from the "background check" closely paralleled an e-mail circulating for more than a year among right-wing circles paranoid about the "Muslim threat" to America. The April 2005 anti-Obama e-mail was titled "The Enemy Within!" and declared, "Obama takes great care to conceal the fact that he is a radical Muslim while admitting that he was once a Muslim, mitigating that damning information by saying that, for two years, he also attended a Catholic school."[27]

The e-mail falsely called Obama's father "a radical Muslim" but added that Obama's real Muslim training came in Indonesia after his mother remarried: "Dunham married another Muslim, Lolo Soetoro, who educated his stepson as a good Muslim by enrolling him in one of Jakarta's Wahhabi schools. Wahhabism is the radical teaching that created the Muslim terrorists who are now waging jihad on the industrialized world." The e-mail concluded, "Since it is politically expedient to be a Christian when you are seeking political office in the United States, Obama joined the United Church of Christ to help purge any notion that he is still a Muslim, which, ideologically, he remains today."[28]

Right-wing columnist Debbie Schlussel began writing about the rumors in December 2006.[29] Schlussel claimed that Obama "is a man who Muslims think is a Muslim, who feels some sort of psychological need to prove himself to his absent Muslim father, and who is now moving in the direction of his father's heritage, a man we want as president when we are fighting the war of our lives against Islam? Where will his loyalties be?"[30] Obama didn't need to be a Muslim in order to have his "loyalties" questioned. Invoking a kind of Islamophobic McCarthyism of guilt by association, Schlussel decreed that Obama was suspect because he had any connections to Muslims, regardless of his religion.

The Truth about Obama's Life in Indonesia

So what was the truth about Obama's "Muslim" background? Obama's father was raised as a Muslim, but like Obama's mother, his father was an atheist. In *The Audacity of Hope*, Obama wrote: "I was not raised in a religious household."[31] However, Obama was exposed to the views of various religious groups by his anthropologist mother. Obama wrote that his stepfather "saw religion as not particularly useful in the practical business of making one's way in the world."[32]

Obama noted, "During the five years that we would live with my stepfather in Indonesia, I was sent first to a neighborhood Catholic school and then to a predominantly Muslim school; in both cases, my mother was less concerned with me learning the catechism or puzzling out the meaning of the muezzin's call to evening prayer than she was with whether I was properly learning my multiplication tables."[33]

Obama did often attend Friday prayers in the local mosque. Zulfin Adi, a close childhood friend of Obama, told the *Los Angeles Times*, "We prayed but not really seriously, just following actions done by older people in the mosque. But as kids, we loved to meet our friends and went to the mosque together and played."[34]

For two hours every week in Indonesia's public schools, students would engage in religious studies. Apparently because his stepfather was nominally a Muslim, Obama was officially registered as a Muslim and therefore went to Koranic studies during the third and fourth grades.[35]

Following up on the story, CNN correspondent John Vause did something unique for the media today: He went to Indonesia and checked on the story by visiting Obama's elementary school. Vause noted, "I've been to madrassas in Pakistan and this school is nothing like that."[36] Obama recalled: "It was an ordinary public school. Kids ran around in short pants and learned math and science and participated in the Boy Scouts. It was comparable to any public school here in the United States."[37] As

Obama noted, "The notion that somehow, at the age of six or seven, I was being trained for something other than math, science and reading is ludicrous."[38]

The Source of the Madrassa Myth

Before it ever reached the mainstream conservative media and received national attention, the madrassa myth was spread by a Chicago lawyer named Andy Martin.[39]

On August 11, 2004, Martin held "simultaneous news conferences in New York and London" to warn the world that "he believes Barack Obama is a political fraud who 'lied to the American people,'" according to Martin's press release, published on PR Newswire. Martin's release demanded that Obama's publisher ban Obama's book from being sold "because of its fraudulent content."[40] Martin's press release quoted himself saying, "I feel sad having to expose Barack Obama, but the man is a complete fraud."[41] Martin also declared in the release, "If he will lie about his mother and father, what else is he lying about? Can we expect 'bimbo eruptions?'"[42] Martin's release claimed that Obama had a "family history of rape, murder, and arson" and that Obama "has treated his Muslim heritage as a dark secret."[43] Finally, Martin added this line that would become the foundation of the madrassa myth: "Obama is a Muslim who has concealed his religion."[44]

So who is Andy Martin? On his own website, Martin describes himself as "the Independent Contrarian Columnist and chief national/foreign correspondent for Out2.com" and "the Managing Director of Andy Martin Worldwide Communications" as well as "Executive Director of the Revolutionary War Research Center" and "Illinois' foremost public interest lawyer" and the author of "The Andy Martin Story."[45] Martin has repeatedly run for office for both parties, from county clerk to mayor to state senator to Congress to governor to U.S. senator to president, in states ranging from Connecticut to Florida to Illinois, always unsuccessfully.[46] Back in 1978, Martin was running as a Democrat in Illinois for the U.S. Senate. A *Chicago Tribune* editorial called him "an absolutely brilliant campaigner" but added that Martin "has no more business in the U.S. Senate than an elk has in a phone booth."[47]

If the *Chicago Tribune* says Martin doesn't belong in the Senate, his reliability as a media source might be questionable as well. Also, according to the *Tribune*, in 1973 Martin was denied admission to the bar in Illinois. The paper reported that he responded to the denial of admission with epithets about the members of the bar review panel.[49] Martin appealed to the Illinois Supreme Court, but the court decision noted that his Selective Service record raised many questions about him. The court said that Martin lacked "responsibility, candor, fairness, self-restraint, objectivity, and respect for the judicial system."[50]

According to the *Chicago Tribune*, in 1980 Martin was sentenced to twelve years in federal prison for mail fraud, but the conviction was overturned.[51] However, the *Tribune* reported that Martin has spent time in prison several times on issues related to contempt of court, and he spent a month in jail in Florida after he was found guilty of damaging a TV station's video camera during his 1996 campaign.[52]

Some of the strangest parts of the madrassa myth spread by Andy Martin are the accusations of Obama's anti-Semitic ties. Martin declared, "It may well be that his concealment is meant to endanger Israel. His Muslim religion would obviously raise serious questions in many Jewish circles where Obama now enjoys support."[53] According to Martin's press release, published on PR Newswire, "Martin says Obama may be a threat to the Jewish community."[54] PR Newswire is a service where anyone can pay to post a press release, which has a disclaimer that it is not responsible for any content posted on the site.[55]

It was especially strange that such questions about Obama would be raised by Martin given his prior statements about Jews and the Jewish community.[56] Many of Martin's statements can be read in the *Chicago Tribune*'s extensive reporting of his remarks from the bankruptcy court records.[57] Just one of Martin's several comments will suffice here. According to the Chicago paper, in an April 21, 1983, court filing, Martin said, "I am able to understand how the Holocaust took place, and with every passing day feel less and less sorry that it did."[58]

Stranger still, on March 13, 2007, Martin announced on PR Newswire that he was "taking public interest legal action against Barack Obama."[59] Martin wrote, "We will be moving shortly in court to block Obama and Random House from marketing his book *Dreams from My Father* as an 'autobiography' or 'biography.' It is fiction, plain and simple."[60]

Martin declared in March 2007 that "Barack Obama is one of the most racist politicians in America today."[61] When Obama's elderly grandmother refused to speak to reporters because of her illness, Martin denounced "Obama's Soviet Union–style attempts to erase his white relatives from public view."[62] Martin asserted that Obama "locked his granny away and refused to allow her to be seen" and added, "America's media have supinely allowed Barry Obama to pretend he has no white relatives."[63]

Martin has asserted that "when the history of the Obama fall-from-media-grace is written, our columns will have been the fuse that exploded the Obama myth and stripped the mask off Barack's face."[64] Perhaps prematurely, Martin claimed, "I am still the 'man who brought down Obama.'"[65] The conservative Illinois blogger ArchPundit agreed that "Andy Martin is the guy who seems to have gotten all this started."[66]

The Media and the Madrassa

But how did such questionable claims about madrassas become fodder for serious discussions in a news cycle? Even after the madrassa story had been thoroughly discredited, *Insight* magazine declared, "Our report on this opposition research activity is completely accurate."[67]

On the morning show of San Francisco radio station KSFO, guest Catherine Moy (coauthor of the book *American Mourning*) declared that Obama "flat-out lied" about the madrassa story. Moy also revealed her source for the information about Obama was Andy Martin. Moy noted that Martin "told me that his research that he did on Barack Obama, that's where Mrs. Clinton got it and leaked it, and that's where you first got your story from *Insight*."[68] In an article for *Contrarian Commentary*, Martin declared, "Even Hillary Clinton began with my research. No surprise; because I was right."[69] Columnist Debbie Schlussel also refused to retract the story and declared, "To whom will he be more sympathetic and loyal—his Muslim family members or you?"[70] Schlussel declared about Muslims: "They hate America and would love one of their own in the White House."[71]

Schlussel's "proof" that Obama's explanations were lies consisted of this inaccurate claim: "Uh, sorry, but public schools DO NOT study the Koran. Islamic schools do." Schlussel also wrote, "Gee, if he wasn't a Muslim, but a Catholic, why would a Catholic identify as a Muslim in a Catholic school? He and his parents were trying to hide his Catholic background from a Catholic school?"[72] Like many students, Obama went to Catholic school even though he wasn't a Catholic, and since his family wasn't religious, he was listed as a Muslim because that was the background of his father.

Insight magazine turned to a traditional conservative trope, blaming the media and then blaming the victim: "The media uproar over our reporting reveals a media establishment choosing not to ask the tough questions about Obama's Muslim past: If he was raised in a secular household (as he claims), why does he have—or retain—Muslim names, Barack and Hussein?"[73] This "tough" question hinted that Obama must change his first and middle names, the names that are his last link to his late father, because they were often perceived as Muslim names. If not, *Insight* was saying, Obama should be suspected of being a covert Muslim—simply because of his name.

The reason why the madrassa myth was believed has much to do with the climate of hate and division in America pushed by the rise of the right-wing media, from Rush Limbaugh to Fox News Channel to *Insight* magazine. *Insight* magazine was utterly shameless about smearing Obama because the far-right media didn't see spreading a lie as anything to feel ashamed about. In a political era when the right-wing media (with help from the mainstream press) successfully smeared John Kerry's honorable service in Vietnam and falsely painted Al Gore as a liar, conservatives have learned that it's better to spread a false smear than try to tell the truth. The madrassa myth was accepted because right-wing media had already absorbed an irrational hatred and suspicion toward Muslims.

Terrorism and Truth

One of the common conservative attacks on Obama was the assertion, similar to one repeated against all Democrats, that Obama's election would be a victory for the terrorists. John Howard, the right-wing prime minister of Australia, directly attacked Obama for urging an end to the war in Iraq: "If I were running al-Qaeda in Iraq, I would put a circle around March 2008 and be praying as many times as possible for a victory, not only for Obama but also for the Democrats."[74]

On the January 29, 2007, edition of Michael Savage's radio show, the far-right talk show host proclaimed, "Are you going to tell me that Obama, Hussein Barack Obama, is going to take our side should there be some kind of catastrophic attack on America? I don't think so."[75] Conservative columnist Star Parker blamed Obama for causing terrorism by his words criticizing the war in Iraq: "They hate us, and they are not going to stop. In fact, they've escalated their terrorism because of comments like Barack Obama's."[76]

The mistake all of these conservatives make is in assuming that terrorism will be defeated by the intensity of their rhetoric, rather than by the use of diplomacy, sound foreign policy, and intelligent military action. They imagine that patriotism must take the form of bloodthirsty rampages around the world, and that anyone who rejects their failed approaches to foreign policy must be on the side of the terrorists.

Struggling to find any basis to attack Obama, the Far Right tried to accuse him of hypocrisy. Dick Morris, in a column for the D.C. newspaper *The Hill*, falsely accused Obama of voting against "a Senate reform banning the increasingly widespread practice of legislators hiring their family members on their campaign or PAC payrolls."[77] In reality, Obama had voted for the bill and Morris admitted misreading the record, but the inaccurate smear against Obama was reprinted by the *Washington Times*, the Salem, Oregon, *Statesman Journal*, and the online *U.S. News and World Report*, NewsMax.com, FrontPageMag.com, Human Events Online, and Family Security Matters.[78]

But Obama was already familiar with the kinds of attacks the right wing launched against him. During his 2004 campaign for the U.S. Senate, he was unfazed by the bizarre outbursts of his Republican opponent Alan Keyes, who declared, "Jesus Christ would not vote for Barack Obama. Christ would not vote for Barack Obama because Barack Obama has behaved in a way that it is inconceivable for Christ to have behaved."[79] Although it is conceivable that Jesus Christ was registered to vote in Chicago in 2004, it is difficult to believe that Alan Keyes would be the only candidate he would vote for.

Obama argued that the conservative name-calling wouldn't affect his campaign: "The American people are smarter than that."[80] Was Obama correct? As Al Gore and John Kerry can report, the right-wing smear machine can be very effective even when promoting absurd anti-Muslim attacks on a Christian candidate. However, the attacks on Obama were so plainly false and so openly racist, and Obama learned to respond to them rapidly and effectively, so that the election wasn't decided by such ignorance.

The Clintons, Obama, and the Conservatives

Conservatives initially struggled to find any substantive objections to Obama, primarily because they focused so little on his candidacy. For conservatives, the 2008 election was all about getting revenge against the Clintons, something the Far Right couldn't accomplish during the 1992 and 1996 elections. The generally positive public opinion about the Clinton administration has been a perpetual thorn in their ideological side, and destroying Hillary Clinton was the only cure.

At the Conservative Political Action Conference in Washington, D.C., in early March 2007 (the leading right-wing conference in the country, which more than 6,000 people attended), the anti-Hillary crusade was on constant display. The tone of the conference was set in the exhibit hall, which featured "Hillary Clinton barf bags," anti-Clinton buttons, and an array of conspiracy theories repeated in the conference lectures. Books such as *The Vast Right-Wing Conspiracy's Dossier on Hillary Rodham Clinton* and *The Clinton Crack-Up* were being promoted to a Clinton-hating audience.

The hatred of Hillary was so overwhelming that some conservatives did not even use her name, reducing her to the female pronoun. Sean Hannity proclaimed, "In the end, we will all unite to stop *her*." He got his biggest applause for saying, "*She* must never be president of the United States." The Far Right even started a website, StopHerNow.com, with the goal of "preventing a Hillary Clinton presidency."

David Bossie, the head of Citizens United, announced that he was creating a documentary on the life of Hillary Clinton. Dick Morris, the former Clinton advisor who was disgraced and turned to the right wing for support after his dalliances with prostitutes were uncovered, planned a documentary attacking Hillary Clinton.

Perhaps the most popular speaker was best-selling right-wing author Ann Coulter, who declared that Bill Clinton was the first black president because he is "half-white, half-trash," a racist remark that was ignored after Coulter caused a storm of controversy when she called John Edwards a "faggot." Coulter largely ignored Obama except to repeat the far-right lies about his background when she proclaimed "B. Hussein Obama" the "perfect candidate" for Democrats: "part atheist, part Christian, part Muslim."

Hillary Clinton drew most of the hatred in the room. Former House majority leader Tom DeLay denounced "the Clinton mafia." Former House speaker Newt Gingrich announced the need to "defeat the Clinton Machine." Michael Barone, a top editor at *U.S. News and World Report*, smeared Hillary Clinton by joking that "one of the leading candidates threw her broom into the ring." The *American Spectator* distributed buttons showing her in a witch's outfit flying on a broom. Conservatives have a hatred of Hillary Clinton that far exceeds anyone else in the world, including Osama bin Laden.

The Far Right has spent so much time demonizing Hillary Clinton and inflating her into a political enemy of gigantic proportions that they could scarcely imagine anyone else winning the Democratic primary. Former House speaker Newt Gingrich has called Hillary Clinton "a nasty woman" and claimed that she runs an "endlessly ruthless" campaign machine. According to Gingrich, "If they think [Obama] is a real threat, they'll just grind him up."[81]

Obama was barely noticed by the right-wingers at the 2007 Conservative Political Action Conference. Kellyanne Conway of the Polling Company proclaimed, "I have not met a single Democrat who knew Barack Obama on 9/11." Of course, not many Democrats knew Bill Clinton or Jimmy Carter seven years before they were elected president. According to Conway, Obama's only attribute worth noticing was his race, and that wouldn't be enough: "Most people are not single-issue voters, and most people are not going to be single-attribute voters."[82]

An index of talk shows (which are overwhelmingly conservative) found that even after Obama announced his plans to run for president, nearly half of all talk segments about the 2008 campaign focused on Hillary Clinton. One conservative blogger observed, "Some of those conservative hosts are not only using their microphones to blast away at Clinton. They are also embracing, or at least saying nice things about, Barack Obama, a liberal Democrat whose primary virtue in their eyes may be that he can defeat Clinton for the nomination."[83] The *National Review* even named its blog about the Democratic presidential primaries "The Hillary Spot," apparently in expectation of her certain victory.[84] Immediately after Obama began exploring a run for president, the right-wing magazine *Human Events* published an article titled, "Hang It Up, Obama—It's Hillary's Nomination."[85]

But many on the right saw Obama as their salvation from another Clinton presidency. Columnist Robert Novak declared that Hillary Clinton "is scared to death of Senator Obama, who is really a very fresh face, and very attractive.... He's a phenomenon."[86]

The Experience Question

Dick Morris proclaimed a vast Clintonesque media conspiracy was being used to prop up an unqualified candidate like Obama: "But soon people will settle down and ask themselves if a freshman senator, with only two years of national office under his belt, can really be president. In the middle of a war, are we going to put a man with absolutely no foreign policy or armed services oversight credentials into the White House? No way. All the media adulation is merely setting Obama up for a nasty fall."[87] By this standard George W. Bush was wholly unqualified to be president because he never held national office (as were Jimmy Carter, Ronald Reagan, and Bill Clinton).

In fighting the war on terrorism, experience isn't the crucial issue. When George W. Bush became president, he had "absolutely no" foreign policy experience. But he put his most experienced buddy, Vice President Dick Cheney, in charge of coordinating the White House antiterrorism efforts. Unfortunately, Cheney was too busy in the summer of 2001 holding secret meetings with energy company executives and never did his job on terrorism.[88] No one knows if the Bush administration could have stopped 9/11, but their failures in this and so many other areas were due to incompetence and indifference, not inexperience.

In the war on Iraq, Bush trusted his two most experienced advisors, Cheney and then secretary of defense Donald Rumsfeld, who had a vast amount of legislative, executive, and business experience stretching back four decades. Yet it was precisely Cheney and Rumsfeld who pushed for war under false pretenses and then mismanaged the war.

The Attack on Liberals

After Obama established himself as a leading contender for the presidency, the right wing began to focus more attacks on him using the traditional attack against a "liberal" Democrat.

Fox News Channel host Sean Hannity declared that Obama has "a bunch of left-wing policy proposals that may frighten moderate Democrats."[89] A *Weekly Standard* writer proclaimed, "If one looks past Obama's rhetoric and at his voting record, it's clear he's far to the left of middle America."[90]

An anonymous conspiracy theorist who writes a political gossip column for the right-wing *Pittsburgh Tribune* declared, "But back in Chicago, the Association of Community Organizations for Reform Now (ACORN) is more important than Iraq or Washington. ACORN and its associated Midwest Academy, both founded in the 1970s, continue to train and mobilize activists throughout the country, often using them to manipulate public opinion through 'direct action.' It's sometimes a code for illegal activities."[91] Obama had little connection to ACORN, and ACORN is a mainstream community organizing group, not a criminal enterprise that in any way promotes illegal activities.

Grover Norquist, head of the right-wing Americans for Tax Reform, described Obama as "a standard-issue, liberal Democrat. What's the difference between Barack Obama and Ted Kennedy on issues? I can't think of one. He wants to raise your taxes and steal your guns."[92] John Fund of the *Wall Street Journal* said, "He has one of the most liberal records in the Senate."[93]

However, Scott Reed, the manager of Bob Dole's 1996 presidential campaign, noted, "Just throwing the 'liberal, liberal, liberal' line at Obama isn't going to work." According to Reed, "Obama is untouchable. He has not made any mistakes. Folks are throwing money at him and his causes. He's wildly popular."[94]

Obama Republicans

The attacks on Obama by the right-wing fringe don't represent the views of most Republicans who know him personally. Perhaps the best testament to Obama's ability to bridge partisan and ideological divides comes from the firsthand experience of conservatives who express their admiration for Obama.

New York Times columnist Frank Rich observed in October 2006, "Search right-wing blogs and you'll find none of the invective showered on other liberal Democrats in general and black liberal leaders in particular."[95] Although the anti-Muslim attacks on Obama changed that equation, it remained the case that Obama was praised by many mainstream conservative politicians and was the most favorably viewed Democratic candidate among Republican voters.

New York Times columnist Bob Herbert suspected a plot behind the niceness: "There's a reason why so many Republicans are saying nice things about Mr. Obama, and urging him to run. They would like nothing more than for the Democrats to nominate a candidate in 2008 who has a very slender résumé, very little experience in national politics, hardly any in foreign policy—and who also happens to be black."[96] However, it is difficult to imagine that Republicans were engaged in some kind of bait-and-switch, hoping to lure Obama into the race in order to crush him. Herbert argued, "The Republicans may be in deep trouble, but they believe they could pretty easily put together a ticket that would chew up Barack Obama in 2008."[97] Many conservatives disagreed. Ramesh Ponnuru of the *National Review* observed, "Right now the conventional wisdom among Republicans is that Obama would be a stronger candidate."[98] Obama sometimes seems to be the only major politician in America for whom bipartisanship is more than an occasional slogan, but instead is a core value. Matthew Dowd, who was George W. Bush's chief campaign strategist in 2004, declared that Obama was the only candidate of either party who appealed to him in 2008 because of his message of unity.[99]

Obama has long been able to appeal to people of all viewpoints. Obama's experience with the *Harvard Law Review* reflects his intelligence and political skill. The members of the *Harvard Law Review* are chosen based on merit for their writing and analytical skills, with only the top 40 Harvard law students out of a class of 540 selected to join in intense competition. The political skills were required to win the vote for president, since Obama was competing against 18 other candidates (three of them were black). Brad Berenson, a former associate counsel to president George W. Bush who also worked with Obama on the *Harvard Law Review,* observed: "Compared to Washington and the White House and the Supreme Court, the *Harvard Law Review* was much more politically vicious." According to Berenson, "The conservatives threw their support to Obama because he could bridge the gap between both camps and retain the trust and confidence of both."[100]

Carol Platt Liebau, a strong conservative columnist who worked with Obama on the *Harvard Law Review*, describes him with great admiration despite her complete disagreement with his ideology. Liebau said that "Barack is a deeply committed liberal, and I am a proud conservative. Even so, he possesses five qualities that are genuinely praiseworthy," calling him "intelligent," "color-blind," "self-confident," with a "sense of humor" and saying that "he listens." Liebau observed, "Unlike many of his left-wing compatriots, he treated his ideological adversaries with respect on a personal level. Indeed, he always offered the small conservative contingent on the *Review* a hearing, even though his decision making consistently showed that he hadn't ultimately been influenced by their arguments."[101]

These are not the words of an Obama devotee, but of someone who fundamentally disagrees with his political viewpoint. It is almost impossible to imagine a prominent conservative columnist speaking in such lauda-tory terms about Bill Clinton or another Democrat. Even John McCain, a maverick Republican widely admired for his military background, found it difficult to get any liberal to praise him in such terms.

New York Times conservative columnist David Brooks noted, "I disagree with Obama on most issues, and I've had several interviews with him. He really hears what you say, and he reflects your argument in its best light."[102] Secretary of State Condoleezza Rice noted that Obama served on the Senate Foreign Relations Committee and observed, "I think he's very appealing and a great person. He's on my committee. And we've always had good exchanges. I think he's an extraordinary person."[103] Republican Congress-man Ray LaHood noted, "I certainly know Senator Obama a lot more, a lot better, because I've worked with him. A week after he was elected two years ago, he was in my office in Peoria, and we were talking about how we could work together for Illinois.... I like the fact that he ... tries to work in a very bipartisan way." According to LaHood, "He's very sophisticated. He's very smart."[104]

Kirk Dillard, a Republican state senator in Illinois who served with Obama, observed: "If Barack has any enemies out there, they come from just sheer jealousy." According to Dillard, "When he first came to Springfield, many resented his good looks, his articulate speaking ability, and his intellect," but Obama won over his colleagues.[105] Dick Lugar, a Republican senator from Indiana, observed: "Barack is studying issues that are very important for the country and for the world."[106] Tom Coburn, the conservative Republican senator from Oklahoma, said "If Barack disagrees with you or thinks you haven't done something appropriate, he's the kind of guy who'll talk to you about it. He'll come up and reconcile: 'I don't think you were truthful about my bill.' I've seen him do that. On the Senate floor." According to Coburn, "What Washington does is cause everybody to concentrate on where they disagree as opposed to where they agree. But leadership changes that. And Barack's got the capability, I believe—and the pizzazz and the charisma—to be a leader of America, not a leader of Democrats."[107]

Conservative and moderate voters shared admiration for Obama. In 2004, Obama got one million votes in Illinois from people who also voted for George W. Bush over John Kerry. One Bush voter, Monica Green, told the *Chicago Sun-Times* that although she was a Republican, she was volunteering for Obama and even donated $250 to his campaign: "I trust him when he says he wants to transform politics. Just call me a Republican voting for Barack Obama."[108]

In 2004, the conservative magazine *American Spectator* dismissed Obama's political future: "We can be confident that a Senator Barack Obama will become the next Paul Wellstone—a nice, bright guy relegated to the back benches of the liberal fringe."[109] By 2007, the same magazine noted in a profile of Obama, "The charismatic freshman senator may just be the Democrat who can beat Hillary—and make liberalism a winning philosophy again. Neither the Clintons nor conservatives should ignore his appeal."[110]

Obama is partisan in the sense that he takes ideological stands that divide people. But for Obama, partisanship is a necessary evil to be avoided, not the foundation of his political approach. Ultimately, any candidate who wants to be elected president and enact a successful political agenda must be able to negotiate a deeply divided government and a deeply divided country. Obama's desire to work with people who disagree with him, even in the face of vicious, hateful attacks by the Far Right, reflects a politician who can rise above partisan divisions.

CHAPTER FIVE

Why Leftists Hate a Liberal

The Far Left Attacks on Obama

If the Democrats can't inspire, if they can't tap into some sense of meaning that goes beyond just dollars and cents, then it's going to be very hard for them to argue against the sort of selfishness and self-interested policies that have come to dominate our politics.

—Barack Obama

The notion that Barack Obama is "too conservative" belongs in the same category as the idea that he is "too white." However, groups in powerless positions tend to turn on their own, whether they are African Americans or progressives dreaming of political power and distrusting anyone who manages to succeed. Among both groups, gaining power is associated far too often with "selling out."

Although the Far Right launched an aggressive attack on Obama, some of the worst denunciations against him came from the leftist wing of his own party, the very group one might expect to be his strongest supporters. And while Obama receives a strong embrace from most progressives, he has also faced sharp attacks from the left. *New York Times* columnist Frank Rich observed, "What little criticism Mr. Obama has received is from those in his own camp who find him cautious to a fault, especially on issues that might cause controversy. The sum of all his terrific parts, this theory goes, may be less than the whole: another Democrat who won't tell you what day it is before calling a consultant, another human weather vane who waits to see which way the wind is blowing before taking a stand."[1]

Progressives have been out of power so thoroughly for so long that they are generally incapable of recognizing the difference between pragmatism and selling out. Under the harsh glare of ideology, all of the shades and nuances so essential to a political understanding are washed away. When so many politicians have lied to you so often before, it becomes difficult to trust anyone in office who makes a promise.

The leftist attacks on Obama began almost immediately after his 2004 speech at the Democratic National Convention. Paul Street wrote in *Z Magazine* online, "The worldview enunciated in Obama's address comes from a very different, bourgeois-individualist and national-narcissist moral and ideological space. Obama praised America as the ultimate 'beacon of freedom and opportunity' for those who exhibit 'hard work and perseverance' and laid claim to personally embodying the great American Horatio Algerian promise." According to Street, "He advocated a more equal rat race."[2] That's true: Obama is no left-wing radical advocating a socialist utopia. Obama is a capitalist, a reformist seeking to improve the system and not a revolutionary trying to overthrow it.

Street also objected to Obama's message of unity: "Real leftists are suspicious of those who downplay internal national divisions, 'patriotically' privileging 'homeland' unity over class differences and over international solidarity between people inclined towards peace, justice, and democracy." Street declared, "[M]any leftists cringed when they heard the newly anointed Great Progressive Hope Obama refer to Americans as 'one people, all of us pledging allegiance to the stars and stripes, all of us defending the United States of America.'"[3]

When Obama talks about pledging allegiance to the flag, he's not bringing us back to a politics appealing to the lowest common denominator and replacing ideas with flag waving. Instead, Obama invokes patriotism for a purpose: to remind us of the ideals that America is supposed to stand for and to promote the concept of a political fight in which one does not question an opponent's patriotism, but can civilly and thoughtfully disagree about policy. Obama's invocation of common symbols and unified people is not merely co-opting the flag cynically to win elections. It serves as a symbol of what he is campaigning for, the idea of unifying a divided country. Although Obama disagrees with the Far Left, he is unusual compared to past leaders in the Democratic Party because he is willing to listen to radicals and understand their point of view. Obama will never embrace the agendas of the Far Left, but he is willing to take valuable ideas and make them part of improving government.

The Left and Obama

The *New Yorker*'s David Remnick told Obama, "Some people on the left, and as you put it in the blogosphere, have been pretty tough on you about being maybe too mild about the Bush administration."[4]

This misunderstands what kind of politician Obama is. Obama is not a crusader, standing up for a lonely, just cause and fighting every opponent to his last breath. He is a compromiser and a uniter at a time when many on the left see compromise as betrayal and unity as suspicious.

Nation columnist Alexander Cockburn denounced Obama as "slithery" and attacked "Obamaspeak" as "a pulp of boosterism about the American dream, interspersed with homilies about 'putting factionalism and party divisions behind us and moving on.'"[5] Leftists were also upset because Obama endorsed prowar incumbent Senator Joe Lieberman over antiwar candidate Ned Lamont in the 2006 Connecticut Democratic primary. Cockburn reported that Lamont supporters were "exceptionally bitter about the role played by Obama, who made the calculation that Lieberman would win and that he would not forfeit political capital by doing anything for his fellow Democrat, Lamont."[6] However, after Lamont won the primary and Lieberman ran as an independent, Obama endorsed Lamont in the general election, donated money to his campaign, and wrote an e-mail supporting Lamont.[7] But it is true that Obama did not aggressively campaign against his conservative friend.

David Sirota, an *In These Times* contributing editor who worked on the Lamont campaign, was one of the progressives who denounced Obama. He wrote about Obama: "[T]his is a person who wants to do the right thing and has genuinely strong convictions. But he also seems to believe that the reason our country has such challenges is because all sides of every issue have not come together in unity." According to Sirota, "[T]here is no 'third way' or 'consensus' way out of many of our most pressing problems, as Obama seems to believe. Why? Because many of our most pressing problems are zero-sum: Someone is benefiting from the status quo, and to change the status quo means someone may lose something."[8] Obama rejects this kind of zero-sum thinking, which regards politics as a fight to the death for resources that cannot be shared. Instead, Obama emphasizes the idea of shared interests. Health care is an example where inefficiency is a key problem and where businesses, and even the wealthy, can benefit from a solution to the broken health care system that is so expensive.

But the disagreements between Obama and progressives are more about tactics, not values and convictions. On the day when it was announced that Obama had gotten more than 100,000 donors in less than three months while banning gifts from federal lobbyists, Sirota framed it this way: "[O]ne of the Illinois senator's biggest donors is the family that owns one of the largest defense contractors in the world, General Dynamics." From this, Sirota concluded: "What a shock, then, that Obama hasn't discussed our bloated military budget.... What a surprise to see Obama triangulating against potential plans to reduce funding for the Iraq War."[9] It's a stretch to imagine that Obama's policies on defense funding are determined by the investments of a family that gave him some donations in the past.

Obama's success at raising money has drawn other attacks. University of Texas at Austin journalism professor and progressive writer Robert Jensen declared about Obama, "He is not presenting any particularly progressive alternative" and accused him of "playing the game" of big money in campaign funding.[10] It is true that Obama played the game (and played it well) of big money. However, until the rules of the game are changed, raising money is part of our political campaign system. Unlike most senators, Obama doesn't come from a wealthy background, and he had to raise money to succeed in politics. Yet Obama became one of the leaders in both the Illinois Senate and the U.S. Senate on campaign reform and efforts to limit big money. Obama ultimately raised $770 million for his campaign along with more than $100 million for a Democratic National Committee fund and another $100 million for convention, transition, and inauguration expenses. Obama's massive fundraising from the general public, with millions of donations online, makes him virtually immune to any demands by big donors for influence.[11]

Civil Unions and Gay Marriages

One of Obama's pragmatic stands troubling to progressives is on gay marriage. In the U.S. Senate debate, Obama opposed the right-wing Federal

Marriage Amendment to ban gay marriage nationally and declared: "I agree with most Americans, with Democrats and Republicans, with Vice President Cheney, with over 2,000 religious leaders of all different beliefs, that decisions about marriage, as they always have, should be left to the states." However, Obama also declared, "Personally, I do believe that marriage is between a man and a woman."[12] At the same time, Obama has strongly supported civil unions, arguing that it is a way to protect equal rights without taking the politically risky approach of gay marriage.

Obama got himself in further trouble by failing to denounce homophobia. As Obama was leaving a 2007 event, a reporter asked him, "What do you think about General Pace's comments that homosexuality is immoral?"[13] Obama responded, "I think traditionally the Joint Chiefs of Staff chairman has restricted his public comments to military matters. That's probably a good tradition to follow."[14] Obama was asked the question again and said, "I think the question here is whether somebody is willing to sacrifice for their country, should they be able to? If they are doing all the things that are needed to be done."[15]

Obama later told Larry King, "I don't think that homosexuals are immoral any more than I think heterosexuals are immoral."[16] But for many Obama supporters, that was too late. Michael Bauer, a gay activist and Obama fundraiser, declared: "I was in disbelief. Totally perplexed that in the face of such bigotry what we were receiving was silence."[17] Jason Zengerle on the *New Republic* website accused Obama of "pandering to bigots" because he didn't directly condemn Pace's view.[18]

Obama has taken a forthright stand calling for the end of the "don't ask, don't tell" policy of discrimination by the military: "It is time to revisit the 'don't ask, don't tell' policy and do what is in the best interests of our national security. At a time when the services are having a tough time recruiting and retaining troops, it seems foolish to kick out good soldiers, sailors, airmen and Marines who want to serve."[19]

Obama and the Middle East

At a rally in Chicago in February 2007, Obama was briefly interrupted by a group of antiwar students who shouted, "Troops out now!" and "Stand up. Cut the funding." Obama declared, "We have a responsibility to be as careful coming out as we were careless getting in." But he later said, "I'm glad they were there. They feel a sense of urgency about a war that should have never been authorized and a war that should have never been fought."[20] Although Obama strongly opposed the Iraq War in 2002, before it ever began, many antiwar progressives have been frustrated by Obama's failure to be a leader in the fight to end the war.

Bill Fletcher of the *Black Commentator* declared himself "very uneasy about some of the senator's foreign policy pronouncements, particularly with regard to the Middle East. To his credit, he opposed the Iraq invasion and had the courage to say so. Yet over the last year, he has displayed a peculiarly uncritical stance when it comes to Israel and has all but ignored the plight of the Palestinians. This past summer, when Israel launched its massive and deadly assault on Lebanon, the senator was quite vocal in his support."[21]

Ali Abunimah, an advocate for Palestinians and the cofounder of the *Electronic Intifada* website, called Obama "a master triangulator." He recalled meeting Obama several times when he was a state senator: "He impressed me as progressive, intelligent and charismatic. I distinctly remember thinking 'if only a man of this caliber could become president one day.'"[22] Abunimah reported that when Obama was running for the U.S. Senate, he told Abunimah, "Keep up the good work!" and said to him, "Hey, I'm sorry I haven't said more about Palestine right now, but we are in a tough primary race. I'm hoping when things calm down I can be more up front." Abunimah told a friend that Obama "was often very progressive about Israel-Palestine. He attended fundraisers in the Palestinian community, one in which the keynote speaker was Edward Said. That's what really made me believe in him at first. But then it all went out the window when he started his climb up the greasy pole."[23]

When Obama gave a speech to the American Israel Public Affairs Committee (AIPAC), he expressed support for Israel as "our strongest ally in the region and its only established democracy" and urged funding missile defense programs to protect Israel. Obama also defended Israel's assault on Lebanon as its "legitimate right to defend itself."[24] When progressive financier George Soros expressed criticism of Israel and support for dealing with Hamas, the elected leaders of Palestine, Obama announced his criticism of Soros's view.[25] According to Abunimah, "His decisive trajectory reinforces a lesson that politically weak constituencies have learned many times: Access to people with power alone does not translate into influence over policy. Money and votes, but especially money, channeled through sophisticated and coordinated networks that can 'bundle' small donations into million-dollar chunks, are what buy influence on policy."[26]

However, Obama's changing rhetoric on Israel reflected the fact that the mainstream media deemed criticism of Israel impermissible for any major presidential candidate. A *New York Times* article called Obama "less experienced" than Hillary Clinton in dealing with Jewish and Middle Eastern politics and declared that "he became a bit tangled in the eyes of some voters" merely because he dared to say, "Nobody is suffering more than the Palestinian people."[27] It apparently did not occur to the *New York Times* reporter that perhaps Obama didn't make a mistake, that perhaps Obama has a different view of the issue and is willing to express it even in front of a potentially hostile audience such as AIPAC, which regards any sympathy for Palestinians as suspect.

Obama and the Bush Doctrine

Obama's failure to condemn all military action led to sharp criticism from some on the left. Leftist blogger Glen Ford declared, "Barack Obama is an imperialist."[28] Left-wing historian and antiwar activist Anthony Arnove, critiquing Obama, noted: "He accepts the Bush Doctrine. He accepts the doctrine of preemptive strikes."[29]

The key part of the Bush Doctrine is the focus on unilateral action and the use of force to spread "democracy" around the world.[30] And the worst part of the Bush administration was not the Bush Doctrine but Bush's implementation of it. Plenty of presidents asserted tough-sounding doctrines, but few ever implemented them with quite so much ruthless incompetence as George W. Bush. As Obama famously declared in 2002, he did not oppose all wars, but he did oppose a "dumb war"—which he foresaw in Iraq.[31] It is often tempting to advocate policies that fix the mistakes of the previous war. Isolationism must not be the reaction to a dumb president and a dumb war.

There is no Obama Doctrine, because Obama is not a doctrinaire kind of leader who operates according to fixed policies. Instead, Obama believes in a set of principles (democracy, security, liberty) for the world and tries to come up with practical measures for incrementally increasing U.S. security and global freedom. He rejects isolationism, and he tries to steer clear of unilateralism.

Barack Obama has noted that the Iranian government is "a threat to all of us" and "we should take no option, including military action, off the table."[32] During the first Democratic debate, in South Carolina on April 26, 2007, this prompted former Alaska governor Mike Gravel to ask, "Tell me Barack. Barack, who do you want to nuke?" Obama replied, "I'm not planning to nuke anybody right now, Mike, I promise."[33] While the idea that Obama would drop a nuclear bomb on Iran is a crackpot notion, his aggressive rhetoric toward Iran raised concerns on the left. Because Obama would not rule out military action against Iran if it acquired nuclear weapons, William Blum in *CounterPunch* declared, "Obama is clearly showing that he's presidential material by meeting the first requirement for that office: no inhibitions about killing large numbers of innocent and defenseless foreign people."[34]

The political realities of a biased media require candidates to talk tough in order to be taken seriously. Obama wrote in 2005 that "our job is harder than the conservatives' job. After all, it's easy to articulate a belligerent foreign policy based solely on unilateral military action, a policy that sounds tough and acts dumb; it's harder to craft a foreign policy that's tough and smart."[35] Obama declared the war on Iraq was a direct consequence of a foreign policy that "sounds tough and acts dumb."[36]

Even when Obama took a tough stand against terrorists in Pakistan, he was denounced by the Washington establishment for violating the unspoken rule against criticizing American allies. Obama promised in a speech to attack terrorists such as Osama bin Laden inside Pakistan if necessary: "If we have actionable intelligence about high-value terrorist targets and President Musharraf won't act, we will."[37] Mitt Romney declared, "I had to laugh at what I saw Barack Obama do. I mean, in one week, he went from saying he's going to sit down, you know, for tea with our enemies but then he's going to bomb our allies. I mean, he's gone from Jane Fonda to Dr. Strangelove in one week."[38] Romney agreed with Obama's "Dr. Strangelove" policy of attacking terrorists, but believed that such truths should not be spoken in public. Hillary Clinton agreed with Obama on attacking terrorists, as did Joe Biden, but she claimed, "It's not something you talk about;

as president, it's something I would do." Obama noted about Clinton, "She said, 'I don't think we should talk about it.' Well, I think we should talk about it. I think the American people ought to have a debate about our foreign policy because it's so messed up and if we don't talk about it we're going to end up repeating the same mistakes."[39]

When Obama told a reporter that he would not use nuclear weapons in precision attacks against Osama bin Laden and other terrorist leaders, Hillary Clinton denounced Obama: "I don't believe that any president should make any blanket statements with respect to the use or nonuse of nuclear weapons." However, Clinton herself had said that about Iran in 2006, "I would certainly take nuclear weapons off the table."[40] Harvard Professor Samantha Power, a foreign policy advisor to Obama, noted, "Barack Obama gave the sensible answer that nuclear force was not necessary, and would kill too many civilians. Conventional wisdom held this up as a sign of inexperience. But if experience leads you to make gratuitous threats about nuclear use—inflaming fears at home and abroad, and signaling nuclear powers and nuclear aspirants that using nuclear weapons is acceptable behavior, it is experience that should not be relied upon."[41]

Another gaffe in the eyes of the Washington establishment occurred when Obama declared about Afghanistan, "We've got to get the job done there, and that requires us to have enough troops so that we are not just air raiding villages and killing civilians, which is causing enormous pressure there." Mitt Romney's spokesperson denounced Obama's statement as an "entirely inaccurate condemnation" of U.S. soldiers, even though Obama was criticizing U.S. policy in order to support the troops, not alleging any intentional killing of civilians. An Associated Press study found that Americans had killed more civilians in Afghanistan in 2007 than the insurgents did.[42]

The attacks on Obama helped to reinforce the myth of his inexperience in foreign affairs. The *CBS Evening News* proclaimed Hillary Clinton "a far better-known candidate with more experience" than Obama.[43] An August 2007 CBS News poll found that 80 percent of Democrats thought Hillary Clinton had "the right kind of experience to be a good president," compared to only 41 percent who thought Obama did.[44] Obama noted that there had been "a premium on reciting the conventional wisdom in Washington" and "that's what passes for experience."[45]

Samantha Power argued that experience is a term used to cover up the flaws of conventional thinking: "It was Washington's conventional wisdom that led us into the worst strategic blunder in the history of U.S. foreign policy. The rush to invade Iraq was a position advocated by not only the Bush administration but also by editorial pages, the foreign policy establishment of both parties, and majorities in both houses of Congress. Those who opposed the war were often labeled weak, inexperienced, and even naive." According to Power, "Barack Obama's judgment is right; the conventional wisdom is wrong. We need a new era of tough, principled, and engaged American diplomacy to deal with twenty-first-century challenges."[46]

But toughness always trumps intelligence in the press. Obama was reminded of this during the first Democratic presidential debate. When moderator Brian Williams asked what he would do if al-Qaeda hit two U.S. cities, Obama responded, "The first thing we'd have to do is make sure that we've got an effective emergency response, something that this administration failed to do when we had a hurricane in New Orleans. And I think that we have to review how we operate in the event of not only a natural disaster, but also a terrorist attack. The second thing is to make sure that we've got good intelligence, (a) to find out that we don't have other threats and attacks potentially out there, and, (b) to find out, do we have any intelligence on who might have carried it out so that we can take potentially some action to dismantle that network." Later in the debate, after John Edwards and Hillary Clinton had given a more militaristic reply to the question, Obama added, "We have genuine enemies out there that have to be hunted down; networks have to be dismantled. There is no contradiction between us intelligently using our military and, in some cases, lethal force to take out terrorists and, at the same time, building the sort of alliances and trust around the world that has been so lacking over the last six years."[47]

After the debate a news report in the *Washington Post* declared, "At issue is whether Obama mishandled a question about how he would respond if two American cities were attacked by terrorists: Did he fail to demonstrate the toughness and resolve that voters want in a president or was his answer a careful and comprehensive checklist for any potential president dealing with an international crisis?"[48] In his take on the debate, conservative columnist Robert Novak declared, "Obama, meanwhile, was extremely disappointing. His fans hold out hope that he will improve in the coming months, but the consensus is that he lost by not winning the debate. All jokes aside, his reputation as an 'articulate' politician comes into some question after this debate, particularly after his failure to state right away that he would retaliate in case of further terrorist strikes against the United States."[49] "Virtually all of the analysis was that Barack stumbled on that question," noted Chicago commentator Bruce DuMont.[50] Columnist Clarence Page declared, "In a moment that called for a blood-stirring vow to avenge America against all attackers, he seemed to change the subject."[51]

After Hillary Clinton attacked Obama as "irresponsible and frankly naive" because he offered in the July 2007 CNN/YouTube debate to meet with controversial leaders of foreign countries, the mainstream press piled on the condemnations.[52] In the world of the Washington consensus, even the slightest deviation from the status quo, no matter how sensible, is treated like a massive blunder. According to the *Washington Post*, "Clinton advisers quickly cast Obama's answer as a rookie mistake," and *New York Times* columnist David Brooks wrote that Obama "continues to make rookie mistakes, like saying he'd talk with Hugo Chávez."[53] Offering to speak to the democratically elected leader of Venezuela isn't a mistake or "insane" as Brooks claimed—it's a different kind of foreign policy from the failed approach of the Bush administration, which refuses to engage in diplomacy with its critics.[54] Obama will be a president who's not afraid of talking to foreign leaders, but the conventional wisdom in Washington holds that America must bully the rest of the world rather than persuade and negotiate.

Obama and the Progressives

Of course, many left-wing critiques of Obama are well deserved and on target. He is an imperfect politician in a corrupt political system. But many attacks were inaccurate. Alexander Cockburn proclaimed, "And so, Obama, the constitutional law professor, voted to close off any filibuster of Alito, and fled Senator Russell Feingold's motion to censure the president."[55] In reality, Obama voted against cloture of the Alito filibuster (and unlike Feingold, Obama opposed the nomination of Chief Justice John Roberts).[56]

The censure of George W. Bush was a perfect example of purely symbolic, divisive legislation that Obama avoids, not evidence of betraying progressive causes. Barack Obama will never be a progressive Don Quixote swinging his rhetorical sword at conservative windmills.

Other progressives challenged Obama's political skills. As liberal blogger Ezra Klein put it, "So far, Obama has proven himself a unifying and consensus-building figure in that a lot of liberals like him. He's not proven himself a unifying and consensus figure able to pass major articles of legislation or defuse traditional opponents to his ideas." According to Klein, "Obama has never passed a major piece of legislation in the United States Senate, after all."[57] Of course, it would be difficult to identify any "major" legislation passed by the previous do-nothing, Republican-controlled Senate of Obama's first term. Despite this, Obama proved that he was a unifying figure who worked with Republicans to pass valuable legislation on arms control and pork-barrel spending.[58]

The progressive suspicion of Obama may also reflect the fact that Obama is leery of embracing labels. Obama said during his 2004 campaign: "When I'm accused of being liberal, really, what's focused on is maybe a handful of votes and in each of those cases I think the position that I took was the right position."[59] Back in 2004, the concern of most political pundits was that Obama might be too liberal even to win the Illinois Democratic primary for the Senate. *Nation* blogger Adam Howard noted that, despite Obama's views, "progressives are skeptical. They assail his voting record, when it's actually one of the most progressive we have to choose from. They question his experience when two of our greatest presidents, Kennedy and Lincoln, could barely boast of having more in their days."[60] As Howard put it, "Americans who are on the left of the political spectrum have been complaining for years now about a lack of an exciting alternative to the Republicans come election time. They held their noses as they cast votes for conventional, safe and experienced candidates like Walter Mondale, Michael Dukakis, Al Gore and John Kerry. All of them were decent, qualified men who inspired practically no one. Why not now, just for a moment, bask in the adoration and admiration that Obama manages to generate, and instead of picking him apart, perhaps we should just be glad that he appears to be on our side."[61]

Media critic Eric Alterman observed about Obama, "He's not a radical by any means, but he is trying to effect change within the system rather than merely master it."[62] Joel Bleifuss, editor of *In These Times*, noted, "Those of us in the Chicago progressive community still believe in Barack Obama. But at the moment we're pretty much taking it on faith."[63]

If Obama appeals to moderate progressives far more than he does to the radical left, that's inevitable in a political system where the Far Left is a tiny minority. No electable presidential candidate will ever satisfy their goals, just as no past president ever did. Even Franklin Delano Roosevelt was, in the eyes of the Far Left, a centrist who undertook progressive policies only under extreme circumstances to save capitalism from its own failures. Obama is a similar kind of politician, and without a Great Depression to push desperate changes, he would never challenge fundamental American institutions because he believes those institutions work well; they just need to work better for all people. One story told about Roosevelt is that early in his first administration, he met with a group of progressives who urged new policies. Roosevelt agreed with them and then told them, "So now, go out there and make me do it."[64]

Even during a financial crisis, Obama alone will not bring a progressive revolution; no single individual can do that, not even a president. But Obama's presidency must be part of a larger social justice movement that not only presses him but also pushes change among the recalcitrant members of Congress in both parties who are deeply attached to the status quo.

Obama among the Kossacks

Obama has not been afraid to argue about his differences with many progressives. Obama posted an entry on the progressive blog *Daily Kos*, arguing, "There is one way, over the long haul, to guarantee the appointment of judges that are sensitive to issues of social justice, and that is to win the right to appoint them by recapturing the presidency and the Senate. And I don't believe we get there by vilifying good allies, with a lifetime record of battling for progressive causes, over one vote or position. I am convinced that, our mutual frustrations and strongly held beliefs notwithstanding, the strategy driving much of Democratic advocacy, and the tone of much of our rhetoric, is an impediment to creating a workable progressive majority in this country."[65]

Obama laid out his opposition to the traditional leftist politics often expressed on *Daily Kos*: "According to the story line that drives many advocacy groups and Democratic activists—a story line often reflected in comments on this blog—we are up against a sharply partisan, radically conservative, take-no-prisoners Republican Party. They have beaten us twice by energizing their base with red meat rhetoric and single-minded devotion and discipline to their agenda. In order to beat them, it is necessary for Democrats to get some backbone, give as good as they get, brook no compromise, drive out Democrats who are interested in 'appeasing' the right wing, and enforce a more clearly progressive agenda. The country, finally knowing what we stand for and seeing a sharp contrast, will rally to our side and thereby usher in a new progressive era."[66]

Obama rejected the Far Left approach: "I think this perspective misreads the American people. From traveling throughout Illinois and more recently around the country, I can tell you that Americans are suspicious of labels and suspicious of jargon. They don't think George Bush is mean-spirited or prejudiced, but have become aware that his administration is irresponsible and often incompetent. They don't think America is an imperialist brute, but are angry that the case to invade Iraq was exaggerated, are worried that we have unnecessarily alienated existing and potential allies around the world, and are ashamed by events like those at Abu Ghraib which violate our ideals as a country."[67]

Obama argued that much of the country views these political fights through a "nonideological lens" and that it's necessary to understand this approach in order to get genuine progressive change: "We won't be able to transform the country with such a polarized electorate." According to Obama, without a pragmatic, unifying approach "we won't have the popular support to craft a foreign policy that meets the challenges of globalization or terrorism while avoiding isolationism and protecting civil liberties. We certainly won't have a mandate to overhaul a health care policy that overcomes all the entrenched interests that are the legacy of a jerry-rigged health care system. And we won't have the broad political support, or the effective strategies, required to lift large numbers of our fellow citizens out of numbing poverty."[68]

Obama's approach is a deeply pragmatic form of progressive politics. Obama is opposed to progressives who think that purity equals power and that any hint of pragmatism is a kind of corruption. Ezra Klein argued (in a piece titled "We Want a Divider, Not a Uniter"): "The question many Democrats must ask before they hitch themselves to the Obama bandwagon is whether he is a progressive or a uniter. . . . I fear that a former community organizer's appetite for consensus leads him to underestimate the depth of opposition, and could possibly lead him to abandon progressive policies in office."[69] But the progressive view that the Democrats must push partisanship is flawed. What Obama understands is that success in pursuing progressive policies comes from uniting the country behind these ideas. Pragmatic politics have long been shunned by progressive adherents who associate it with the betrayals of the Clinton administration. But pragmatism is fundamentally different from Clintonesque triangulation. Triangulators sacrifice their principles to achieve political power. Pragmatists use the best feasible means to achieve political goals. *New Republic* literary editor Leon Wieseltier observed, "As an antidote to polarization, he seems to be proposing what used to be called, when Bill Clinton did it so well, triangulation: He is running another end-of-ideology campaign."[70] Yet Obama has noted, "Let me be clear: I am not arguing that the Democrats should trim their sails and be more 'centrist.'" Obama explicitly rejects the Clintonesque strategy of triangulation: "Too often, the 'centrist' label seems to mean compromise for compromise's sake, whereas on issues like health care, energy, education and tackling poverty, I don't think Democrats have been bold enough. But I do think that being bold involves more than just putting more money into existing programs and will instead require us to admit that some existing programs and policies don't work very well."[71]

Alexander Cockburn also accused Obama of being in "the right-center segment of the political landscape inhabited by the Democratic Leadership Council."[72] But when the DLC listed Obama as one of the young leaders to watch, Obama had it take his name off the list because he didn't want to be associated with the centrist group that was strongly linked to Bill Clinton. Obama also recalled, "I remember back in 2004, one of the candidates had made a proposal about universal health care, and some DLC-type commentator said, 'We can't propose this kind of big-government costly program, because it'll send a signal we're tax-and-spend liberals.' But that's not a good reason to not do something. You don't give up on the goal of universal health care because you don't want to be tagged as a liberal. People need universal health care."[73] This is why Obama should be described as a pragmatic progressive rather than a centrist, even if sometimes his rhetoric and his policies may seem to be moving to the middle.

Does Obama's pragmatism work as a political strategy? Because no charismatic politician has ever really tried it, we don't know. Perhaps Obama's approach doesn't succeed in every case, in every time. But for America in the twenty-first century, having suffered through the failed presidency of George W. Bush, Obama's approach is more than a breath of fresh air. It's an opportunity to bring forth a new form of politics, one that is simultaneously progressive and popular and politically effective. Pragmatism will never satisfy those who think the progressive movement is all about positing a utopian society rather than achieving social change. Obama has rarely sponsored a bill that progressives would regard as perfect. In fact, he probably never sponsored a bill that he himself regarded as perfect. Obama's goal was always to pass a bill to achieve social change, not to make a merely symbolic stand.

As a community organizer, Obama met plenty of people who could talk the talk about injustice and criticize the status quo. But changing the system required a lot of hard work and lowered expectations. To Obama, progress doesn't come from imagining some utopian ideal and waiting around for someone to bestow it upon us; progress comes from incremental steps toward an ideal that will never be reached.

Liberals often embrace candidates who sound progressive because they run to the left for the primary and then run to the right during the general election—and end up undermining any authority they might have and distancing the voters who want integrity. Obama generally has not played this political game, and it is part of what makes him different from traditional politicians.

Conservatives and liberals have learned different lessons from losing. In 1964, when Barry Goldwater was trounced by Lyndon B. Johnson, it actually launched today's conservative movement that culminated in the election of Ronald Reagan in 1980. In 1972, when George McGovern was trounced by Richard Nixon (largely because the centrist Democratic machine elites abandoned McGovern), the progressive movement in the Democratic Party was dead. Democrats starting with Jimmy Carter always ran to the center and avoided a progressive agenda like the plague. After the miserable failures of Al Gore and John Kerry employing this approach, many progressives have argued that Democrats need to follow the conservative approach post-Goldwater and win by standing for something. Obama is trying to bridge these two approaches, to have integrity and progressive values, while simultaneously presenting a more centrist face that appeals across political boundaries.

Obama has also rejected the idea popular among political consultants of smearing opponents. Obama argued, "I firmly believe that whenever we exaggerate or demonize, or oversimplify or overstate our case, we lose."[74] Obama's approach was certainly counterintuitive to many progressives who had witnessed the success of conservative forces in exaggerating, demonizing, and oversimplifying the case against Democratic candidates, to the point of creating a new word to describe the process of lying about a candidate to defeat him or her: swiftboating. It would be tempting to turn the same tactics against the Right. But Obama was right to criticize demonizing as a political tactic for progressives. The Left doesn't have a vast media empire of talk shows and pundits to sustain a campaign of hate and lies. Progressives aren't given the benefit of the doubt by the mainstream press when they engage in these attacks, as the right wing has been. Obama argued, "Whenever we dumb down the political debate, we lose. A polarized electorate that is turned off of politics, and easily dismisses both parties because of the nasty, dishonest tone of the debate, works perfectly well for those who seek to chip away at the very idea of government."[75]

The Republicans win elections by driving down the number of average citizens voting while activating their own base. They know that if Americans ever voted at the 85 percent levels common in France and many other countries, the Republicans today would never win another presidential election. The Republican vote depends upon a discouraged electorate that doesn't vote. That's why part of the bag of Republican dirty tricks is to banish voters by challenging their registration or expunging imagined "ex-felons" from the voting rolls. The Republicans know that they can win only if most Americans don't vote.

Obama's experience registering voters and organizing disillusioned people who are the most alienated from our political system has educated him about the power of the discouraged voter. Obama did more than activate the base; he inspired a few million new voters to participate in the political process, and that transformed the political system.

Politicians have largely been accustomed to ignoring the interests of young people and the poor. Why? They don't vote, they don't give, and they don't lobby. And in a corrupt political system that revolves around money, inspiring a new generation of voters to take political power amounts to an incredible transformation.

Progressives have failed so often and so badly in recent political races that they have lost the capacity to understand the American political process. Instead, progressives career wildly from hopeless optimism for unelectable candidates (remember Nader?) to naive hope in centrist career politicians (remember Kerry?) who lose anyway. All of the disappointment progressives have felt about both the winners (Clinton) and the losers (Gore) keeps being repeated in every election cycle. Part of the leftists' distrust of Obama stemmed from their frustration with a flawed two-party system in which progressives have little influence compared to corporate power.

Thomas Frank, in his book *What's the Matter with Kansas?* argues that the Republican Party has seduced cultural conservatives by promoting social policies against gays, abortion, and other "evil" ideas, while actually enacting the big business policies that favor a wealthy elite. The truth is that the Democratic Party is not much different. Every four years, Democratic candidates will make the obligatory promises for progressive policies. But once the pollsters and the consultants and the lobbyists have their way, these progressive policies are left by the wayside. Cultural conservatives are indeed betrayed by a Republican Party that gives lip service to conservative social and moral issues and then focuses on serving corporate interests. But few people realize that the Democratic Party gives lip service to liberal social and moral issues and then focuses on serving corporate interests.

Why Does the Left Fail So Badly and So Often?

Contrary to what most conservatives think, it's not because progressive values are inimical to the American majority. Most progressive ideas are more popular than most conservative policies. But contrary to what most leftists think, it's not because progressives have simply failed to "frame" their ideas properly in the battle of the political sound bites. Obama's approach is fundamentally different from "framing," as he explained: "This is more than just a matter of 'framing,' although clarity of language, thought, and heart are required. It's a matter of actually having faith in the American people's ability to hear a real and authentic debate about the issues that matter."[76] Obama rejected the idea that his approach would allow Republican attacks to go unanswered: "I am not arguing that we 'unilaterally disarm' in the face of Republican attacks, or bite our tongue when this Administration screws up. Whenever they are wrong, inept, or dishonest, we should say so clearly and repeatedly; and whenever they gear up their attack machine, we should respond quickly and forcefully. I am suggesting that the tone we take matters, and that truth, as best we know it, be the hallmark of our response."[77]

Nor does Obama think that progressives must give up their values to succeed in elections: "I completely agree that the Democrats need to present and fight for a clearly stated set of core convictions, and that we have not done so as effectively as we need to over the past several election cycles. We can insist on being principled about the ends we are trying to achieve (e.g., educational opportunity and basic health care for all Americans, honest and accountable government, etc.), without sacrificing our commitment to open debate, intellectual honesty, and civility."[78] According to Obama, "I also agree that it is the job of Democratic elected officials to help shape public opinion, and not just respond passively to opinion that's been aggressively shaped by the Republicans' PR machinery. I am simply suggesting, based on my experience, that people will respond to a powerfully progressive agenda when it's couched in optimism, pragmatism and our shared American ideals."[79]

Sometimes, Obama strays too far toward this pragmatic tendency when he presumes that public opinion is opposed to his progressive politics without making any effort to persuade the American people (and their representatives) to change their minds. But Obama's approach is not merely to marry the left wing of his party with the center. Plenty of politicians have aspired to this tactic, most recently George W. Bush and his "compassionate conservative" fraud. Usually, this political approach involves some form of deception, whether it is Democrats such as Bill Clinton lying to the Democratic wing of their party to win the primary and then inevitably lurching to the right to win over the center in the general election, or Republicans such as George W. Bush lying to the centrists in order to win and then satisfying his far-right constituents once in office.

American elections are not all about who has the most popular ideas or the best rhetoric. Political skill matters. A charismatic individual can reshape an election beyond ideology and political machinations. Although Obama has been compared to many politicians—Lincoln, John F. Kennedy, Bobby Kennedy—the political figure he most resembles is Ronald Reagan. The phrase "Reagan Democrats" entered the political vocabulary to describe how Reagan's charming personality and inclusive rhetoric were able to bring over traditional Democratic voters who normally would disagree with his policies.

Obama declared, "I'm not an ideologue. Never have been." He even said, "There's a part of me that's a little bit conservative."[80] Obama is a distinct individual holding a variety of different positions, and there is no way that every progressive could agree with every position he takes. But Obama represents the first politician in a long time who is willing to embrace progressive values while utilizing a rhetoric that appeals across political boundaries. If Obama can succeed, he may usher in a new era of progressive politics, one that the Far Left may not recognize as such, but that could transform our political system.

Announcement of Presidential Candidacy

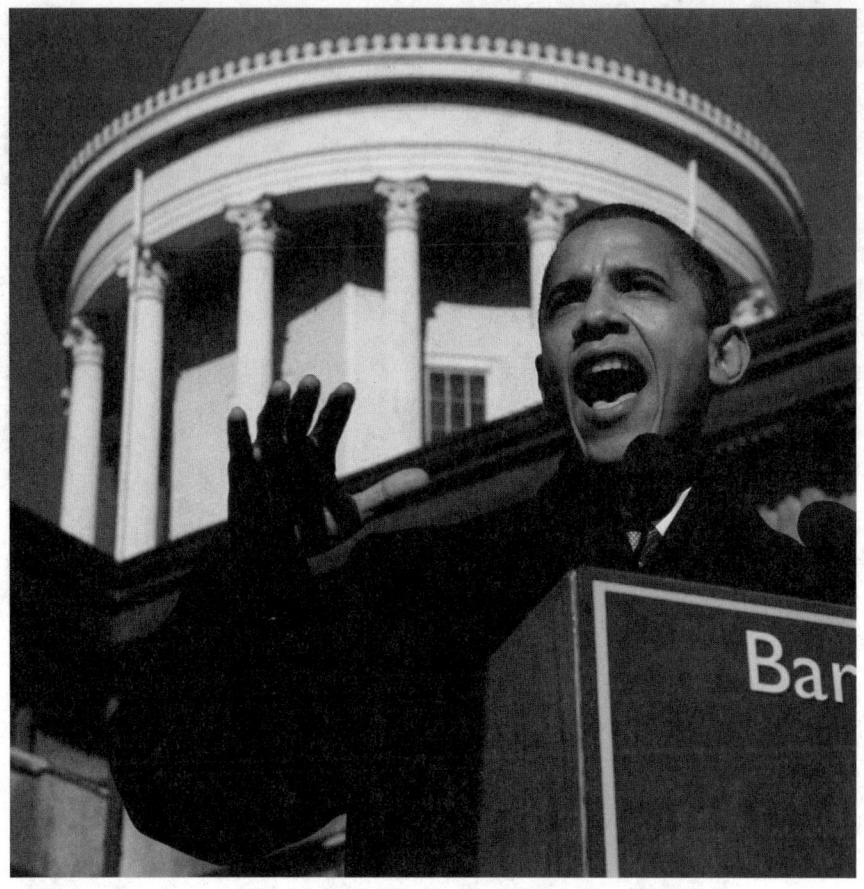

U.S. Senator Barack Obama (D-Ill.) announces his candidacy for president of the United States at the Old State Capitol in Springfield, Illinois, February 10, 2007 (AP Photo/Charles Rex Arbogast).

Generation Obama

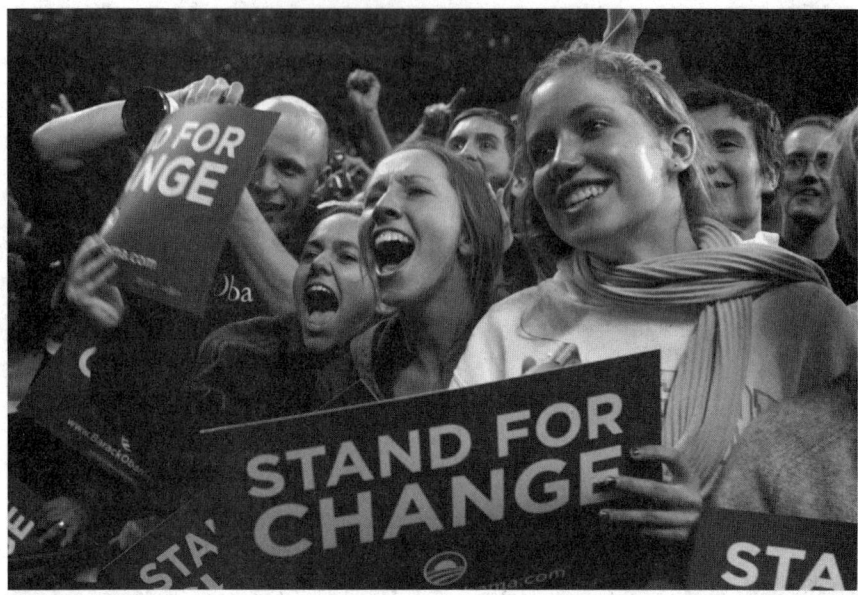

Students were among the most active supporters of the Obama campaign, registering to vote in record numbers and using the Internet to mobilize campaign volunteers, contributions, and policy discussions. Young people have applied in droves to work for the Obama administration. (AP Photo/Rick Browner)

The Media and Obama

Obama was not only named Person of the Year by *Time* magazine, but appeared on *Time*'s cover 15 times since 2006. Media coverage of Obama both helped and hurt over the course of the campaign, but ultimately, the candidate used the media to his advantage. (Reuters/Shephard Fairey/*Time*)

Obama on the World Stage

Foreign policy is one area in which Obama was criticized for lack of experience, but his multiethnic background and targeted travels to Africa, Russia, and the Middle East showcased his potential to bring the world together in contrast to Bush era divisiveness. (AP Photo/Les Neuhaus)

Obama at Church in Selma, Alabama

As the first post–baby boom presidential candidate, Obama distanced himself from the politics of the 1960s, yet embraced the continuing importance of the Civil Rights movement. Here he appears at a church in Selma, Alabama, making that connection clear while affirming the role of religion in his life. (AP Photo/Rob Carr)

"A More Perfect Union"

In response to sharp criticism over controversial pastor Jeremiah Wright, Obama delivered one of the most profound speeches ever given by a presidential candidate on March 18, 2008, in Philadelphia. Hearkening to words from the Constitution, Obama spoke eloquently about the role of race in the past, present, and future United States. (AP Photo/Matt Rourke; inset photo of Jeremiah Wright, Jr. AP Photo/Paul Sancya)

Mile High History

Barack Obama accepts the nomination of the Democratic Party on an Athenian-style stage set in the middle of Invesco Field in Denver, Colorado, on August 28, 2008. Having the nomination ceremony in an open air arena packed with record-breaking crowds heightened the security risk, and critics accused the candidate of grandstanding. As the first African American candidate to receive the nomination of a major U.S. political party—on the 45th anniversary of Martin Luther King Jr.'s "I Have a Dream" speech—Obama made history in more ways than one. (AP Photo/Alex Brandon)

Change Comes to America

Election night in Chicago's Grant Park found the new first family the embodiment of American hopes and dreams at home and a world of possibility abroad. (AP Photo/Pablo Martinez Monsivais)

CHAPTER SIX

"*This Is My House, Too*"

Obama and the Liberal God

*Secularists are wrong when they ask believers to leave their religion at
the door before entering into the public square.*

—Barack Obama

On December 1, 2006, Barack Obama stood in front of thousands of suspicious and perhaps even hostile evangelical leaders at the Saddleback Church
in Lake Forest, California. He had been invited by its pastor, Rick Warren,
the best-selling author of *The Purpose Driven Life,* to speak at Warren's
"Global Summit on AIDS and the Church" and take an AIDS test.[1]

Sam Brownback, the Republican senator from Kansas running for
president, preceded Obama on the stage and recalled how both of them
had recently spoken to the National Association for the Advancement of
Colored People, with Brownback getting a polite reception while Obama
received raucous applause. Brownback declared that it would be different
here: "Welcome to *my* house." Obama had one correction to offer Brownback: "Sam, this is my house, too. This is God's house."[2]

Obama's mere appearance at the church was controversial. Conservatives hounded Warren for allowing Obama to speak. Right-wing talk
show host and columnist Kevin McCullough denounced the "inhumane,
sick, and sinister evil" of Obama and proclaimed that "Barack Obama has
a long history of defying the intended morality of scripture" because he
supports abortion rights, hate crimes legislation, and equal rights for gays
and lesbians. McCullough claimed that Obama "represents the views of

Satan" and his "wickedness in worldview contradicts nearly every tenant [sic] of the Christian faith that Warren professes."³ McCullough organized a letter, signed by Phyllis Schlafly, Tim Wildmon of the American Family Association, Judie Brown of the American Life League, Joe Scheidler of the Pro-Life Action League, Peter LaBarbera of Americans for Truth, and representatives of Operation Rescue, Christian Action for the Preborn, and Missionaries to the Preborn, denouncing Warren for not banning Obama from the event.⁴

Reverend Patrick J. Mahoney, director of the Christian Defense Coalition, declared: "Having Senator Barack Obama speak on issues of social justice is like having a segregationist speak on civil rights."⁵ Mahoney argued that because Obama is prochoice, he "supports violence against women and children." Reverend Rob Schenck, president of the National Clergy Council, declared that "Senator Obama's policies represent the antithesis of biblical ethics and morality, not to mention supreme American values."⁶

But Obama had the courage to appear before a conference of conservative evangelicals and openly attack their opposition to condoms, and he still received a standing ovation. This wasn't a campaign event—Obama wasn't running for president yet, and virtually everyone in the room was a Republican who would never, ever vote for a prochoice candidate like Obama. Obama's appearance impressed many conservatives. Michael Gerson, an evangelical Christian who worked as one of George W. Bush's closest aides in the White House, declared: "Someone like Obama has at least a feel for the religious basis that a lot of people bring to these issues.... I think it was an important moment when Senator Obama went to Rick Warren's church. It was well received."⁷

Obama is accustomed to attacks on his faith from the Right. Not only did Alan Keyes proclaim that "Jesus Christ would not vote for Barack Obama," but after Obama warned that "faith got hijacked" by the Republican Right, Ann Coulter joked that Obama should not use "religion" and "hijack" in the same sentence.⁸ But it wasn't only the right-wingers who opposed Obama's appearance at Rick Warren's evangelical conference. One left-wing blog objected to "an evangelical suck-up like Barack Obama."⁹ And writer Kym Platt of *Ask This Black Woman* saw Obama's appearance as a "red flag" and worried that "the tenets of his evangelical Christianity are a cause for concern."¹⁰ But Obama is not an evangelical seeking converts to his religion. He is evangelizing for a very different cause: to acknowledge faith as a part of people's lives and the values that drive their political views.

Obama's message on religion has drawn other attacks from the Left. According to David Sirota, a writer for the *Nation* and senior editor at *In These Times*, "Obama has used his star power to attack his own party's base—in this case, progressives."[11] And how does Sirota think that Obama attacked progressives? Because Obama said: "I think we make a mistake when we fail to acknowledge the power of faith in the lives of the American people and join a serious debate about how to reconcile faith with our modern, pluralistic democracy."[12] Even an atheist could agree that Obama is right to point out the political mistake of dismissing faith, and some progressives have certainly done so. As Obama shows us, a religious progressive has an incredible power to expand progressive values beyond the left-wing base. As Obama puts it, "There are some liberals who dismiss religion in the public square as inherently irrational or intolerant, insisting on a caricature of religious Americans that paints them as fanatical, or thinking that the very word 'Christian' describes one's political opponents, not people of faith."[13] Obama wants to reclaim religion as part of the liberal faith, which represents a quiet majority of the progressive base for the Democratic Party.

Blogger Joe Garcia on *Daily Kos* wrote, "Obama and other Democrats have accepted the contrived right-wing agenda on so-called social issues. Every Democrat believes they must wear their religion on their sleeves. Discussion of values is no longer cast as civic virtue but framed by Judeo-Christian tenets."[14] Obama was well aware of the tension within the Democratic Party, as candidates "are scrambling to 'get religion,' even as a core segment of our constituency remains stubbornly secular in orientation, and fears—rightly, no doubt—that the agenda of an assertively Christian nation may not make room for them or their life choices."[15] However, Obama recognizes that it is possible for a politician to speak about faith without threatening the secular basis of our government. Obama speaks openly about faith but also embraces separation of church and state. Obama is a rationalist who genuinely respects religion, giving him enormous power to sway a vast number of Americans who support Democratic policies but regard the Republicans as more in line with their religious views. Of course, Obama has never wavered from his principled stand for individual freedoms. But he gave the Democrats the first opportunity in a generation to take back religious voters from the Republicans.

The Attack of the Phantom Muslim

It is precisely because of Obama's ability to appeal to centrist believers without alienating most secular liberals that he has been seen as such a threat to political opponents. That may explain why conservatives aggressively attacked Obama by falsely claiming that he was a Muslim. This kind of "swiftblogging" was reminiscent of the Swift Boat Veterans for Truth, who smeared John Kerry during his 2004 presidential campaign.

The attacks were disturbing not only because they were so obviously false, but because of what they implied if they were true. The idea that the religious background of an eight-year-old child should permanently exclude him from the presidency is disturbing. The fringe elements of the conservative coalition seemed to imply that Obama was some kind of Muslim Manchurian candidate, awaiting election to the presidency before he unveiled his secret Islamic plot to destroy Christian America. This kind of bigotry combined racism with a smear campaign.

It is interesting that the religious right became obsessed with the possibility that Obama was raised a Muslim, but no one spoke out against the very real fact that Obama was raised by skeptics and atheists. When atheism is regarded as a tolerable alternative to Islam, it indicates the serious extent of prejudice against Muslims in America today. According to Obama, his biological father from Kenya had been raised as a Muslim but was "a confirmed atheist, thinking religion to be so much superstition."[16] His Indonesian stepfather was a Muslim but had an "equally skeptical bent, a man who saw religion as not particularly useful in the practical business of making one's way in the world."[17]

As a child in Indonesia, Obama attended a Catholic school for two years, followed by a public school that was predominantly Muslim and included two hours a week of religious studies. Obama spent his time in the Koranic studies session probably because his father was a Muslim. None of this formal education in religion had much impact on Obama. His mother had "a faith that she would refuse to describe as religious, that, in fact, her experience told her was sacrilegious: a faith that rational, thoughtful people could shape their own destiny."[18] In *Dreams from My Father*, Obama calls her "a lonely witness for secular humanism."[19]

Obama recalls his grandmother's "flinty rationalism" and the stories she told of "sanctimonious preachers" she encountered in small-town middle

America. He remembers his grandfather's kindheartedness, which would never accept an exclusionary tradition. Obama's grandparents, with whom he lived during his adolescence, were skeptical Christians who became Unitarians. But it was Obama's mother who provided him with "a working knowledge of the world's great religions."[20] His mother taught him that religion was "just one of the many ways—and not necessarily the best way—that man attempted to control the unknowable and understand the deeper truths about our lives."[21] Obama writes, "My mother viewed religion through the eyes of the anthropologist that she would become; it was a phenomenon to be treated with a suitable respect, but with a suitable detachment as well."[22] This is exactly how Obama treats religion, although he does so from within a religious tradition rather than from the outside.

Obama's secular upbringing has also shaped his approach to religion today: "My faith is complicated by the fact that I didn't grow up in a particular religious tradition. And so what that means is when you come at it as an adult, your brain mediates a lot, and you ask a lot of questions."[23] Obama is living proof that you don't need to be raised religious to be virtuous. He recalls how his mother, without a religious text, taught him "the values that many Americans learn in Sunday school: honesty, empathy, discipline, delayed gratification, and hard work. She raged at poverty and injustice, and scorned those who were indifferent to both."[24] Obama has never abandoned what he calls "my mother's fundamental faith—in the goodness of people and in the ultimate value of this brief life we've each been given."[25]

A Rational Conversion

In 1985, when Obama was making $13,000 a year as a 25-year-old community organizer on the South Side of Chicago, he made a decision: "I was finally able to walk down the aisle of Trinity United Church of Christ on 95th Street in the South Side of Chicago one day and affirm my Christian faith. It came about as a choice, and not an epiphany. I didn't fall out in church. The questions I had didn't magically disappear. But kneeling beneath that cross on the South Side, I felt that I heard God's spirit beckoning me. I submitted myself to His will, and dedicated myself to discovering His truth."[26]

Obama's religious faith was inspired by the good works of the black churches, not by some kind of mystical revelation. Working with the ministers and laypeople in churches on job training and after-school programs, Obama discovered that "what had been more of an intellectual view of religion deepened."[27] According to Obama, "I became much more familiar with the ongoing tradition of the historic black church and its importance in the community. And the power of that culture to give people strength in very difficult circumstances, and the power of that church to give people courage against great odds. And it moved me deeply."[28] Obama wanted "a vessel for my beliefs"[29] and he turned to the black church in his community because "I was drawn to the power of the African American religious tradition to spur social change."[30] According to Obama, his choice was "just a moment to certify or publicly affirm a growing faith in me."[31]

Obama did not turn to religion because he imagined that God spoke to him, or because he believed the story of the Bible is factually accurate, or because he thought religion is necessary for morality, or because he had some personal problems he needed help to cure. Instead, Obama sought religion because he was lonely: "I had no community or shared traditions in which to ground my most deeply held beliefs." As Obama put it, "Without an unequivocal commitment to a particular community of faith, I would be consigned at some level to always remain apart, free in the way that my mother was free, but also alone in the same ways she was ultimately alone."[32] Obama was drawn to religion because he recognized the power and achievements of the black church in the Civil Rights movement. The black church also showed Obama that "faith doesn't mean that you don't have doubts, or that you relinquish your hold on this world."[33]

Religion didn't change Obama's fundamental values. Obama came to religion because of what he already believed, and because he saw in the black church a model for community and activism. As Obama put it, "Religious commitment did not require me to suspend critical thinking, disengage from the battle for economic and social justice, or otherwise retreat from the world that I knew and loved."[34] For Obama, Jesus isn't a magical creature to be worshipped blindly; he's a real person to be imitated for his moral example. What's important to Obama about Jesus is not the "Night of the Living Dead" aspects of Christian belief in a resurrection, but the moral lessons about self-sacrifice for a larger cause.

The Politics of Faith

Ever since Jimmy Carter admitted to *Playboy* magazine that he sinned by lusting in his heart for women other than his wife, political candidates have been wary of discussing the details of their religious views. Obama's frank thoughts about religion are surprising in an age when God is treated as just another political expediency to be carefully managed by polls and focus groups. That is part of what makes Obama's approach to faith so powerful.

Unlike George W. Bush and other politicians who invoke God, Obama said, "I think there is an enormous danger on the part of public figures to rationalize or justify their actions by claiming God's mandate."[35] For Obama, God is a source of doubt and self-questioning, not a way to assert certitude: "I think that religion at its best comes with a big dose of doubt."[36]

A question must be asked about Obama and every other politician: Does he really believe in God, or is his professed faith just the theological equivalent of kissing babies? Politicians are particularly willing to manipulate what they believe when public opinion is overwhelming. Only 14 percent of Americans say that this country is ready for an atheist president.[37]

However, there are many reasons to believe that Obama is telling the truth about his faith. Most politicians who fake religion choose a very conventional approach and invoke it only for ceremonial and political purposes. By contrast, Obama writes in depth about his struggles over religion and the doubts that he has. If Obama wanted to deceive the public about his faith, he could have mouthed the usual platitudes about religion at the appropriate moments and avoided the topic otherwise. Or a deceitful politician might have chosen the over-the-top approach of George W. Bush, who declared that he was a sinner who had a magical conversion, claimed the Bible is his favorite book, signed the resolution for Jesus Day in Texas, and proclaimed that Jesus is his favorite political philosopher.[38]

Obama is also skeptical about politicians who use religion for political purposes. "I am not suggesting that every progressive suddenly latch on to religious terminology—that can be dangerous. Nothing is more transparent than inauthentic expressions of faith."[39] If Obama was trying to fake faith, he also wouldn't be so quick to embrace secular morality: "Because I do not believe that religious people have a monopoly on morality, I would rather have someone who is grounded in morality and ethics, and who is also secular, affirm their morality and ethics and values without pretending that they're something they're not."[40]

Unlike most politicians, Obama uses God not to confirm certainty but to instill doubt. For Obama, God is the great questioner forcing himself to align his actions with his values. When Obama prays, he says, he is engaged in an "ongoing conversation with God."[41] But this conversation is not a delusional belief that a supernatural being is talking directly to him. Instead, Obama uses God as a way to check his own ego. He uses prayer to "take stock" of himself and maintain his "moral compass." He has a conversation with God in order to ask himself, "Am I doing this because I think it's advantageous to me politically or because I think it's the right thing to do?"[42] Obama refuses to accept the idea that true believers must shout at God, babble in tongues, and seek to force everyone else to agree. Obama does not measure the degree of religious faith by the intensity of the desire to impose it on others. To the contrary, he sees true religious belief as something rationally understood.

Doubting Faith

Obama is promoting an uncommon kind of Christian faith, at least in the mainstream media where religious devotion is often synonymous with fundamentalism and extremism. Obama noted, "We have come to define religion in absolutist, fundamentalist terms. So to be a believer is to be a fundamentalist in some fashion."[43]

Obama refuses to agree that his God is a lesser God, that his religion is a watered-down religion merely because it includes doubt and reason and questioning. Obama believes in "a faith that admits doubt, and uncertainty, and mystery. Because, ultimately, I think that's how most people understand their faith. In fact, it's not faith if you're absolutely certain. There's a leap that we all take, and, when you admit that doubt publicly, it's a form of testimony."[44] Obama said, "There are aspects of Christian tradition that I'm comfortable with and aspects that I'm not. There are passages of the Bible that make perfect sense to me and others that I go, 'Ya know, I'm not sure about that.'"[45] Sometimes, Obama is explicit in rejecting the fundamentalist view that everything in the Bible is literal truth. As Obama said, "There are still passages that I read in the Bible, that I say, well, this doesn't make any sense."[46]

Obama's doubt-filled faith is also representative of most Americans. The overwhelming majority of Catholics don't believe that abortion and contraception and homosexuality should be banned, despite the official position of the Catholic Church. The same is true of many Americans of all faiths who question and doubt and reconcile life with ancient religious texts rather than pretending to believe every letter of every word is divine commandment.

Obama doesn't believe in the idea that people must accept Jesus or be condemned to hell: "I find it hard to believe that my God would consign four-fifths of the world to hell."[47] Likewise, Obama is skeptical of heaven: "What I believe in is that if I live my life as well as I can, that I will be rewarded. I don't presume to have knowledge of what happens after I die." But he believes that "whether the reward is in the here and now or in the hereafter, aligning myself to my faith and values is a good thing."[48] For Obama, tucking in his daughters and knowing that he has helped to make them kind and honest and curious people, "that's a little piece of heaven."[49] That expression is much more than the heartwarming platitude of a doting father. For Obama, it's a theological statement. He cannot know if there is a heaven, and he sees the closest thing to heaven on earth in his daughters. The heaven of an afterlife is neither believed nor disbelieved by Obama; it's ignored because it's an unknowable factor that shouldn't affect what we do on earth. We do good, Obama believes, because it is the right thing to do, not because God is threatening us.

The Commonality of Religions

Obama also brings his mother's anthropological viewpoint to his ideas about religion: "I believe that there are many paths to the same place, and that is a belief that there is a higher power, a belief that we are connected as a people, that there are values that transcend race or culture, that move us forward, and that there's an obligation for all of us individually as well as collectively to take responsibility to make those values lived."[50]

Obama sees a common moral basis to the major religions: "My mother was a deeply spiritual person and would spend a lot of time talking about values and give me books about the world's religions and talk to me about them. Her view always was that underlying these religions was a common set of beliefs about how you treat other people and how you aspire to act, not just for yourself but also for the greater good."[51]

Obama even regards his public discussion about faith as a way to bridge the gap between believers and nonbelievers. By expressing one's religious doubts, Obama said, "it allows both the secular and the religious to find some sort of common space where we say to each other, 'Well, I may not believe exactly what you do, what you believe, but I share an experience in wondering what does my life mean, or I understand the desire for a connection to something larger than myself.' And that, I think, is in the best of the United States religious tradition."[52]

This diverse training about religion has shaped Obama's approach to politics: "To be effective, you have to be able to listen to a variety of points of view, to synthesize the viewpoints."[53] Because he was never forced to adopt a religion, Obama developed a skepticism toward all assertions of absolute truth, including his own: "I retain from my childhood and my experiences growing up a suspicion of dogma, and I'm not somebody who is always comfortable with language that implies I've got a monopoly on the truth, or that my faith is automatically transferable to others."[54]

Church and State

Obama wears his religion on his sleeve, but he doesn't shove it in your face. He does not demand that others believe as he does. More important, he embraces a government that does not wear a religion of any kind. As Obama put it, "I am a big believer in the separation of church and state."[55] Obama believes in the separation of church and state, but not the separation of religion and politics. He rejects the ideology of secularism that sees religion as a purely private activity that must be kept away from politics lest it poison our common well of government.

It's tempting, when watching the violence in Iraq between different Muslim sects, to agree that religion must be kept on a short leash to maintain a peaceful society. As Obama said, "There's an enormous amount of damage done around the world in the name of religion and certainty."[56] But Obama recognizes how the public discussion of religion and our values can help us maintain a pluralistic democracy rather than driving it apart.

Obama is skeptical about the use of religion by politicians: "I think there is an enormous danger on the part of public figures to rationalize or justify their actions by claiming God's mandate. I don't think it's healthy for public figures to wear religion on their sleeve as a means to insulate themselves from criticism, or avoid dialogue with people who disagree with them."[57] Obama is walking a delicate line between speaking honestly and openly about his religion without trying to be a religious politician.

Obama's theology parallels his political viewpoints. He believes that religion represents what unites people, not what divides them. Much has been made of how Obama's race shaped his political approach, how an African American living in a predominantly white world not only learned how to embrace his racial background and its history but also how he used that knowledge to shape the political view of an outsider looking in, always willing to listen to those different from himself.

Obama's religious upbringing may have been an equally important influence. As someone brought up as a rational secularist, exposed to many religions but never indoctrinated into any of them, Obama could have chosen a path rejecting religion. He could have rebelled against his upbringing and become a fundamentalist of the Christian or Muslim variety. Instead, Obama sought out faith, but a kind of faith that mirrored and also influenced his approach to politics.

Obama's religion, like his politics, is deeply felt but highly tolerant of different perspectives. It is an inclusive religion, but not a watered-down religion. His willingness to listen to the political views of others is drawn from a lifelong willingness to hear different religious ideas. It is a testament to Obama's political and intellectual skills that he can speak about religion with more depth and candor than any other presidential candidate in recent memory, yet satisfy most people ranging from atheists to fundamentalists that his perspective on God is a thoughtful, decent approach to religion. It's a reminder that Obama's religion, like his politics, rejects the idea that we must choose between a hard-core devotion that will never hear the other side or a watered-down wishy-washy centrism that ultimately believes in nothing. Obama, in both his faith and his political ideology, has found a third way that embraces an open mind with committed values.

CHAPTER SEVEN

From Quest to Reality

Politics and Policy in an Obama Administration

We know that government can't solve all our problems—and we don't want it to. But we also know that there are some things we can't do on our own. We know that there are some things we do better together.
—Barack Obama

Obama has been criticized by pundits and progressives for having more lofty rhetoric than specific policies. Obama responded to this criticism: "They say, well, we want specifics, we want details, we want white papers, we want plans. We've had plans, Democrats. What we've had is a shortage of hope."[1] However, Obama is more than just a candidate of abstract hope. He's also developed many policies. *Chicago Tribune* columnist Eric Zorn wrote: "Obama's somewhat wonky new book, his speeches and his voting record in the Illinois Senate and U.S. Senate reveal plenty about his political philosophy."[2]

Obama was slower than some candidates to put out a comprehensive policy agenda in 2007 because he tried to measure what policies public opinion and political realities will allow. As Obama observed, "I'm one of those folks—I wouldn't probably fit in with the (Bush) administration—who actually thinks that being informed is a good basis for policy."[3] However, Obama's history of bills proposed and enacted in the Illinois Senate and the U.S. Senate reveals a great deal about the kind of vision he has for America.

Obama in Springfield

Obama's record as a state senator in Illinois is a good indication of his development as a political leader and the values that he stands for. Elected in 1996 (after he successfully challenged the petitions of the other candidates and ran unopposed), Obama spent eight years working in the capital of Springfield.

Not surprisingly, his past is now a matter of debate. Former House majority leader Tom DeLay called Obama's record in the Illinois Senate "on a par with a Marxist leftist."[4] Like many things that ever came out of DeLay's mouth, this wasn't true. In reality, Obama's record as a state senator reveals a pragmatic politician learning how to work among the difficult dilemmas posed by standing up for principles while making political progress.

As a state senator in Illinois for eight years, despite being in the minority for most of that time, Obama was well regarded for his legislative skills. He sought to have health care treated as a basic right. He was the driving force behind legislation to create a state earned income tax credit, expand early childhood education programs, crack down on predatory lenders, require videotaping of police interrogations, and other measures for which he was able to create bipartisan support for progressive policies.

Obama recalled, "To some degree, the experiences in the state legislature are identical to Congress, except that there are a lot of reporters around in Washington and there are virtually none in the state capitol. But the pattern of legislative activity is very similar, and the political dynamic was similar, because when I first arrived at the state legislature, we had an old guy who was the senate president, named 'Pate' Philip. And he was not a neoconservative but the original paleoconservative. He was a big, hulking guy. He looked like John Murtha, but had very different politics, and would chomp on cigars and make politically incorrect statements."[5]

Pate Philip ran the Illinois Senate with an iron hand until the Democrats finally won back the majority in the 2002 election. Under Philip's control, no Democrat had much hope of passing any progressive legislation. Philip was called the "David Duke of DuPage County" for good reason. In 1983, Philip took a free vacation from the South African government, whose apartheid state he supported. Philip declared about state employees who are minorities, "Some of them do not have the work ethics that we have. Secondly, they don't tend to turn on or squeal on their fellow minorities. I don't know what you do about that, but it's kind of a way of life."[6] Philip reportedly opposed a high-speed rail system in the Chicago suburbs because "it brings in the niggers. I'm against them."[7]

Obama in the Minority

Despite working in the Democratic minority in Illinois, Obama cosponsored a bipartisan package of reform legislation in 1998, including the Gift Ban Act, that dramatically overhauled ethics laws in a state full of corruption. In 1999, Obama led the drive in the senate to increase child support payments for poor parents, although the Republican governor vetoed it.[8] Obama was able to get a state earned income tax credit passed in 2000, and then made it permanent in 2003. The earned income tax credit was particularly important because income taxes in Illinois are much more regressive than federal taxes, and the working poor in Illinois often paid more in state income taxes than for federal income taxes.

After Democrats finally took control of the state senate in the 2002 elections, Obama launched a tidal wave of legislation. However, even without Pate Philip blocking legislation, it was difficult to get new progressive laws passed in Illinois. One example was Obama's bill to help stop police abuse. Chicago had become infamous for use of torture by police to help frame innocent people.[9] Thirteen innocent men on death row were exonerated and released, some of them victims of these tortured confessions. Illinois desperately needed some action to restore confidence in the police. Obama's proposal was to require videotaping of interrogations of suspects in capital cases. When Obama began, the idea of a bill was opposed by police, prosecutors, most of the senate, and Democratic governor Rod Blagojevich. Blagojevich, a Democrat with delusional ambitions of running for president, was determined not to appear soft on crime and had promised to veto any proposal for mandatory tapings. But by the time Obama finished his work, the police and prosecutors embraced the bill, and it passed in the Illinois Senate by a vote of 58–0. Governor Blagojevich took the unusual step of reversing himself to sign it, and Illinois became the first state in the country to require such tapings.[10]

Despite initial opposition, Obama won widespread approval for his racial profiling law in 2003. Senate Bill 30 required that law enforcement officers identify the race of people pulled over for traffic stops in order to allow for studies on the issue of racial profiling. Obama's moderate proposal not only allowed police to identify officers engaging in racial profiling, but also helped restore confidence in the police by proving when they weren't engaged in profiling. As Republican state senator Kirk Dillard put it, "Working on issues like racial profiling was contentious, but Barack had a way both intellectually and in demeanor that defused skeptics."[11]

Ted Street, president of the Illinois Fraternal Order of Police, endorsed Obama in 2004, in part because of his work on death penalty reform. Laimutis Nargelenas, a lobbyist for the Illinois Association of Chiefs of Police, observed that although Obama sometimes voted for "individual rights" rather than "the ability of law enforcement to get things done," he was always thoughtful on law and order and on supporting funding for police programs. According to Nargelenas, "When he said he was going to do something, you could always trust him on his word."[12]

Most people like the idea of a politician who votes for "individual rights," but the fact that Obama could do so and still maintain the respect of notoriously conservative law enforcement groups in Illinois shows his political skills. Obama's recognition of the importance of civil liberties and a just criminal system is reflected in his votes on these law-and-order issues, when he refused to take the easy stand of toughening penalties. Obama voted against a 1998 proposal to criminalize contact with a street gang for any convicts on probation or out on bail. In 2001, Obama opposed making gang activity eligible for the death penalty: "There's a strong overlap between gang affiliation and young men of color.... I think it's problematic for them to be singled out as more likely to receive the death penalty for carrying out certain acts than are others who do the same thing."[13] In 1999, Obama opposed mandatory adult prosecution for youth who discharge a firearm near a school, declaring, "There is really no proof or indication that automatic transfers and increased penalties and adult penalties for juvenile offenses have, in fact, proven to be more effective in reducing juvenile crime or cutting back on recidivism."[14] In 2001, Obama questioned the harsh penalties for drug dealing, noting that selling 15 tablets of ecstasy was the same Class X felony as raping a woman at knifepoint.[15] In 2002, Obama sponsored an unsuccessful measure to create an employment grant program for ex-criminals, who often return to a life of crime because no one will hire them.

Sundiata Cha-Jua, director of the African American Studies and Research Program at the University of Illinois, observed that in the Illinois Senate, "Obama was clearly one of the best African American politicians in terms of speaking to African American issues."[16] Obama's years in the state senate convinced African American leaders and voters that he was not just another slippery politician seeking to promote the interests of himself and his donors. Salim Muwakkil concluded, "His legislative record during his eight years as the state senator from Illinois' thirteenth district convinced them that he had the black community's interest at heart, even as he cultivated alliances with other political forces."[17]

The Conservative Attack on Obama in Illinois

Far from being "Marxist leftist," Obama's record in Illinois represents that of a pragmatic progressive who pushed for moderate reforms and opposed right-wing legislation. But conservatives have tried to attack Obama for his liberal votes in Springfield. John Fund of the *Wall Street Journal* wrote, "His record as a state legislator is even more liberal. In 1996, he spoke out against the Defense of Marriage Act, which the Senate approved 85–14 and Mr. Clinton signed into law. He twice voted 'present' on a bill to ban partial-birth abortions. In 1999 he was the only state senator to oppose a law that prohibited early prison release for sex offenders. Is anyone naive enough to believe Mrs. Clinton wouldn't use those positions as evidence that he couldn't win?"[18] In the Illinois legislature, voting "present" is the equivalent of voting "no" because a majority of "yes" votes are required for passage. Many Illinois legislators use the "present" vote as an evasion on an unpopular choice, so that they can avoid being targeted for voting "no." During the 2004 Democratic primary, an opponent mocked Obama's "present" vote on abortion bills with flyers portraying a rubber duck and the words, "He ducked!"[19]

According to "Barack Obama Exposed!," an attack by the right-wing magazine *Human Events*, "Explaining these votes could be uncomfortable for Obama, who has never been made to answer for his controversial decisions."[20] As *Human Events* observed, these votes show that "no matter what lip service Obama gives to conservative principles, at the end of the day he reliably comes down on the liberal side."[21] But what they reflect is Obama's support for progressive positions that represent the majority of the American people.

On abortion, Obama voted against SB 230 (1997), which would have turned doctors into felons by banning so-called partial-birth abortion, and against a 2000 bill banning state funding. Although these bills included an exception to save the life of the mother, they didn't include anything about abortions necessary to protect the health of the mother, which the U.S. Supreme Court required until 2007. The legislation defined a fetus as a person and could have criminalized virtually all abortion.

Obama's record also revealed concern for the rights of everyone, including criminals. He voted against SB 381 (1997), which required prisoners to pay court costs for frivolous lawsuits against the government (and would have discouraged legitimate litigation). He was the only vote against SB 485 (1999), which required sex offenders sentenced to the county jail to serve their full terms without any "good time" off offered to other criminals. Of course, there's no good reason why minor sex offenders should serve longer sentences than anyone else, and removing the "good time" rules makes it more difficult to ensure order in jail. The fact that Obama didn't pander to voters with these politically popular but unwise bills showed his integrity as a politician.

Obama supported the right of workers to choose unions, by voting for HB 3396 (2003), which allows 50 percent of workers to select a union by signing a card, and SB 1070 (2003), which gives graduate student instructors at universities the right to unionize.

On culture war issues, Obama was willing to stand up against the religious right. In 2003, Obama cosponsored legislation banning discrimination based on sexual orientation. Obama supported measures to fight HIV, such as SB 880 (2003), to allow the purchase of hypodermic needles. Obama opposed SB 609 (2001), which banned any stores with pornographic video tapes within 1,000 feet of any school, park, church, or residential area, effectively banning such stores in all urban areas. Obama also voted against HB 1812 (1999), which would force school boards to install software on computers to block sexually explicit material.

Obama sought moderate gun control measures, such as a 2000 bill he cosponsored to limit handgun purchases to one per month (it didn't pass). He voted against letting people violate local weapons bans in cases of self-defense (2004), but also voted in 2004 to let retired police officers carry concealed handguns.

Critiques from the Left

Obama has also been attacked by the Left for his record in the Illinois Senate. Leftist blogger Nathan Gonzales accused Obama of "a number of occasions when Obama avoided making hard choices" because he voted "present."[22]

Obama voted "present" many times in the Illinois Senate, including on several anti-abortion bills. In some cases, these votes reflected Obama's support for only part of the bill. In other cases, Obama was providing "cover" for legislators who faced political challenges as part of a political strategy; by having other legislators voting "present" along with them, their votes would seem less like political expediency.[23]

Obama has a strong record of getting progressive legislation enacted. He embraced campaign finance reform by pushing for SB 1415 (2003), to create public funding for supreme court races. Obama supported SB 1725 (2003), to restore the Illinois estate tax. He voted in 2004 to end $300 million worth of tax breaks for businesses, and in 2000 he voted against repealing the state's gasoline tax. Obama opposed various efforts to cut unemployment taxes on businesses, including SB 777 (1999), SB 879 (1999), and SB 795 (2001). He supported SB 796 (2003), which increased the state minimum wage.

Obama also has a record of success on health care in Illinois. He sponsored the legislation expanding Kid Care and Family Care that added 20,000 children to the state health insurance program.[24] Obama was a cosponsor of SB03, the Senior Citizen Prescription Drug Discount Program Act, which enabled senior citizens and people with disabilities to obtain prescription drugs at discount rates negotiated by the state's Department of Central Management Services. Obama also cosponsored smaller reforms such as SB 989, which allowed Medicaid money to care for mentally or emotionally disturbed children as outpatients rather than the far more expensive option of institutionalizing them, and SB1417, which required all insurance companies operating in Illinois to pay for screenings of colorectal cancer. Obama also voted in 2004 to endorse embryonic stem cell research in Illinois.

Obama proposed amending the Illinois Constitution's bill of rights to add health care as an inherent right, mandating universal health coverage by 2006, but his proposal was killed in committee. However, Obama was able to get HB 2268 (the Health Care Justice Act) approved, which created the Bipartisan Health Care Reform Commission to create a plan for universal health care in Illinois.

In the state senate, Obama sponsored more than 780 bills, and about 280 were passed.[25] However, in his early years in the senate, he struggled to find success. Rich Miller, the leading independent journalist who covers Illinois politics, observed in 2000, "Barack is a very intelligent man. He hasn't had a lot of success here, and it could be because he places himself above everybody. He likes people to know he went to Harvard."[26] But after Obama had his ambitions for higher office crushed by his loss to Bobby Rush, he focused more intensely on state politics and building coalitions. According to Miller, "I just can't emphasize enough how much this guy became respected, and how transformative it was. By 2004, he just had this aura about him."[27] Miller concluded, "He was a little off-putting at first—that whole Harvard thing. But the bottom line is pretty much everybody I know had a high opinion of him, Republican or Democrat. In this state it's hard for anyone to get along, and even though he was very liberal, he was able to pass a hell of a lot of bills."[28]

Emil Jones Jr., the Democratic leader in the state senate, reported about Obama: "He was very aggressive when he first came to the senate. We were in the minority, but he said, 'I'd like to work hard. Any tough assignments or things you'd like me to be involved in, don't hesitate to give it to me.'"[29]

Obama was able to pass so much legislation so quickly because of the strong ties he had built with fellow Democrats and Republicans and the respect he had earned in Springfield. Cynthia Canary, director of the Illinois Campaign for Political Reform, noted about Obama, "He wasn't a maverick. There were other legislators I would turn to if I just wanted to make a lot of noise. That wasn't his style."[30]

Obama's style was to forge close ties with moderate Republican legislators. Kirk Dillard, Republican minority whip in the Illinois Senate, even recorded a campaign ad for Obama in 2007, declaring that "Senator Obama worked on some of the deepest issues we had and was successful in a bipartisan way." Dillard declared, "Republican legislators respected

Senator Obama." Dillard later said, "I'm a stalwart Republican, I support John McCain for the presidency."[31] But he noted, "Republicans may admire Senator Obama."[32]

Other Republicans in the state senate admired Obama's work. Carl Hawkinson, former Republican chair of the Judiciary Committee, said: "Obviously, we didn't agree all the time, but he would always take suggestions when they were logical, and he was willing to listen to our point of view. And he offered his opinions in a lawyerly way. When he spoke on the floor of the senate, he spoke out of conviction. You knew that, whether you agreed with him or disagreed with him."[33]

Obama was also unusual because he never became hostage to a particular political machine. Denny Jacobs, a former Democratic senator in Illinois, noted about Obama, "He's an enigma. He's not the mayor's guy. He's not the alderman's guy. He's not the county board chairman's guy. He's nobody's guy. Usually you're somebody's guy. In Chicago, that's a way of life."[34] Because of Obama's easy electoral victories and his widespread support, he's never been subservient to any political leader or movement. While Obama is sometimes criticized by progressives for endorsing some mainstream establishment candidates (such as Chicago Mayor Richard Daley and various aldermen), he's never been under their control. As *Chicago Tribune* columnist Eric Zorn observed, "He hasn't acquired his political capital by spending years swapping favors and grandstanding in lesser offices or by climbing the coattails of his politically powerful father."[35]

Obama's success as a state legislator did more than just establish a strong record for his run in 2004 for the U.S. Senate. It was in Springfield that Obama learned how to negotiate and compromise and bring together bipartisan alliances, which have become his strongest political skills.

Obama and the U.S. Senate

Obama entered the U.S. Senate in 2005 as one of its biggest celebrities and one of its politically weakest members. He had zero seniority, and he had to overcome resentment from colleagues who didn't appreciate being ignored by the media in favor of a newcomer. Obama also had to learn the ropes of an arcane political institution, in which once again he was part of the minority party struggling to get anything accomplished.

Obama encountered exaggerated expectations from journalists who complained that he didn't accomplish enough in the U.S. Senate. One writer noted in the *Progressive,* "He has been in the U.S. Senate since only 2004, and he has a thin legislative record to boot."[36] Leon Wieseltier in the centrist *New Republic* claimed, "In his few years in the Senate he found time to write a big book but almost no legislation."[37] The conservative *Investor's Business Daily* editorialized, "Obama doesn't have much to show. No legislative triumphs that offer a glimpse into how he would lead, no defining efforts of statecraft that reveal the core of his character.... there's nothing new here."[38] Despite this agreement across the ideological spectrum about Obama's legislative failings, the truth is that Obama produced more legislation in the Republican-controlled Senate of 2004–2005 than most of his colleagues.

Although ranking at the bottom of the U.S. Senate in seniority and trying to keep a low profile in the face of his media celebrity, Obama introduced bills to reduce mercury and lead pollution, improve security at chemical plants, help develop alternative energy, protect drinking water from terrorist attacks, improve the safety of spent nuclear fuel, increase rail and transit security, improve emergency evacuation and aid procedures, help the victims of Hurricane Katrina, speed up background checks for immigrants, make employers verify the legal status of employees, aid innovative school districts and summer programs, increase the Pell Grant and make higher education more affordable, guard against an Asian flu epidemic, protect genetic privacy while increasing genetic research, increase the efficiency of the health care system, provide housing for homeless veterans, improve ethics on Capitol Hill by limiting the revolving door and ending lobbyist gifts, prevent voter intimidation, and create an Office of Public Integrity.

However, this work couldn't satisfy the high expectations of critics. According to left-wing writer David Sirota, "Considering that he's one of the most famous politicians in America, the accomplishments are fairly mundane."[39] But the same could be said of the legislative accomplishments of John Edwards and Hillary Clinton, despite the fact that they had more time in the Senate and the advantage of a Democratic majority during their terms. Celebrity status doesn't get progressive legislation passed in a Republican-controlled Senate.

John Heilemann wrote in *New York Magazine,* "Substantively speaking, Obama hasn't even made the most of his brief time there. The legislation he has offered has been uniformly mundane, marginal, and provincial—securing additional funding for veterans, to cite but one example."[40] But most people don't think that helping veterans makes you mundane and provincial—veterans, for example, appreciate such a law. In addition, much legislation these days is aimed at veterans because of the war in Iraq—an important and entirely appropriate policy focus.

It would be difficult to find many Democratic senators in the 109th Congress who accomplished more than Obama legislatively, despite the fact that he lacked experience working within the often byzantine Senate politics and had no seniority to control committees. As *Chicago Tribune* columnist Eric Zorn noted, "Obama has served in the minority party in the U.S. Senate for two years—not a position with much leverage. Still, he managed to get his name on sunshine legislation to track and search government spending online, action to send additional humanitarian relief to the Congo and a nuclear threat reduction program. He's also promoted the interests of military veterans."[41]

As a U.S. senator, Obama disappointed some progressives by not being the champion of hopeless causes that we have come to expect from Dennis Kucinich, a candidate who fights the good fight even if he always loses. Heilemann wrote, "How many times has he used his megaphone to advance a bold initiative or champion a controversial cause? Zero."[42] But Obama is more interested in results than symbolic stands, and that requires political compromise, not grandstanding.

Obama and Liberal Politics

Obama has been attacked for his progressive politics. Former Clinton advisor (turned conservative consultant) Dick Morris proclaimed, "So far, Obama seems very conscious that his left-wing, party-line voting record is not a good foundation for his national ambitions. He seems aware that the country wants more of a postpartisan, embodying the consensus to which Americans have come over these recent dangerous and bitter years."[43]

It's certainly true that Obama is a liberal. In 2006, Obama had an 86 rating from *National Journal*, making him tied for 10th most liberal senator; in 2005, Obama ranked 16th with an 82.5 liberal rating.[44] By contrast, Hillary Clinton's liberal rating dropped from 79.8 in 2005 to 70.2 in 2006 as she ran for reelection and sought to position herself as a centrist for president.

In 2006, Obama received 100 percent ratings from the AFL-CIO, League of Conservation Voters, Americans for Democratic Action, and Planned Parenthood, and an "A" grade from the National Education Association.[45] He got an 83 percent rating from the ACLU. Meanwhile, right-wing groups gave Obama low ratings: a 6 percent rating from National Taxpayers Union and an 8 percent rating from the National Taxpayers Limitation Committee and the American Conservative Union.[46]

Obama's Legislative Agenda

Obama sponsored 152 bills and resolutions and cosponsored 427 bills in the 109th Congress during 2005 and 2006. Beginning with a bill to increase funding of Pell Grants to help poor students attend college, Obama proposed a wide range of progressive legislation.

Obama and Senator Chuck Schumer (D-N.Y.) introduced the Deceptive Practices and Voter Intimidation Prevention Act of 2007, which would ban people from knowingly lying about elections (such as the time and place of an election, or qualifications to vote) in order to deceive voters.

Steve Ellis, an official with Taxpayers for Common Sense, noted, "He's certainly been willing to reach across the aisle, and you could say far across the aisle."[47] Obama cosponsored John McCain's Secure America and Orderly Immigration Act and supported security improvements along the border with Mexico.

Rich and Poor in America

After Hurricane Katrina decimated the New Orleans area, Obama was a leading advocate for improving federal emergency responses. Obama noted about the Bush administration, "The incompetence was color-blind. What wasn't color-blind was the indifference."[48] Obama called for the devastation to spark "a serious conversation about poverty."

However, Obama was also suspicious of wasteful government spending. Obama called for a chief financial officer to oversee Katrina spending, and he voted with fiscal conservatives who opposed an earmark for the expensive relocation of a railroad line as part of Katrina rebuilding. Obama joined with conservative Senator Tom Coburn (R-Okla.) to denounce a $192 million no-bid contract FEMA made with Carnival Cruise Lines to house evacuees on cruise ships. Obama and Coburn noted that the cost was "$2,550 per guest, per week, which is four times the cost of a $599 per tourist 7 Day Western Caribbean Cruise from Galveston, Texas."[49]

Obama has been an advocate for the poor, both as a community organizer and as a legislator. Obama cosponsored the Standing with Minimum Wage Earners Act of 2006, which would make wage increases for members of Congress tied to increases in the minimum wage. Obama has expressed strong support for the Employee Free Choice Act, which makes it easier for workers to unionize without fear of retaliation from their employers.[50]

Obama is not an orthodox left-winger. Obama voted against the Central American Free Trade Act, primarily to send a message to the Bush administration urging greater concern for environmental and labor regulations. However, he voted to support a minor free trade deal with Oman. Obama voted for the Class Action Fairness Act of 2005, a Republican bill to limit class-action lawsuits that was supported by 18 Democrats. Ken Silverstein argued in *Harper's Magazine* that the bill "was lobbied for aggressively by financial firms, which constitute Obama's second biggest single bloc of donors."[51] However, one of Obama's leading sources of donors is lawyers, who strongly endorsed the measure. One important aim of the law is to reduce the kind of class-action suits where lawyers get millions in settlements, while the alleged victims receive mostly worthless coupons.

In his 2005 commencement address to Knox College in Illinois, Obama described the conservative philosophy of government as "to give everyone one big refund on their government—divvy it up by individual portions, in the form of tax breaks, hand it out, and encourage everyone to use their share to go buy their own health care, their own retirement plan, their own child care, their own education, and so on. In Washington, they call this the Ownership Society. But in our past there has been another term for it—Social Darwinism—every man or woman for him or herself. It's a tempting idea, because it doesn't require much thought or ingenuity."[52] Obama has rejected this "free market" vision of government, preferring to see the power of the state as something that can serve the public interest.

According to Obama, "We've got to put a lot more money into education than we have. We have to invest in human capital."[53]

Obama said, "Domestically, our national debt and budget constrain us in ways that are going to be very far-reaching and long lasting. And I think whoever is elected in 2008 is going to be cleaning up the fiscal mess that was created as a consequence of the president's tax cuts."[54] Obama opposed repealing the estate tax: "Let's call this trillion-dollar giveaway what it is—the Paris Hilton Tax Break. It's about giving billions of dollars to billionaire heirs and heiresses at a time when American taxpayers just can't afford it." Obama has proposed to "reverse some of those tax cuts that went to the wealthiest Americans." As Obama put it, "It's not as if rich people were suffering under Bill Clinton."[55] After two terms of a president and vice president devoted more to serving the bottom line of companies like Halliburton than to helping the people at the bottom of our society, the American people are looking for a dramatic change with Obama.

Health Care

No issue affects so many Americans, in terms of their lives and their pocket-books, as health care. As Obama noted, "We have reached a point in this country where the rising cost of health care has put too many families and businesses on a collision course with financial ruin and left too many without coverage at all."[56]

Obama has already embraced minor legislation to improve health care. Legislation proposed by Obama and Hillary Clinton would address medical malpractice costs by helping hospitals to develop programs to disclose medical errors.[57] An Obama amendment passed by the Senate required the Environmental Protection Agency to stop delaying the writing of rules dealing with disposal of lead paint during renovations.[58]

After a Democratic forum on health care in Las Vegas, the conservative *Economist* magazine editorialized, "Barack Obama resorted to empty waffle, endorsing the idea of universal coverage but confessing that he had not yet produced a health care plan. An odd failure, given that the forum was devoted to the subject—and that this is one of the most important issues for Democratic voters."[59] Was it really an "odd failure" that a candidate two months into his campaign, and two years before any Democrat could pass a health care plan, hadn't developed a detailed solution to what may be the most expensive and intractable public policy problem facing America? It wasn't long ago that no one paid much attention to a presidential race 21 months before the next inauguration; this past election, the pundits demanded detailed, comprehensive plans for every policy immediately after a campaign was launched. In an era of 24-hour cable news and Internet blogs, the idea of thinking about a plan for a while was unthinkable, and talking to people before one formulated a policy was unnecessary when push polls and focus groups told you everything you needed to know. A few weeks later, Obama released his health care proposal, which aimed to make universal health care coverage available by the end of his first term. To pay for the plan, Obama proposed restoring tax rates for the wealthiest individuals back to the levels during the Clinton administration.

Although Obama has expressed interest in single-payer health care systems, he believes that the American political system is not ready to pass such an idea. Because of $1 billion in campaign contributions over the last ten years from the health care industry, Obama noted, "We need to overcome that." However, his health care plans do show that a more efficient system can be found for America.

It's clear that current health care corporate interests will fight against Obama's plans. For example, obamatruth.org, a website started by Joe Novak, a Republican political consultant known as "low blow Joe," accused Obama of hypocrisy because he doesn't denounce his wife's employer, the University of Chicago Hospitals, which makes millions of dollars while charging poor people for medical services. Novak worked for insurance millionaire J. Patrick Rooney, a leading GOP donor and opponent of health care reform. According to Novak, "What some people consider a dirty trick, I would argue is many times the legitimate dispersal of information."[60] But Obama noted about health care reform, "We are not in 1992. We are not in 1993. We are not in 1994. We don't have to be intimidated."[61]

Filmmaker Michael Moore noted about Obama's health care plan, "Many parts of his proposal are good." The problem, Moore noted, is that it doesn't guarantee coverage to every American.[62] Obama's plan doesn't force all Americans to purchase health insurance, but it's not clear that compulsory policies do much more than enrich insurance companies. Obama urged that our health care system invest more money in prevention: "We spend less than four cents of every health care dollar on prevention and public health."[63]

Obama's health care proposals won't satisfy everyone, and they won't fix every problem in the expensive disaster of health care in America. But Obama's ideas are a comprehensive start to solving the problem of health care.

Obama's Environment

One environmental magazine called him "a bona fide, card-carrying, bleeding-heart greenie."[64] As a student at Columbia University, Obama worked for three months as an environmental activist to promote recycling in Harlem. As a community organizer in Chicago, he fought against environmental racism by helping public housing residents demand to have their apartments tested for asbestos and repaired. As Obama noted, "Environmentalism is not an upper-income issue, it's not a white issue, it's not a black issue, it's not a South or a North or an East or a West issue. It's an issue that all of us have a stake in."[65]

In the 2004 Democratic primary race, Obama was endorsed over his six opponents by both the Sierra Club and the League of Conservation Voters (LCV) (which also named him an Environmental Champion). One League official declared in 2004, "I've been playing national politics for more than 20 years and I quite literally can't remember one person I've met—even on a national level—who was more in command of facts, more eloquent, and more passionate on these issues than Senator Obama."[66]

In the Illinois Senate, Obama introduced a bill requiring more pollution controls at coal plants to block the Bush administration from rolling back the Clean Air Act in Illinois. He cosponsored a bill to require that 10 percent of electricity in the state come from renewable sources by 2012, and supported measures to increase energy efficiency codes. Obama sought tougher standards for diesel engines, and he proposed protecting wetlands and stopping toxic dumping.[67]

Jack Darin, director of the Sierra Club's Illinois chapter, noted about Obama in 2004, "He's an incredibly quick study. He's not a scientist, but remarkably adept at analyzing the details of complex environmental issues, asking the right questions, and ultimately making the right policy decision for public interest."[68]

In 2007, Obama joined with John McCain and Joe Lieberman to propose legislation that would help stop global warming by reducing greenhouse

gases by 2 percent per year for the next several decades, imposing manda-
tory caps on emissions by power plants, refineries, and industrial facilities.[69]
Tiernan Sittenfeld, legislative director for the League of Conservation
Voters, noted about Obama: "He's really been a champion on a number of
environmental issues," such as opposing oil drilling in the Arctic National
Wildlife Refuge.[70]

Obama has proposed regulations to make gasoline cleaner to reduce greenhouse gas emissions from cars by 5 percent in 2015 and 10 percent in 2020 by
increasing use of biofuels.[71] In 2005, Obama supported a mandate that would
require automakers to average 40 miles per gallon by 2017. Obama, joined by
two Democrats and four Republicans, proposed mandating 4 percent increases
in automobile fuel economy each year.[72] Obama's "Health Care for Hybrids"
plan offered to "pay 10 percent of the $6.7 billion in annual health costs for
retirees that are weighing down General Motors, Ford and Chrysler if they'll
commit to building more fuel-efficient cars."[73]

Obama's environmental efforts went beyond the high-profile issues such
as global warming to include other serious global threats, such as mercury.
Obama declared, "There are affordable and available alternatives to mercury. We just need to take the steps necessary to keep it from being shipped
around the world where we lose track of it, because ultimately it will make
its way back to the United States in the food that we eat and put our kids
at risk."[74] Obama also noted the problem of mercury pollution caused by
so-called cleaner coal from western states.

After environmentalists objected to Obama's support for coal liqui-
fication subsidies, Obama changed his position to say that he would
only support the subsidies if it would lower carbon dioxide emissions
compared to petroleum fuels. Environmentalists have also criticized
Obama's strong embrace of corn-based ethanol, because its environmental benefits have been questioned. But as Obama declared in 2006,
"If we truly want to harness the power of these fuels and the promise
of this market, we can and must generate more cellulosic ethanol from
agricultural products like corn stocks, switch grass and other crops our
farmers grow."[75] Obama also cosponsored legislation to encourage the
use of biodiesel and the development of cellulosic feedstock, which is
expected to provide a more efficient form of ethanol than corn, but he
wants to ensure that a domestic fuel market is created for oil security
as well as environmental reasons.[76]

However, Obama has recognized that environmental protection and energy security have a price tag: "If we have a real energy plan, it's going to cost something. There's not a magic energy store where we can buy a new gadget; we're going to have to invest and make some tough decisions."[77] Rather than seeking symbolic measures on the environment, Obama has proposed efforts to reach bipartisan compromise on important changes.

Foreign Policy

In 2007, Hillary Clinton reportedly told Democrats about Obama that "she believed the threat of his candidacy will diminish as voters learn how inexperienced he is in government and foreign affairs."[78] However, Obama's experience in foreign affairs may be his strongest attribute.

Obama wrote the law signed in 2006 that provided $52 million in U.S. assistance to help stabilize the Congo, and he worked to approve $20 million for the African Union peacekeeping mission.[79] Obama also worked with Sam Brownback (R-Kan.), writing an op-ed in the *Washington Post* criticizing the Bush administration's failure to stop genocide in Darfur.

Obama worked with Richard Lugar (R-Ind.) to pass legislation to help secure dangerous conventional weapons, especially from the former Soviet Union. In December 2006, the Senate passed the Lugar-Obama bill to restrict the global spread of conventional weapons. Obama noted, "The Lugar-Obama initiative will help other nations find and eliminate the type of conventional weapons that have been used against our own soldiers in Iraq and sought by terrorists all over the world."[80]

Obama has long been an advocate of human rights, but he recognizes today that it is more than a humanitarian effort; global protection of rights is a national security necessity. Obama's chapter on Indonesia in *The Audacity of Hope* is a key example of how incisive his political analysis of foreign policy is. Few Americans understand the nuances of how America is perceived abroad.

Instead of surrounding himself with campaign workers or people who take polls, Obama has convinced global experts to help him shape policy. Samantha Power, a Pulitzer Prize–winning Harvard authority on human rights, worked in Obama's Senate office. Former assistant secretary of state Susan Rice noted, "I've been around long enough not to waste my time trying to talk to politicians who just aren't educable. Obama's different. He has judgment and intelligence, but he knows how to listen and take on insights from other people too."[81]

Ethics and Money

Barack Obama has been a unique figure in American political history: an amazing fundraiser who wants to limit the influence of money. There have always been a few "good government" types in Washington, D.C., demanding ethics reform. And there have already been a few prolific fundraisers who could hold million-dollar meet-and-greets with the wealthy. But until Obama, they've never been the same person.

As Obama declared, "The fact that I'm raising obscene amounts of money for this presidential race doesn't make me a hypocrite. I want to see those systems implemented, and I have a track record of doing it."[82]

Some critics tried to identify hypocrisy in Obama's pledge to reject donations from lobbyists. The *Los Angeles Times* reported, "While pledging to turn down donations from lobbyists themselves, Sen. Barack Obama raised more than $1 million in the first three months of his presidential campaign from law firms and companies that have major lobbying operations in the nation's capital."[83] However, this money never came from any companies. It came from individuals who worked for these corporations. An absolute purity against lobbying would be almost impossible. Nearly every American works for a company, or belongs to a union, that engages in lobbying of some kind. The fact that less than 5 percent of Obama's money could be traced to people at firms engaged in lobbying indicates how little dependence he had on the traditional sources of campaign funding that end up corrupting our political system.

Obama's campaign did accept money from state lobbyists because they weren't involved in federal lobbying, and he also accepted money from former lobbyists. But overall, the Obama campaign represented a sharp attack on the power of lobbyists. By banning direct donations from lobbyists, Obama sent a signal that influence couldn't be bought. By raising money from millions of individual donors during his campaign, Obama made it impossible for special interests to have a claim over his success.

In his political past, Obama often struggled to raise money on a par with other candidates, even though he did take PAC money and lobbyist donations. His 2004 election to the U.S. Senate came despite being vastly outspent by one of his opponents. And because he wasn't planning to run for president, Obama used his campaign funds to help other Democrats get elected in 2006 rather than building up a $10 million treasure chest like Hillary Clinton did. So Obama's refusal to take PAC or lobbyist money in his presidential campaign represented a real risk. He had no idea whether he could raise enough money to compete against experienced fundraisers such as Hillary Clinton who would take money from lobbyists. As it happened, his campaign broke all fundraising records.

Ethics Reform in Congress

Lobbyist Jack Abramoff, who pled guilty to tax evasion, fraud, and bribery in 2006, helped spur a new crusade for congressional ethics. In 2006, Obama was put in charge of the Democratic efforts for ethics reform.

Because Obama proposed to have ethics reform go through the normal committee procedures rather than be negotiated by an informal bipartisan group, John McCain exploded in anger, writing Obama a sarcastic letter accusing him of lying: "I would like to apologize to you for assuming that your private assurances to me regarding your desire to cooperate in our efforts to negotiate bipartisan lobbying reform legislation were sincere.... I'm embarrassed to admit that after all these years in politics I failed to interpret your previous assurances as typical rhetorical gloss.... I hold no hard feelings over your earlier disingenuousness."[84]

It is a measure of Obama's diplomatic skills that McCain's rude letter didn't faze him or provoke a similar reaction. Instead, Obama responded, "The fact that you have now questioned my sincerity and my desire to put aside politics for the public interest is regrettable but does not in any way diminish my deep respect for you nor my willingness to find a bipartisan solution to this problem."[85] Two days later, they publicly made up.

Obama's decision reflected McCain's failure to have any influence among his fellow Republicans in pushing for lobbying reforms. Obama determined that working within the committees and pursuing a specific bill would be more effective than trying to pursue a bipartisan task force whose recommendations would be ignored by most Republicans anyway. Forcing politicians to vote against a popular ethics reform would work better than trying to come up with a compromise that would achieve broad bipartisan consensus, which was impossible in the face of Republican opposition.

Obama has suggested public financing of elections, reduced-cost TV advertising for candidates, and limits on the revolving door for congressional staffers who become lobbyists. He sought to ban gifts from lobbyists and corporate-financed travel. To show his commitment to the cause, Obama even gave up one of his favorite perks: low-cost travel on private planes donated by lobbyists. He announced that he would "pay the full costs of a flight taken on someone else's private plane, rather than pay the much cheaper price of a first-class ticket."[86]

Obama supported numerous reforms that his colleagues would not embrace, including proposals to prohibit paid coordination of lobbying, ban lawmakers from negotiating future employment as lobbyists, prohibit earmarks in which a member of Congress has a financial interest, and ban the use of earmarks to buy votes.[87] Obama's ideas for ethics reform included requiring bills to be available online for 24 hours before a vote, opening conference committee meetings for the public to watch, and forcing members of Congress to immediately disclose any future employment negotiations.[88] Obama was one of eight senators to oppose a bill aimed at improving lobbyist rules because it was not restrictive enough. Obama joined Senator Russ Feingold's bill calling for greater public financing of campaigns.

Obama called for a "nonpartisan, independent ethics commission" to replace the current inactive, politicized system in Congress.[89] He noted, "We cannot change the way Washington works unless we first change the way Congress works."[90] Mary Boyle of Common Cause noted, "I couldn't look for more of a hot potato—a bill to sponsor that will not win you the love of your colleagues—than an outside independent ethics commission. In that sense, it was clear he was looking to do the right thing and wasn't overly concerned with how it would play with his colleagues."[91]

Although most of Obama's goals for ethics reform have not been passed by his colleagues in Congress, he was able to get one important piece of legislation enacted into law despite opposition from the old guard. On September 18, 2006, Congress passed S. 2590, the Federal Funding Accountability and Transparency Act introduced by Obama and Senator Tom Coburn (R-Okla.). This bipartisan legislation created a searchable database on the Internet for all federal contracts and grants, and it has won praise from reform groups on both the left and the right.

America has never before elected a president who has been a leader in promoting ethics reform in Congress. After the revolving door between government and industry during the Bush administration, America needs a president who will impose strong ethical standards on the federal government. Good government can be more than just a naive slogan of utopian dreamers; it can become a guiding philosophy for the Obama administration.

CHAPTER EIGHT

The Victory

Barack Obama's Improbable Triumph

I realize that I am not the likeliest candidate for this office. I don't fit the typical pedigree, and I haven't spent my career in the halls of Washington. But I stand before you tonight because all across America something is stirring. What the naysayers don't understand is that this election has never been about me; it's about you.

—Barack Obama

Standing among a crowd of 200,000 cheering people in Grant Park on the night of November 4, 2008, I could sense how dramatic Barack Obama's victory was. This was much more than hometown pride, much bigger than the political equivalent of the White Sox winning the World Series. And the Grant Park gathering was only a small part of the celebration going on throughout the country, and around the world.

How did Obama win? How did he defeat Hillary Clinton, the most powerful political force in the Democratic Party, and John McCain, the most popular and admired Republican politician in the country?

As a former community organizer who helped lead a massive voter registration drive in Chicago in 1992, Obama put together the biggest grassroots organizing campaign ever seen. Obama's campaign also understood the importance of the Internet. Obama's presence on the web and social networking sites blew away the competition, creating a powerful force of volunteers and supporters. It turned Obama into the greatest fundraiser in American political history.

After Obama won the Democratic primary, the attacks on him grew even more intense. Conservative books full of errors and misrepresentations filled the best-seller lists, and conservative talk radio went into overdrive spreading lies about Obama. From crazed conservatives claiming that Obama's birth certificate was a fake to the bigoted e-mails about Obama being a Muslim that roamed around the Internet like mosquitoes, no presidential candidate in history has ever had to overcome more negative attacks than Obama did. John McCain promised to run an "honorable" campaign and then relied on guilt-by-association smears and red-baiting attacks on "socialism" to dominate his agenda.

By contrast, Obama ran one of the most disciplined, well-organized, and effective political campaigns in American history. And during an era of negative campaigns, Obama didn't lie about his opponent or engage in sleazy attacks.

As *Newsweek* noted, "In South Carolina, the Obama campaign refused to indulge in the time-honored, if slightly disreputable, practice of dispensing 'walking-around money' to activists and preachers in the black community. The Clintons, by contrast, continued to hand out the usual favors and cash. Obama not only won the black vote overwhelmingly, he also won the state of South Carolina by 30 points."[1] Obama's victory may have seemed improbable, but the fact that he did it while taking the political high road must have seemed even more improbable to the political pundits.

The pundits and the press have repeatedly underestimated Obama during his political career, and the campaign for president was no exception. In understanding how Obama won, it's essential to look at a key factor downplayed by the press, the youth movement for Obama, as well as the negative factors of race and media coverage, which were twisted by the press and presented as advantages for Obama.

Ultimately, it was Obama's positive attributes that attracted the support of donors, volunteers, and voters. For the first time in many years, Americans felt inspired by a presidential candidate. Instead of being embarrassed by George W. Bush, they imagined Obama as someone they could be proud of as president.

How Generation Obama Won the Election

The vote for Obama broke numerous records. With more than 132 million votes cast, Obama received 69.5 million votes (the largest vote for a president in history by a margin of more than 7 million votes), and he won by almost 10 million votes.[2]

According to an analysis in the *Boston Review,* "Voters under the age of 30 made up 18 percent of the electorate in 2008, compared to 17 percent in 1996, 2000, and 2004, nowhere near the historic highs of 1972 and 1992. Had Obama relied only on a surge among young voters, holding other groups at the 2004 voting behaviors, he would have fallen short of victory."[3]

None of this is true. In fact, the youth vote was critical to Obama's victory. According to exit poll data, after a low of 37 percent in 1996, youth voting (18–29) grew to 48 percent in 2004 and 52 percent in 2008, the highest ever recorded in exit polls. Once census-based data is compiled, the 2008 youth turnout might rival the 55.4 percent in the 1972 election.[4]

However, even that number understates youth voting in 2008. Although 55.4 percent of registered young voters went to the polls in 1972, this reflected lower voter registration rates. In 1972, young people 18 to 29 were 24.2 percent of voters and 28.6 percent of citizens. But in 2008, young people were approximately 18 percent of voters and just over 20 percent of citizens, the smallest gap ever recorded.[5]

Almost 24 million Americans under 30 voted in 2008, growing by 4 million votes compared with 2004. Young voters supported Obama 68 percent to 32 percent, compared to those over 60, who supported McCain 51 percent to 47 percent. That's an age gap of 40 percentage points, the biggest margin ever found.[6] Obama won the youth vote by more than 8 million votes, accounting for most of his margin of victory.

Yet the mainstream press downplayed the importance of the youth movement for Obama. An MSNBC.com story titled "Young Voters Not Essential to Obama Triumph" claimed: "AnaMaria Arumi, who directs the exit poll desk for NBC, MSNBC and Telemundo, has done the calculations based on the exit poll data and here is what she found: On a state-by-state level, when she reran the numbers as if there were no voters under 30, the only states that would switch to Republican presidential candidate John McCain are Indiana and North Carolina."[7] The MSNBC blog *First Read* added a snarky aside, "(Never mind the cynics among us who may now send all these 'young voters did it' press releases into their junk email folder.)"[8]

Perhaps those cynics should have held on to their press releases. Obama won more than just Indiana and North Carolina due to young voters. He also won Florida and Ohio thanks to the votes of young voters, along with an extra electoral vote in Nebraska.

Now it is true that Obama's landslide was so overwhelming that he would have still won the election without these four states (or even Virginia, which he would barely win without young voters). But Obama's margin of victory without young voters would have been cut in half in Nevada, Pennsylvania, New Hampshire, and Iowa, putting him perilously close to losing if McCain had been able to stage a comeback.

Without the youth vote, Obama's popular vote victory would have been cut to less than 1 percent, essentially destroying Obama's mandate for change. Young voters inspired by Obama were also absolutely essential in U.S. Senate races in Minnesota, Oregon, and Alaska, not to mention numerous close races in the House as well as local and state elections.

The Obama campaign was far more effective than McCain's at reaching out to young people. Among all voters, 13 percent reported being contacted by the Obama campaign and 6 percent were contacted by the McCain campaign. But among young voters, 16 percent had been contacted by the Obama campaign and only 4 percent were contacted by the McCain campaign.[9]

Generation Obama was also a critical force in the organization Obama used to win the election. Whether they were schlepping to Florida or coming out in droves to the Iowa Caucus, young voters won this election for Obama.[10] They were the core of the volunteers who drove the enthusiasm for the Obama campaign. They were the people convincing their neighbors and relatives to vote for Obama. They were the bulk of the volunteers and low-paid campaign workers who did the essential grunt work of this campaign. They were the ones who utilized the web and social networking and cell phones and on-the-ground canvassing to turn what might have been another election stolen by Republicans into a landslide for Obama.

The cynical journalists can twist the poll numbers and dismiss the importance of Generation Obama, but the truth is that Obama transformed the youth numbers in this election to astonishing levels, and in doing so, he may have helped establish the foundation for a permanent progressive majority.

Racism and the Obama Candidacy

Racism was a powerful force in the 2008 presidential election, and often bigotry lurking underneath the surface bubbled up to the top. Around the country, Obama's skin color sparked racist reactions. Four North Carolina State University students wrote anti-Obama comments in a free expression tunnel, including "Let's shoot that nigger in the head." A noose was hung at Baylor University on Election Day, and Obama campaign materials were burned in a pit. At Purdue University, racist anti-Obama graffiti was written near a place where black students often gather. A poster of the Obama family on a University of Alabama professor's office door was ripped apart, and a death threat and a racial slur were written on a replacement poster.[11]

Obama has received more threats than any other presidential candidate. In Standish, Maine, the Oak Hill General Store started the "Osama Obama Shotgun Pool" where customers bet $1 on a date when Obama would be killed: "Stabbing, shooting, roadside bombs, they all count.... Let's hope someone wins." In Rexburg, Idaho, young children on a school bus chanted, "assassinate Obama."[12] Obama received Secret Service protection earlier than any candidate ever because of the racist e-mails sent to his Senate office.[13] In the media, racist responses to Obama were also common. In Tennessee, an elementary school principal wrote a column in the local newspaper suggesting a song for Obama to the tune of *The Jeffersons'* theme: "Well we're movin' on up,/To Washington, D.C./To a deee-luxe pimp pad,/Painted whiiiite."[14]

Throughout the campaign, conservative talk show host Rush Limbaugh made several racist attacks on Obama. Limbaugh claimed that Obama did not have the intellectual capacity to write his own books: "Obama didn't even write these books; Ayers did."[15] Limbaugh called Obama "stupid" and asserted that Obama "probably didn't get out of Harvard without affirmative action."[16] The notion that Barack Obama could not have graduated from Harvard Law School without preferential grading was one of the most racist assertions made during this campaign. No one can possibly imagine that

Obama's success—including selection to the *Harvard Law Review,* election as its president, graduating magna cum laude in the top 10 percent of his class, passing the bar, and becoming a top teacher at the University of Chicago Law School—was all somehow granted to him by a conspiracy of Harvard law professors to raise his grades. But to a racist like Limbaugh, such nonsense becomes believable if it's a black person who is succeeding.

Limbaugh regularly played a parody song, "Barack the Magic Negro," that said about Obama, "he's black but not authentically." Limbaugh was oddly obsessed about Obama's racial background and bizarrely made the false claim that Obama was an Arab: "Do you know he has not one shred of African American blood? ... He's Arab. You know, he's from Africa. He's from Arab parts of Africa.... He's not African American. The last thing that he is is African American."[17]

Yet Limbaugh additionally claimed that Obama was obsessed with race: "Almost all of his beliefs are founded in race and anger and racial division."[18] Limbaugh claimed, "It is clear that Senator Obama has disowned his white half, that he's decided he's got to go all in on the black side."[19]

Limbaugh was fond of using racial insults against Obama, calling him "a Chicago street thug,"[20] "Halfrican American,"[21] "a half-minority,"[22] and even "the little black man-child."[23]

Ironically, Limbaugh also accused Obama of "inciting racism" and "inflaming racial hatred."[24]

When the leading conservative commentator in the country makes openly racist (and obviously false) attacks on a black candidate, without any protests or serious media coverage, it shows how far America still has to go in achieving racial equality.

The Continuing Significance of Racism

Conservative activist David Horowitz wrote, "I am glad he won by a big enough margin so that only cranks will continue to claim that the words racism and America can ever be reasonably linked."[25] The mainstream press was equally anxious to proclaim racism dead and buried as Obama became the president-elect. *Time* magazine claimed, "Barack Hussein Obama did not win because of the color of his skin. Nor did he win in spite of it." Unfortunately, this simply isn't true.

Most analysts have downplayed the role of race in the 2008 election results. The common view about race in the election was given by *ABC News*: "Race was perhaps a surprisingly minor factor. Nineteen percent of all voters called it at least somewhat of a factor in their vote; 80 percent said it was not a factor at all. But Obama's margin was essentially the same among those who called race a factor—53–45 percent—and those who said it was not, 51–46 percent. There were, however, differences by race. Seventeen percent of whites called race a factor, and favored McCain by 61–37 percent. Whites for whom race was not a factor voted for McCain by a narrower 53–44 percent. Meanwhile one in three blacks called race a factor in their vote, and, like all blacks, favored Obama almost unanimously."[26]

These are alarmingly high levels of self-reported racism, although reports in the national exit poll (with 19 percent listing race as a factor and 9 percent giving it as a significant factor) turned out to be inaccurate.[27] In reality, 13.24 percent of voters nationwide told the exit pollsters that race was an important factor (including the small number who said it was the single most important factor), and 21.4 percent of voters said race was a factor (including those who called it a minor factor). Interestingly, 53 percent of these votes where race mattered were for Obama, a contrast with the primaries where race-based voting hurt Obama much more.[28]

Racism and the Democratic Primary

During the final weeks of the Democratic primary, Hillary Clinton played the race card by citing a *USA Today* poll and explaining that it showed "how Senator Obama's support among working, hard-working Americans, white Americans, is weakening again, and how whites in both states who had not completed college were supporting me."[29] But what Clinton said was true: Obama's support was weak among less-educated whites.

It is notable that racism and sexism seemed disconnected in the primary race. In the West Virginia primary, 20 percent of voters said race was a factor in their vote, and they supported Clinton over Obama 84 percent to 10 percent. But gender was a key factor helping Hillary Clinton. Overall 18 percent of the voters said gender was a factor, and they supported Clinton 73 percent to 22 percent. The men who said gender was a factor in their voting also supported Clinton 59 percent to 34 percent. This indicates that bigotry can be a divided concept. White people, and even white men, can support a female candidate enthusiastically while simultaneously revealing their dislike of black people to pollsters.

Surprisingly, racism mattered more than sexism in the Democratic primary race. On Super Tuesday, more Democratic voters admitted to racist motivations in opposing Obama (an average of 2.88 percent of the voters) than admitted to sexist motivations in opposing Clinton (an average of 1.83 percent). Overall, the racist vote outweighed the problack vote for Obama by an average of 0.5 percent. By contrast, the prowoman vote for Clinton outweighed the sexist vote by an average of 5.0 percent.[30] This disparity was repeated throughout the Democratic primary. Clinton's entire margin of victory in the Pennsylvania primary came from racist whites who openly opposed Barack Obama because he is black.

What's remarkable about these numbers is that they represented a reversal of the polling data only a year earlier. A July 2007 *Newsweek* poll found that only 4 percent of Americans said that they would not vote for an African American president, and only 30 percent thought that the rest of America would not. By contrast, 10 percent said they would not vote for a woman, and 14 percent said they would not vote for a Latino. The same poll found that if the Democratic race came down to Hillary Clinton and Barack Obama, only 34 percent of whites would vote for Obama, and an astonishingly low 29 percent of nonwhites said they would support Obama.[31] Obama's campaign dramatically changed the personal support for him. But it also increased the willingness of Americans to tell pollsters that they opposed Obama because of his race.

Racism in the General Election

It is a mistake to imagine that the exit polls showed race was a positive factor for Obama. Many of the voters for Obama who said race mattered were African Americans, who vote for Democrats anyway by a large margin. Obama slightly increased the Democratic percentage of the African American votes and slightly increased African American turnout. But for the most part, the people voting for Obama who said that race mattered were almost certain to vote for a Democrat. And it is much easier to admit that race matters and say that you voted for the black candidate than the opposite. There was also an unknown number of people who voted against Obama because of race and refused to admit it to the pollsters.

Also, included among this 53 percent were many people who held racist feelings against Obama but voted for him nevertheless due to party loyalty or concerns about the economy and the war in Iraq. For example, in nearly all-white West Virginia, the proportion of people who said race mattered but who nevertheless voted for Obama grew from 9 percent in the primary to 39 percent in the general election.

There are some who argue that voters of any race who supported Obama and said race was a factor are all racists. But that's like saying the NAACP is the same as the KKK because they both are concerned about race. It's not racism to support electing the first African American president. It is racism to oppose doing so based on race.

The "racist" vote was anyone who said race was a factor and voted against the black candidate. The nationwide average of the 36 states where voters were asked about race in the exit poll (correcting for population) was 7.13 percent racist (as an important factor) and 11.5 percent racist as any factor. The most racist state in these polls was Louisiana, where 14.84 percent of voters against Obama felt race was an important factor, while 23.78 percent of anti-Obama votes said race was a factor in their vote. Closely following Louisiana were Alaska (14.0 percent and 21.08 percent) and Kentucky (14.3 percent and 19.8 percent).

The least racist state in these polls was California, where only 3.78 percent of voters were opposed to Obama and said race was an important factor, and only 5.92 percent overall said race was a factor and opposed Obama. Close behind California were New York (3.41 percent and 7.44 percent), Washington (3.51 percent and 6.84 percent), and Illinois (3.96 percent and 7.68 percent). The biggest surprise might be Georgia, where the numbers were only 4.81 percent and 8.4 percent. Maybe it's notable that the Obama campaign fought hard for Georgia, while the most racist states had few Obama commercials or campaign workers. However, we shouldn't discount the power of racism just because Obama won. In presidential elections, 11.5 percent of the electorate isn't a small factor; it's a massive group of voters (more than 14 million people).

How big of an influence was racism? The following states would have shifted to Obama if all of the McCain voters who said race was an important factor had switched sides: Arizona (10), Missouri (11), Montana (3), South

Carolina (8), and West Virginia (5). That's a total of 37 electoral votes. In addition, the following states would have turned to Obama if the Mc-Cain voters who said race was a factor of any kind had supported Obama: Georgia (15), Kentucky (8), Louisiana (9), and Tennessee (11). That's 43 more electoral votes. Speculating among the states without exit polls on race but considering the racism in surrounding states, it seems likely that Texas (34), Mississippi (6), South Dakota (3), and North Dakota (3) would have gone for Obama without racism. That's 46 more electoral votes.

Altogether, without the influence of racism, the only states McCain would have clearly won are Alaska (3), Idaho (3), Wyoming (3), Utah (5), Alabama (9), Arkansas (6), Oklahoma (7), Nebraska (4), and Kansas (6): a total of 46 electoral votes, compared to Obama's 492. And Obama's popular vote margin would have easily been in double digits.

There has been far too much attention given to the Bradley effect, which many commentators declared dead on election night. The Bradley effect only refers to racists who lie to pollsters, which apparently didn't happen on November 4. But we should be far more concerned about the large number of Americans who are openly willing to admit their racism to pollsters (or those who are influenced by race without saying so). Frank Rich proclaimed in the *New York Times* that the election proved "while there are still bigots in America, they are in unambiguous retreat."[32]

It is indeed a sign of progress in this country that "only" one-tenth of Americans openly admit to being racist in choosing a president. Only a few decades ago, a black candidate for president was unthinkable in America. But these levels of racism are far from a sign that racism is over. Obama was the perfect candidate to overcome racist views among voters, and 2008—with an economic crisis and a failed Bush presidency—provided the perfect circumstances for this to happen.

There is some reason for hope. In West Virginia, during the Democratic primary, 21 percent of voters said that race was a factor, and only 9 percent of them voted for Obama. In the general election 31 percent said race was a factor, and 39 percent voted for Obama. In a state where blacks are 3 percent of the population, this obviously wasn't a case of African Americans supporting Obama for racial reasons. These figures also contradict any notion that "white guilt" was behind the white voters for Obama who said race was a factor. It's highly unlikely that a massive number of West Virginians who were openly racist in the Democratic primary suddenly decided that a black man needed to occupy the White House. It's equally unlikely that Republicans voting in the general election were supporting Obama and did so due to white guilt. What is more likely is that Democrats who opposed Obama because of race in the primary couldn't bring themselves to vote for a Republican, despite the continuing significance of race to them. Openly racist whites voted for Obama in spite of their bigotry, not because they had any white guilt. Whether it was due to party loyalty or simply a belief that Obama was the better candidate, many racist whites (perhaps 5 percent of all voters) decided to cast a vote for Obama even though race was clearly a negative factor for them.

According to one analysis in the *Boston Review,* "Obama won because of race—because of his particular appeal among black voters, because of the changing political allegiances of Hispanics, and because he did not provoke a backlash among white voters."[33] In reality, Obama won in spite of race, not because of it. Racist white voters, not pro-Obama minorities, were the outliers in the voting.

Hispanics are the key to understanding the racial dimension of the 2008 election. Latinos are not a core Democratic constituency. Only 56 percent of them voted for Kerry in 2004. Nor do Hispanics have any particular allegiance to Obama. During the Democratic primary, Hispanics supported Hillary Clinton, often by overwhelming margins, leading some pundits to fear that antiblack bigotry among Latinos might cost Democrats the election. Yet Obama won 67 percent of the Hispanic vote in 2008, an 11 percentage point increase over 2004. That number actually exceeded the gain in black voters for Obama (from 88 percent to 95 percent). The Latino vote indicates that race wasn't the reason for Obama's appeal among Americans.

The only racial group that didn't match the overall electorate's dramatic shift in support for Obama was whites, where voting for the Democratic candidate only grew from 41 percent in 2004 to 43 percent in 2008. This suggests that the primary racial effect in the 2008 election came from racist whites who refused to support the black candidate.

The Republican Party's rise to power in recent decades has largely depended upon the fact that impoverished whites blame blacks rather than corporations for their problems. Without these racist whites, Republicans such as Richard Nixon and Ronald Reagan and George W. Bush could never have won. The biggest hope for the future of the Democratic Party is having the old racists who helped bring the Republicans to power die off.

Many commentators assumed that Obama's success with the young and well-educated was because of some "elitist" support he had among the latte-sipping crowd. The real reason is racism. Younger people are less likely to embrace racist views. Well-educated people are less likely to embrace racist views. And that makes all the difference in America, where the continuing significance of race can be measured with alarming detail in exit polls.

The fact that racism played an important part in the 2008 campaign actually bodes well for Obama's reelection chances in 2012. As the public becomes more familiar with Obama and accepts him in the role of president, the initial resistance of some racists will be overcome, as in the case of bigots who oppose racial diversity in their neighborhood but grow to accept one black family on a personal basis after they have lived there for a while. However, it should not lead anyone to grand conclusions about the end of racism.

A More Perfect Union

On March 18, 2008, in response to the controversy over Rev. Wright's sermons, Obama made a speech in Philadelphia at the Constitution Center.[34] Obama himself wrote the speech about race, and it reflected his values more than any other speech he gave during the campaign.[35] Although much of his campaign staff had tried to steer Obama away from talking about race, Obama declared, "Race is an issue that I believe this nation cannot afford to ignore right now."

In his speech, Obama called the Constitution "ultimately unfinished" because "it was stained by this nation's original sin of slavery." But he added that it was "a Constitution that promised its people liberty and justice and a union that could be and should be perfected over time." Perfection, to Obama, is the struggle "to narrow that gap between the promise of our ideals and the reality of their time."

Obama criticized Wright for making the same mistake of seeing America as unchanging: "The profound mistake of Reverend Wright's sermons is not that he spoke about racism in our society. It's that he spoke as if our society was static; as if no progress had been made." According to Obama, "America can change. That is the true genius of this nation." Obama sought to define a middle ground between the racially oblivious who naively define America in utopian terms and the racial radicals who see racism as a permanent, unending stain on America.

Obama's speech about the Constitution was fundamentally about race, but it was also about much more than just race. The speech reflected Obama's approach to politics as well, and it explained what he meant by "change." For the conservative fundamentalists who hate Obama, perfection is something granted by God, and the Constitution is its political equivalent. For Obama, perfection is something attained gradually by hard work within the political process.

For Obama, this "more perfect union" cannot be attained by wishing away our problems or refusing to recognize them. Perfection first requires the acknowledgment of sin and the realization that our country is not perfect, our Founding Fathers were not perfect, and our political system does not inevitably lead to the best results. As Obama put it, "This union may never be perfect, but generation after generation has shown that it can always be perfected."

Obama's victory on November 4, 2008, showed that America has made dramatic steps toward that model of perfection. But as Obama noted, "I have never been so naïve as to believe that we can get beyond our racial divisions in a single election cycle, or with a single candidacy." If someone as highly qualified as Obama still faces this kind of racism, imagine what happens to African Americans in this country who don't have sterling academic credentials, who are not among the most eloquent speakers in American history, who do not happen to be the greatest fundraiser and campaign organizer in the history of politics, and who do not have the opportunity of massive media coverage for two years to enable racists to overcome their doubts.

Obama's election as president surpassed the hurdle of racism only because he was able to leap so high and because the racial barrier is somewhat lower than it once was. But the barrier of race is still there. Racism turned a double-digit Obama victory into a seven-point margin. Racism turned a massive electoral vote landslide that could have exceeded LBJ's victory over Barry Goldwater into a moderate landslide.

Racism still matters in America. Racism substantially affected the November 4 election, and severely hurt Obama's pursuit of the presidency. We need to recognize the continuing significance of race in America, not only to continue the fight for racial equality but also to appreciate how truly amazing Obama's substantial victory was in the face of this racism.

The Myth of Media Bias for Obama

Perhaps the most widely believed assumption of the 2008 election was that the media loved Barack Obama. Rush Limbaugh declared that the media were following Obama with "their tongues dragging along the concrete to the floors."[36] "Lenin, Stalin never got this kind of coverage from their media," Limbaugh claimed, which he blamed on the "chicki-fication of our culture and our news business."[37] After Obama won the presidency, Limbaugh blamed it on "blatant imbalance and unfairness" in the media.[38]

Joseph McQuaid, publisher of the conservative *New Hampshire Union Leader,* wrote an editorial headlined "Obama Orgy" that denounced "the outrageous imbalance in the major media's coverage of the candidates."[39] Such proclamations bolstered a GOP offensive against what the McCain campaign called the media's "bizarre fascination with Barack Obama. Some may even say it's a love affair." A Republican National Committee fundraising letter two days later decried "the fawning, one-sided coverage Barack Obama and Democrat candidates receive from the mainstream media." ABCNews.com columnist Michael S. Malone wrote, "The sheer bias in the print and television coverage of this election campaign is not just bewildering, but appalling."[40]

Former speaker of the House Newt Gingrich declared that "coverage of this election has been among the most dishonest and one-sided by the mainstream media in American history."[41] Crowds at McCain rallies yelled at reporters, "When are you going to stop lying to America?"[42]

The accusations of media bias for Obama weren't limited to conservatives. The *New York Times Magazine* called the campaign an "extended journalistic valentine" for Obama and noted, "Both the Clinton and McCain campaigns charged repeatedly that Obama enjoyed an easy ride from the press, as have a smattering of postelection assessments from within the news media."[43] The most influential media critic in the country, Howard Kurtz of the *Washington Post* and CNN's *Reliable Sources,* repeatedly attacked the press as pro-Obama and even started an "Obama Adulation Watch."

After the election, *Time* magazine's Mark Halperin claimed, "It's the most disgusting failure of people in our business since the Iraq war. It was extreme bias, extreme pro-Obama coverage."[44] But the example cited by Halperin was very odd: "The example that I use, at the end of the campaign, was the two profiles that the *New York Times* ran of the potential first ladies. The story about Cindy McCain was vicious. It looked for every negative thing they could find about her and it cast her in an extraordinarily negative light. It didn't talk about her work, for instance, as a mother for her children, and they cherry-picked every negative thing that's ever been written about her." By contrast, Halperin claimed, the story about Michelle Obama was "like a front-page endorsement of what a great person Michelle Obama is." However, one newspaper's coverage of the candidate's wives proves absolutely nothing about media bias, especially since Cindy McCain was the only candidate's wife who used a charity to supply her drug addiction, and the media's fixation on Michelle Obama's "really proud" comments showed no signs of a pro-Obama bias.

In fact, the anti-Obama bias was evident in the willingness of influential reporters like Halperin and Kurtz to denounce the press for being pro-Obama. By contrast, the media's support for McCain (who once referred to the press as his "base") went unmentioned by anybody in the mainstream media.

Not surprisingly, most Americans have come to believe these repeated declarations of pro-Obama media bias. A Rasmussen poll in July 2008 found that 49 percent of respondents believed that reporters would try to help Obama win, while 14 percent believed most would try to help McCain. Strikingly, "45 percent say that most reporters would hide information if it hurt the candidate they wanted to win," while only 30 percent disagreed.[45]

Such polls reveal the power of the right-wing media in America. The myth of the pro-Obama media is the same as the myth of the liberal press, and it has been created by a standard strategy: Right-wing pundits declare repeatedly and vociferously that the media is biased in favor of liberals; centrist media pundits, who generally prefer critiques from the right because they don't make a structural challenge to their work, concede that they have a point; and progressive critics, excluded from both the proestablishment and the right-wing talk shows that dominate the media, go unheard.

The Conservative Media Attacking Obama

In reality, the clear bias of the media in the 2008 election was against Obama, not for him. The biggest source of the media bias against Obama was right-wing talk radio. There is simply no left-wing equivalent to Rush Limbaugh's three-hour assaults on Barack Obama every weekday. Limbaugh reaches nearly 20 million people a week, double the ratings of any network TV newscast, and he spews his venom for 15 hours per week, six times the time of any news broadcast.[46]

The few liberal outlets where McCain is critiqued systematically, such as Air America or MSNBC's *Countdown with Keith Olbermann*, are vastly outnumbered in airtime and audience by Limbaugh, Sean Hannity, Michael Savage, Glenn Beck, Laura Ingraham, Bill O'Reilly, and many more right-wing talk show hosts who use their platforms to launch regular attacks against Obama. A study by the Center for American Progress and Free Press found that 91 percent of weekday talk radio is conservative.[47]

A postelection Annenberg Public Policy Center poll of 3,000 adults found startling levels of ignorance, noting that 19 percent of the people believed that Obama is a Muslim, a higher figure than that found during the campaign, and 22 percent believed that Obama is half Arab, a bizarre theory promoted by Rush Limbaugh and other racists on the Far Right. The ignorance wasn't limited to perceptions about Obama: 46 percent agreed that Saddam Hussein played a role in the attacks of September 11.[48]

This poll revealed how little of a proliberal bias can be found in the media. Surely, if the press was really so opposed to conservative ideas, there's no way that nearly a majority of Americans would believe one of the fundamental lies about the war in Iraq, even while most Americans oppose that war. The poll also showed the power of the right-wing media in America. The idea that Obama is a Muslim or half Arab was consistently pushed by conservative talk shows and embraced by tens of millions of people even though these racist attacks were false and widely refuted.

According to a July 22–23, 2008, *Fox News* poll, 49 percent of respondents had heard friends or neighbors say there is something about Obama that scares them, compared to only 36 percent for McCain. Yet 46 percent believed Obama was receiving more positive coverage, compared to only 6 percent for McCain.[49] The public's belief in media bias for Obama was largely propelled by the lies about Obama told on conservative talk radio and spread via gossip and e-mails. Because these false stories about Obama were not reported in the mainstream press, many people imagined that some kind of bias was at work.

The Media Coverage of Obama

As with most myths, one part of the "Obama lovefest" story is true: There has been substantially more coverage of Obama than of any other candidate. Numerous stories claiming proof of a pro-Obama media bias focused on studies of the network news broadcasts by the Tyndall Report, a news-monitoring service, which revealed that in the first half of 2008, McCain received 52 percent as much network coverage as Obama (203 minutes versus 389 minutes).

The amount of coverage for both candidates was unprecedented, but the advantage held by Obama in overall coverage was nothing unusual, as shown by figures compiled by the Tyndall Report. The report noted that, in measuring the first six months of each election year, Democratic challenger Michael Dukakis got only 31 percent of the coverage garnered by former vice president George H. W. Bush in 1988, and incumbent Bill Clinton got only 28 percent of the coverage Republican challenger Bob Dole received in 1996. In every year Tyndall studied except 1988, the candidate of the party that didn't hold the White House has gotten more coverage. It's logical for the media to give more coverage to a less familiar candidate; having a longer, contested primary campaign also helps. Considering that Obama's primary nomination battle continued for a full four months after media commentators pronounced McCain's primary victory, the 2008 coverage gap was in fact surprising for how small it was.

The coverage gap also reflected greater public interest in Obama. In a July 23, 2008, *NBC News* poll asking "Who are you focusing on?" 51 percent of respondents said Obama and only 27 percent said McCain. As CNN *Headline News* conservative host Glenn Beck wrote (July 24, 2008), "'The Media' aren't around for their health, they're around to make money, and if Obama drives sales or ratings, then I can't really blame them for continuing to tap that well until it runs dry." Obama was on the cover of magazines because his face sold more magazines than McCain's picture. That's a proprofit bias, not a liberal bias. Even *Fox News* anchor Shepard

Smith called the claims of a bias toward Obama by the mainstream media "preposterous": "The mainstream media reflected what was happening in this nation. It did not drive it."[50]

Flawed Measures of Media Bias

A 2007 study by the Project for Excellence in Journalism (PEJ) and the Shorenstein Center found that in the first five months of 2007, Obama received 47 percent "positive" coverage and 16 percent "negative," better than any other candidate. McCain, by contrast, had 12 percent "positive" coverage and 48 percent "negative" (October 29, 2007).

But such positive/negative studies are a flawed measure of media bias. Not only do they rely on researchers' interpretations of what is positive and negative, they implicitly assume that reality is neutral, and that fair coverage will produce comparable numbers of "good news" and "bad news" stories. Obama received "positive" press coverage in the same way that a winning sports team gets "positive" coverage from sportswriters reporting on its victories; without an independent measure of how well a candidate is doing, calculating "positive" or "negative" coverage won't tell you anything about media bias.

Another study by PEJ found that from September 8 to October 16, 2008, stories about Obama were more positive (36 percent) than negative (29 percent), while stories about McCain were more negative (57 percent) than positive (14 percent).[51]

But a majority (53 percent) of the news coverage was about the horse race where Obama's lead was growing. Even the policy coverage (20 percent of the total), because it tended to focus on the economic crisis, was also negative toward McCain because of how he mishandled the issue, first proclaiming that "the fundamentals of the economy are strong" and then suspending his campaign (and trying to postpone a debate) because the economy was so weak before he flip-flopped and decided to continue campaigning. When the press is obsessed with the horse race and one candidate is winning, the reporting will inevitably reflect that fact. The PEJ study also excluded all talk radio stories, where the bias was overwhelmingly anti-Obama.

Obviously, when Obama was running the better campaign, winning all of the debates according to instant polls, and consistently leading in the polls, it was not media bias for the press to report these facts. To the contrary, the media tended to be biased against Obama by suggesting that McCain might be closer than he really was (based on a few outlier polls) or by ignoring the instant polls and calling the debates a draw. Nor was the media coverage of Obama extraordinarily positive; in fact, it was more negative than that of John Kerry in 2004.[52]

Moreover, a study by the conservative Center for Media and Public Affairs of the first month of the general election campaign in the summer of 2008 found that McCain received more positive network newscast coverage than Obama.[53] If the media were truly biased toward one candidate or one party, we would expect to see consistent favoritism, not these wild swings in media analysis in different periods. Instead, these studies of media coverage reflect the success of the campaigners, not the bias of the press.

The problem with any attempt to measure media bias is the complexity and diversity of the media. Certainly, some parts of the media (such as youth-oriented late-night comedy shows) were biased for Obama, just as other parts (such as the much larger talk radio segment) were biased for McCain. But analyzing the media by counting stories and assigning them negative or positive ratings is a tricky business prone to ideological bias.

The far-right Media Research Center (MRC) released a report in August 2008 declaring that it found overwhelmingly positive media coverage of Barack Obama in the network evening news broadcasts.[54] According to MRC, in the last month of the primary race, 43 percent of the network news stories were positive about Obama and only 1 percent was negative. From May 7 to June 3, there were 90 network news stories about Obama, so according to the MRC, there was only one story in the entire month on all three networks that was negative about Obama. Out of all of these stories— about Michelle Obama's "proud" remarks, about Obama's overwhelming losses in West Virginia and Kentucky, about John McCain and George W. Bush denouncing Obama on Iran and comparing it to appeasement of Nazis, about Michael Pfleger's speech at Obama's church denouncing Hillary Clinton—the MRC claimed that only one story was negative.[55] And Howard Kurtz concluded in a story about the study, "Barack Obama has gotten awfully good coverage from the media in this campaign, and plenty of it."[56]

It's true that most reporters are liberal, and surveys may show that a majority of them, like the overwhelming majority of urban Americans, voted for Obama. That's because the bulk of journalists are well-educated and low-paid, which was a top-performing demographic for Obama. However, the key mainstream media decisions are made by owners, editors, and elite media stars, who reflect a far different demographic. For example, when Obama and McCain appeared before newspaper editors in a meeting hosted by the Associated Press, McCain received a box of doughnuts with sprinkles and got a standing ovation. Obama got no ovation, and was accidentally called "Osama" by AP Chair Dean Singleton.[57] Ron Fournier, the Washington bureau chief for the Associated Press (which might have been the single most influential media position during the election), was a McCain supporter who had actually interviewed with the McCain campaign in 2006 and 2007 to consider taking a high-level position. In 2004, Fournier e-mailed Karl Rove about the war in Iraq, urging him to "keep up the fight."[58]

In the most commonly cited example of media bias for Obama, Chris Matthews may have embarrassed himself by talking about that "thrill going up my leg" at an Obama speech (a thrill shared by many Americans), but Matthews is fond of making oddball positive comments about candidates of both parties, whether it's comparing John McCain to Martin Luther or pondering the "sex appeal" of Fred Thompson: "Can you smell the English leather on this guy?"[59]

The Media and Guilt by Association

The clearest example of media bias against Obama was the disparity in coverage of the guilt-by-association attacks on the two candidates. A Media Matters study of the major media outlets found 76 reports about Obama and Tony Rezko, but only 7 stories about McCain facilitating land deals that benefitted major donors.[60] The *Washington Post* and *New York Times* published 99 articles and 62 editorials/op-eds about Obama and his controversial pastor Jeremiah Wright. The same papers printed only 8 articles and 4 op-eds/editorials mentioning McCain and his links to controversial pastor John Hagee.[61]

Obama's distant acquaintance with Bill Ayers (whose role decades ago in the Weather Underground Obama condemned) became the basis of absurd accusations of "terrorist" connections, while the press completely ignored McCain's endorsement of Oliver North, a criminal who actually sold weapons to Iran when it was officially designated as a state supporter of terrorism. North then illegally used the profits to fund the Contras, a guerrilla group in Nicaragua that engaged in rape, murder, and kidnapping of civilians. Not one mainstream media outlet ever mentioned the fact that McCain personally donated money to the Contras after their human rights violations were widely publicized.

Media Matters discovered that there were 311 reports during the campaign mentioning Obama and Bill Ayers, but only 5 reports (nearly all referencing David Letterman's questions) about McCain's links to G. Gordon Liddy.[62] Liddy was a McCain donor who hosted a fundraiser for McCain in the 1990s. In 2007, McCain called Liddy "an old friend," declaring, "I'm proud of you." Liddy's criminal past during Watergate never bothered McCain, nor did his 1994 comments that his radio listeners should murder federal agents: "Go for a head shot." Liddy also plotted the assassination of journalist Jack Anderson and the firebombing of the Brookings Institution, although these terrorist attacks were never carried out. Both Liddy and Ayers were unrepentant criminals with some distant links to the two candidates, but only Obama was ever investigated and questioned by news reporters about his past association.

The *Politico* reported that many potential scandals investigated by the press about McCain were simply never published: "John McCain's press shop and legal teams spent a lot of time answering questions about—and preparing to rebut—exposes that never ran, according to the campaign's top lawyer, Trevor Potter."[63] And in the rare case when an anti-McCain story was published, the pundits quickly rose to his defense. When the *New York Times* (after delaying the story until after the Republican primary race was over) reported that John McCain was so close to one lobbyist that his former campaign manager feared he was having an affair with her, the rest of the press eviscerated the newspaper for daring to even mention this obviously newsworthy story.[64]

Obama and the Myth of Inexperience

The biggest negative for Obama in the 2008 election was his perceived inexperience. As CNN anchor T. J. Holmes declared about Obama, "He doesn't have that much experience when it comes to foreign policy. Do we really want to put this country and this war on terror in the hands of this inexperienced guy?"[65]

A campaign of misinformation greatly exaggerated Obama's alleged inexperience. Fred Thompson's September 2 speech to the Republican National Convention proclaimed that Obama was the "most inexperienced nominee to ever run for president." The next night, Rudy Giuliani repeated the accusation about Obama: "He is the least experienced candidate for president of the United States in at least the last 100 years." Giuliani and Thompson seemed to be conveniently forgetting that George W. Bush in 2000 had served only six years as governor, far fewer years of experience as an elected public official than Obama's twelve years of experience (eight as state senator, four as U.S. senator). Nor did they seem to care that McCain's vice presidential pick, Sarah Palin, had only two years of experience as governor of Alaska.

Obama's experience in state and national politics also exceeded that of Ronald Reagan (eight years as governor), Jimmy Carter (four years in state senate, four years as governor), Dwight Eisenhower (no political experience), and Harry Truman (ten years as U.S. senator, one year as vice president). In fact, Obama's total political experience exceeded Thompson's eight lackluster years as a senator or Giuliani's two terms as mayor of New York City, which they felt made them qualified to be president. Yet not one media outlet challenged this lie spread by Giuliani or Thompson, or even presented a contrary point of view.

I conducted a quick study of presidential experience and discovered that out of 42 presidents, only 20 had more experience as an elected public official than Obama does now. Only 22 presidents had more experience than Obama as an elected official in Washington, D.C.[66] In terms of his experience, Obama would be a typical president. Yet you didn't find anyone in the media reporting on the fact that Obama had more foreign policy experience than four out of the last five presidents.

However, even if Obama were inexperienced, that would be no reason to vote against him. History shows us that an experienced politician usually makes a lousy president. In fact, the most consistent variable to predict a failed presidency is experience. The *Wall Street Journal* and the right-wing Federalist Society in 2005 surveyed an "ideologically balanced" group of 130 prominent professors to rank the best and worst presidents.[67] Out of the top ten presidents ranked as great and near great, only three had more experience as an elected political official (or more experience in Congress) than Obama does now. Out of the five worst presidents ranked as failures, all of them had more experience than Obama. Obama's depth and breadth of experience, both as an elected official and as a citizen committed to public service, far exceeded the norm for a president. Yet the media repeatedly attacked Obama as inexperienced and never refuted these false charges by Republicans against him.

Obama and the Myth of the Broken Pledge

One attack by John McCain on Barack Obama became an article of unquestioned faith repeatedly declared in the mainstream media: Obama broke a promise to accept public financing in the general election. The mainstream press was nearly unanimous in falsely claiming that Obama had broken a promise to take public financing.

The *New York Times* wrote about his "decision to break an earlier pledge to take public money."[68] NPR claimed, "Earlier, Obama had said he would participate in public financing if his Republican rival, Arizona Sen. John McCain, did the same."[69] Chris Matthews claimed it was "breaking his principles, breaking his word.... It sounds like he's changed his tune ... something he promised before."[70] The *New York Post* headline was, "Going Barack on His Word."[71]

The press repeatedly called Obama's decision a "flip-flop." "It was a flip-flop of epic proportions," said Mark Shields, and David Brooks added that it was "the low point of the Obama candidacy" and "epic hypocrisy."[72] *CBS News* reported that Obama "abandoned a campaign pledge." *NBC News* claimed that Obama "did promise to observe the limits if his opponent did." But the most extensive misinformation came from *ABC World News*. On June 19, Charles Gibson proclaimed, "This is a direct contradiction to what Obama said." George Stephanopoulos proclaimed this a "flip-Flop" and added, "this is a clear flip." Continuing the same story for a second day, Gibson titled the opening segment of the *ABC World News* on June 20, "Flip-Flop Flack: Mounting Criticism of Barack Obama for Refusing Public Financing."

And according to *ABC News'* Jake Tapper, "Obama's stark abandonment of a pledge he repeatedly made during the Democratic primaries has dinged his reputation as a government reformer, and it clearly gave his critics ammunition to attack his character and paint him as a Democratic flip-flopper."[73]

But Obama never made such a pledge. Even in February 2007, before Obama's massive fundraising became evident, staffers were explicit in stating that public financing in the general election was an "option" and not a commitment.[74] In response to a November 2007 questionnaire from the Midwest Democracy Network and Common Cause, Obama wrote: "My plan requires both major party candidates to agree on a fundraising truce, return excess money from donors, and stay within the public financing system for the general election.... If I am the Democratic nominee, I will aggressively pursue an agreement with the Republican nominee to preserve a publicly financed general election."[75] No one could read this answer as suggesting that Obama would accept public financing under any condition. Obama explicitly "required" a promise by the Republican to adopt a "fundraising truce"—meaning not using the parties or 527s as a way to cheat the system.

In a February 20, 2008, op-ed for *USA Today*, Obama explained that such an agreement would have to be carefully negotiated to produce "a meaningful agreement in good faith that results in real spending limits. The candidates will have to commit to discouraging cheating by their supporters; to refusing fundraising help to outside groups; and to limiting their own parties to legal forms of involvement. And the agreement may have to address the amounts that Senator McCain, the presumptive nominee of his party, will spend for the general election while the Democratic primary contest continues."[76]

Obama told reporters in February 2008, "If I am the nominee, then I will make sure our people talk to John McCain's people to make sure we abide by the same rules.... My folks will sit down and see whether we can arrive at commonsense ground rules."[77] However, when the Obama campaign contacted a top McCain lawyer to negotiate spending restrictions, the McCain camp refused to go along with these limits.[78]

Obama was completely consistent from the beginning of his campaign on public financing: He would only accept it if the Republicans were willing to meet his conditions for restraining spending by the parties and outside groups.

Even though the mainstream media was falsely attacking Obama for breaking a pledge he never made, the press failed to report that McCain had actually violated campaign finance laws.[79] McCain used the promise of public financing in the primary to obtain a crucial bank loan for his campaign and then failed to follow spending limits as required by law. Yet it was the false charge of a broken pledge by Obama, not the real fact of a law broken by McCain, that received overwhelming media attention.

How Obama Beat the Media

A candidate like Barack Obama could not have won the Democratic nomination even a decade ago against the power of the media elites. If Obama had depended on the press to win, he would have been dismissed long ago as "too inexperienced," "too intellectual," "too liberal," and, of course, "too black." Instead, the Internet allowed Obama to create a national community organizing model on the web, an unprecedented grassroots fundraising operation, and a place to provide direct access about who he is without the media's distorting mediation. Obama's speech on race in response to the Wright controversy was immediately summarized by some in the press as "Obama refuses to reject his preacher," but millions of people watched Obama's speech on YouTube and saw the brilliance that could not be reduced to a soundbite.

It's no surprise that Obama's support was strongest among those people (the young, the well-educated) with the best access to the Internet, who can do an end run around the media gatekeepers and get direct access to what a candidate thinks. As the mainstream press becomes increasingly irrelevant to the voters, they are obsessed with every empty "scandal" that they can use to create arguments to drive their ratings up.

Because the right wing (and the mainstream media) so effectively peddled the myth of a pro-Obama press, the Obama administration will face a constant disadvantage from the public assuming that press coverage is favorable while journalists are anxious to attack him in order to avoid seeming too friendly (a perceptual problem they never had under George W. Bush, even while the coverage of Bush was far more positive than an incompetent administration deserved).

The bias of the press against Obama only magnifies how overwhelming his victory in 2008 was. The press anointed Hillary Clinton as "inevitable," ran endless stories about every leftist acquaintance of Obama, and ignored countless negative stories about McCain, but in the end Obama created a campaign that overcame these disadvantages.

Obama and the Progressive Movement

What may be most surprising about Obama's victory is that the left had surprisingly little to do with it. Many leading progressives never recognized (or openly mocked) Obama's transformational abilities. In the exit polls, Obama, Edwards, and Clinton all roughly split equally among liberals, moderates, and conservatives in the Democratic Party. On Daily Kos and other progressive websites, activists initially favored John Edwards over Obama. Leftists such as Paul Krugman, David Sirota, Ralph Nader, and Rick Perlstein all favored Edwards for his anticorporate rhetoric; Krugman continued attacking Obama even after Edwards had left the race, and most progressives reluctantly embraced Obama as better than Hillary Clinton. The failure of the left to embrace the most progressive presidential nominee in American history reflects the practical ineptness of today's progressive movement. The left has been out of power for so long and is so easily accustomed to ideological sniping on grounds of purity that most of its leaders never saw the groundswell of a new generation moving past them to join the Obama campaign. To this day, cynical grumbling is the preferred leftist stance toward Obama, even though he has the potential to be the Ronald Reagan of liberals, putting a popular face on progressive politics and leading a landslide to the left never seen before in contemporary American politics.

Some progressives were upset that Obama's appointments included some more centrist figures such as Larry Summers, Hillary Clinton, and even Republicans such as Robert Gates and Ray LaHood. However, Obama always ran as a candidate willing to work with people of all views. And many of his cabinet appointees have learned from the failures of the Bush era and shifted their views to the left. The key question is: What policies will Obama implement? He has established a cabinet of highly capable people, even if none of them might match the dreams of a progressive.

Despite the complaints of some leftists, Obama is preparing for the most dramatic shift to the left of any presidency in American history. In the midst of an economic crisis, Obama has offered his own version of the

New Deal: a plan for a massive public works program to create 2.5 million jobs, repairing the infrastructure of America, and improving energy efficiency. He has repeated his pledge to end the war in Iraq. And he rapidly assembled a plan for his administration that involves rolling back hundreds of bad policies from the Bush administration.

The future of the Obama administration will depend upon his skills and the capabilities of the people he appoints. After eight years of an incompetent president who surrounded himself with right-wing ideologues and sycophants, Obama will easily seem like an improvement to the vast majority of voters. But the past is quickly forgotten, and if Obama proves too cautious in bringing change to a country desperate for it, his approval ratings will fall.

But the success of the Obama administration will also depend on the rest of the country. A president is not a dictator with a four-year term. Obama will be constrained by Congress and the opinions of experts as well as the general public. That's why a progressive movement must accompany the Obama administration, not be replaced by it. For almost a decade, the progressive movement has been stifled by a president impervious to the weight of public opinion against him, and the result has been hopelessness and cynicism. The Obama administration promises a president who will listen to the people and hear the progressive voices that form a majority in this country. Now we need to make sure those voices are heard.

The Obama Presidency

Now that Barack Obama has won the presidential election, there's a big question left unanswered: How will he govern as president? Throughout his campaign, Obama repeatedly called for change; not just change in who holds power in Washington; not only change in the policies being proposed but also change in the way government itself works.

There will always be the temptation to follow the beaten path of political insiders and pollsters. But Obama has the opportunity to be different from his predecessors and to chart a new approach for his presidency.

One big advantage for Obama is technology. The Internet has transformed American culture and the nature of political fundraising and campaigning, but it hasn't done much to change American politics—yet.

As the first president to come out of the Internet era and the first presidential candidate to embrace networking and online communications as a fundamental part of his campaign, Obama can use the Internet to make government more transparent, more efficient, and more responsive to the needs of the people.

Obama has promised to appoint a chief technology officer for his administration, and he used his transition website (change.gov) to provide a mechanism for more public involvement, including a "Your Seat at the Table" web page.[80]

But the other key component of technology will be if Obama can move beyond the bubble of the Beltway and get information that challenges the conventional wisdom of Washington. Doing this requires an active progressive movement that can mobilize people and put pressure on Obama and Congress from the left to counteract all of the pressures from the right.

CHAPTER NINE

The Obama Administration

Turning Hope into Change

*Change happens because the American people demand it, because they rise up
and insist on new ideas and new leadership, a new politics for a new time.*
—Barack Obama

Barack Obama has faced many challenges in his life, but none of them can
compare to his current challenge. Nothing is more difficult than convert-
ing a campaign based upon hope into an administration prepared to take
on the worst economic turmoil facing America in decades. Obama must
rebuild an executive branch left in tatters by eight years of mismanagement
and reconstruct the world's biggest economy similarly in shambles from
the Bush administration. Obama must try not only to fulfill his many
campaign promises but also expand his thinking to deal with the global
economic crisis. And while a recession afflicts America's domestic side,
Obama must return the country to a position of respect around the world
after George W. Bush's tremendous failures in global politics. No president
entering office has ever faced so many challenges, fighting multiple wars
along with domestic turmoil.

Foreign Policy and the Myth of the Surge

To remake America's image in the world, Obama must rethink its foreign policy, including much of the conventional wisdom he embraced

during his run for president. Obama's worst error during the campaign was his admission during an interview with Bill O'Reilly that the surge in Iraq had worked: "The surge succeeded beyond anyone's wildest dreams."[1]

Admittedly, Obama was caving in to the conventional wisdom about the surge that was pushed relentlessly in the press. By contrast, Bob Woodward's book, *The War Within: A Secret White House History, 2006–2008*, rejected the myth of the surge alone winning the war and instead identified four reasons for the reduction of violence in Iraq: use of better tactics and covert warfare; the increased number of troops; the shift by Moqtada Al-Sadr to restrain the Mahdi Army, and the Anbar Awakening, where Sunnis turned against al-Qaeda and worked with the Americans. According to Woodward, "85 to 90 percent of the successful operations and 'actionable intelligence'" came from factors other than the surge.[2] Another factor in the decline in violence was the ethnic cleansing of Baghdad, and the fact that killings only dropped six months after the surge began was another indication that the surge had little impact.[3]

Obama was completely right when he declared back in 2007, "My assessment is that if we put an additional 30,000 of our outstanding troops into Baghdad that that's going to quell some of the violence in the short term. I don't think that there's any doubt that as long as U.S. troops are present they are going to be doing outstanding work. It doesn't change the underlying assessment that there's not a military solution to the situation in Iraq. The underlying political dynamic has not changed."[4]

Even without the surge, this improvement in military tactics, the Anbar Awakening, and the Al-Sadr brigade truce would have dramatically decreased violence in Iraq. In fact, if Obama's plan for withdrawal had been implemented earlier, it would have caused this reduction in violence to take place well before 2007 because the reduction in troops would have forced the U.S. military to change its tactics and improve them and it would have forced the Iraqis to undertake the political deals that led to the reduction in violence in Iraq.

The debate about the surge in Iraq is much more than some historical argument. Obama will not repeat the same mistakes of the Bush administration, but he may find new mistakes to make. In Afghanistan, there is a danger that Obama may embrace the misleading idea that more troops on the ground will lead to more security. A "surge" in Afghanistan will only work if it is accompanied by the same political and military changes and agreements that resulted in improvements in Iraq.

By giving in to the misguided notion that a surge worked in Iraq, Obama runs the risk of deluding himself that an increase in troops will solve the problems in Afghanistan. If Obama thinks that "more troops" are the solution to every foreign policy problem, he will eventually find himself in a Vietnam-style quagmire abroad.

The Israeli/Palestinian Conflict

The most difficult foreign policy challenge facing the Obama administration will be the same one that presidents for decades have tried, but failed, to resolve: Israel and Palestine. The Israeli invasion of Gaza in January 2009 was clearly undertaken at that time because of the Bush administration's unrelenting support for Israeli policies. Israel hoped to avoid forcing Obama himself to take any stands early in his presidency, knowing that Obama would follow the strong tradition of a president-elect refusing to undermine the stance of a departing president.

To try to solve the Israeli-Palestinian conflict, Obama must turn to lessons learned from the key national event in his life: the Civil Rights movement. Even though Obama was too young to remember it personally, the civil rights movement made his candidacy possible. And the Civil Rights movement should be Obama's model for solving this intractable dispute in the Middle East.

This is not to equate the Palestinian liberation movements with the American heroes fighting for civil rights. The Palestinians have turned to terrorism rather than nonviolence, and some Palestinians seek the destruction of Israel rather than justice and equality. But it would be easy to imagine that the Civil Rights movement might have morphed into a violent struggle if peaceful resistance had not brought some progress such as the Civil Rights Act of 1964.

The reason the Civil Rights movement succeeded was that presidents from Eisenhower to Kennedy to Johnson used the National Guard (however reluctantly) as an outside force of law imposed upon the South. Without this external force of law, southern politicians would have continued to deny African Americans their basic rights because doing so was popular.

The same solution is needed in Palestine, albeit in radically different circumstances. Israel will never allow the Palestinians to have an independent state as long as there are any rocket attacks or terrorist bombings aimed against its people, even if it means killing more innocent Palestinian civilians in the process.

Because of this, the idea of a truly Palestinian state with complete self-government is a mere illusion. The Palestinian state is too weak to control everyone who commits acts of violence, and its leaders have too many political incentives to allow attacks on Israelis. The Israelis and the Palestinians also need an external force that can impose international law, prevent attacks from one country against another, and stop the inevitable cycle of retaliation that makes peace impossible.

The only realistic solution for Palestine is to make it a demilitarized UN protectorate occupied by UN troops (including those from Arab countries) who aggressively target and attack any terrorist activities. At the same time, Israel must be prevented from attacking Palestine and from imposing the blockades and border closings that have destroyed the Palestinian economy.

Whether you believe that the Palestinians cannot be trusted to secure their own borders, or that the Israelis cannot be trusted to respect Palestinian authority, it is clear that the existing system does not work. Palestinian independence is meaningless if Israel can simply invade its territory at any moment for any reason. And because Palestinian independence is a joke, it's time to give it up completely and accept the fact that at least when it comes to national security, an international body is necessary in Palestine to maintain peace. No one likes the idea of UN soldiers occupying a country and enforcing the peace, but if the only alternative is an endless chain of Israeli attacks and invasions, even the Palestinians will accept this as a far better solution.

Israelis, too, may worry that a UN force will be unable to stop every attack upon Israel. That's because it is impossible for anyone to prevent terrorist bombings or rocket attacks completely. But Israel will understand that a UN body trying to stop these attacks from within Palestine is a much better and more effective option than the use of Israeli soldiers.

The question is, can Obama see this solution that satisfies no one completely and manage to get all sides to agree to it? Or will he embrace the same old approaches of negotiations and promises and mutual attacks that have proven to be a failure for decades?

The Obama Appointees

Obama has sparked anger from many progressives who believe that his cabinet selections are far too centrist, reflecting a return to the Clinton administration rather than a voice for change. But Obama's selections reflect the total reversal of the Bush administration approach that put loyalty and ideology far above competence. After George W. Bush was anointed the winner of the 2000 election by the Supreme Court, the right-wing Heritage Foundation urged him to "make appointments based on loyalty first and expertise second."[5]

Obama has instead chosen to put highly experienced people into key positions, even when they were his political rivals (such as Secretary of State Hillary Clinton) and critical of Obama's methods. In doing so, Obama is following his long-standing belief in using pragmatic approaches to pursue progressive policies. Ultimately, the test for Obama will be the success of what he accomplishes, not the means he uses to achieve it.

The Obama Court

Perhaps the most important choice Obama will make during his presidency is the selection of Supreme Court appointees. With a Supreme Court dominated by conservatives (seven out of nine justices are Republicans), it is critical for Obama to appoint progressive nominees who share his commitment to constitutional rights. Many experts expect at least three Supreme Court appointments during the Obama presidency, especially replacing some of the older liberal judges. Obama's tendency toward centrism and consensus must be overcome in these appointments, or the rightward tilt of the Court will be institutionalized for decades to come. Unless Obama recognizes that the Supreme Court has lurched to the right after the heyday of the Warren Court, he may repeat the mistakes of previous presidents who allowed conservatives on the Supreme Court to be the dominant force.

Obama realized this fact when he voted against Samuel Alito and John Roberts as George W. Bush's Supreme Court appointees even though he never questioned their qualifications. Obama was explicit in declaring that their conservative ideology, particularly on a Supreme Court that leans right, made it impossible for them to receive his vote. Obama needs to apply the same logic to his Supreme Court appointments and recognize that ideology matters. This doesn't mean that Obama will apply a narrow litmus test or demand particular stands from his appointees, but rather that he should seek out progressive legal thinkers who have a sound judicial philosophy.

From the beginning of his presidency, Obama must cultivate a "farm team" of good judges in the lower courts—young, brilliant, progressive legal scholars on the district courts and U.S. courts of appeal who can become likely candidates for a Supreme Court opening.

Ideally, Obama should be looking for legal thinkers like himself—progressives who believe in the idea of civil rights, who reject the right-wing ideology of originalism and the conservative attempts to use "original intent" to destroy civil rights and civil liberties, true scholars who understand the hypocrisy of attacks on "judicial activism" by conservative judicial activists and who see the Constitution as a living institution.

Obama has always been skeptical of the idea of bringing progressive change solely through judicial action. He has criticized the Civil Rights movement for relying too much on lawsuits rather than activism to transform the country. And he pursued a career in activism and politics, rather than becoming a full-time lawyer or judge, because he believed that democratic politics was more essential to transformational change. However, the Supreme Court remains very important not only because it could, as at the beginning of the New Deal, stand in the way of progressive change, but also because a progressive Supreme Court can help defend individual rights against threats of a future president who might follow in George W. Bush's ideological footsteps.

Media Diversity

Both throughout and after the 2008 campaign, conservative talk shows and blogs spouted a grand conspiracy theory that Obama's victory would lead to the reinstatement of the fairness doctrine in an attempt to silence conservative talk radio by demanding that all sides be heard on public airwaves. The fact that during the presidential campaign Obama had opposed reinstating the fairness doctrine has not diminished the enthusiasm on the Far Right for conspiracy theories about a liberal plot to silence conservatives.

Progressive groups such as Free Press have pushed aggressively for limits on media ownership, but with limited success and even fewer practical results. Unfortunately, it makes little difference whether a media outlet is owned by a large corporation or an enormous corporation. Media ownership rules only prevent companies from acquiring large numbers of broadcast outlets; nothing prevents large corporations such as General Electric from owning media outlets. And the corporate influences created by advertising also affect media attitudes.

Instead of trying to regulate content or ownership, as some on the left advocate, Obama needs to take a new approach to the problem by greatly expanding the role of community media. Obama can begin by reforming the 1995 Telecommunications Act, which was the greatest single legislative mistake of the Clinton administration. This enormous giveaway of public resources to telecommunications companies was a disaster for the public interest.

The shift of television from analog to digital signals presents an incredible opportunity to open up television to the public interest. With new TV channels now available, over-the-air television stations have a vast new territory available and very little substance with which to fill it. The danger is that our TV airwaves will soon be taken over by even more infomercials and reruns, rather than programming that genuinely serves the public interest. Rather than using unenforceable threats to force commercial networks and stations to serve the public, the government should seek to put more media in the hands of the public through nonprofit community organizations. Low-power FM radio stations and other efforts can expand access, but it is the TV spectrum that offers a unique but limited window of opportunity to rebuild and revolutionize the public media system.

But media reform shouldn't be limited to broadcasting. The economic crisis has hit the news business particularly hard, with newspapers facing massive cuts by owners who seek to maintain ridiculous profit margins in the face of a recession and a long-term shift from paper to Internet sources of news for most people. There is no economic model likely to maintain a solid newsgathering presence in the corporate media during the Internet age. That's why a new commitment to community media should include a role for public financing of community media, local investigative reporting, and sound journalism following the nonprofit models of National Public Radio and the Public Broadcasting System. These broadcast sources are already the leading models for substantial news coverage, far exceeding what the corporate media achieve. And apart from some attempts by the Bush administration to impose ideological control over PBS, these government-supported media have been remarkably successful at avoiding government censorship.

We need a similar model for print and Internet journalism as the failures of the corporate press become more and more obvious to news consumers. A simple 1 percent tax on media advertising revenues would provide funds for nonprofit community media and public journalism around the country. Without a greater commitment to real media diversity, the public will be trapped in the downward spiral of corporate media that is becoming more and more devoted to celebrity "news," make-believe "reality" TV, and dumbed-down right-wing pundits.

Obama's vast e-mail network helped him evade some of the constraints imposed by the media dominance over the political debates. Obama can directly contact his supporters and mobilize them to lobby for his policies, all without the filter of the media getting in the way. But Obama still needs the media to reach out to the masses of the American people, and that's why media reform is critical for his success.

The Crisis in Higher Education

Perhaps the most critical domestic promise for Obama to fulfill will be his commitment to make a college education accessible for all Americans. The greatest mistake of Franklin Delano Roosevelt and the New Deal was the failure to expand access to higher education as a response to the Great Depression. Job creation programs such as the Works Progress Administration and safety net programs such as Social Security provided a valuable and necessary response. Economic growth was dramatic (9 percent to 10 percent annually) during the New Deal and unemployment fell every year except during the 1938 recession caused when conservatives convinced Roosevelt to cut spending in a misguided effort to balance the budget.[6]

Many scholars believe that World War II brought the end of the Great Depression, as the nation's industrial might was finally mobilized by the necessities of war. But it is difficult to imagine how building devices for mass killing could provide the foundation for economic growth. Nor can the theory that World War II led to economic growth explain what happened when the war ended and America returned to the free-market system that had been mired in recession. Indeed, the immediate postwar effect was a serious recession in 1946. But unlike during the Great Depression, after World War II the economy recovered and went on to a postwar boom.

The most fundamental difference between government policy before and after World War II was the G.I. Bill, a small piece of legislation designed not for economic growth but as a politically popular way to reward veterans. No one imagined at the time how enormous the G.I. Bill (officially called the Servicemen's Readjustment Act of 1944) would be. The G.I. Bill provided two essential components for long-term economic recovery. First, it provided an outlet for unemployed veterans in the postwar recession. Second, the G.I. Bill dramatically increased the levels of education in America, giving it the most educated populace in the world and setting up America as the economic and intellectual leader it became in the 1950s and 1960s. By 1950, 500,000 Americans were enrolled in college, triple the prewar figure. Ultimately, 7 million veterans received education and training under the G.I. Bill, with 2.2 million attending college.[7]

In December 2008, the Carnegie Corporation took out an ad in the *New York Times*, signed by 36 higher education leaders, asking for Congress to fund billions of dollars in new higher education infrastructure spending.[8] New "green" buildings on campuses may be good for the economy and good for higher education in the long term after years of government cutbacks, but the most important and immediate need for federal funding is to help students pay for their education. The recession has hit higher education with a double whammy: The stock market freefall has sent endowments plummeting while severe state cutbacks in funding higher education are expected as states follow laws that require balanced budgets. In New York, Governor David Paterson announced plans to cut $348 million from state universities, while California plans to cut $464 million from higher education.[9] To make matters even worse, the tightening of the loan market has made it more difficult for students to get private loans they need to meet all of their college expenses.

Traditionally, higher education is a recession-proof business; in fact, when the economy hits a downturn, college enrollments usually go up as unemployed workers seek to improve their skills. But the opposite may be true in this recession. The Modern Language Association meeting at the end of 2008 reported a decline of over 20 percent in employment listings, the worst in the organization's history.[10] Even though demand for higher education may grow, the budget cutbacks and high tuition will make it impossible for many Americans to get the access to colleges they desire.

Some conservatives have opposed the expansion of higher education. Charles Murray wrote an op-ed in the *New York Times* calling for "discrediting the bachelor's degree" and arguing that "a large majority of young people do not have the intellectual ability to do genuine college-level work."[11]

Obama understands the importance of higher education. Colleges don't need a bailout, but they do need public investment in the education of students. A recession is the perfect time for unemployed and underemployed individuals to improve their skills, but it will only happen if the federal government takes decisive action to make that financially feasible.

The Fate of the Reserve Officer Training Corps (ROTC)

As higher costs put college out of reach for more Americans, young people have turned to programs like ROTC to help finance their education. At a September 11, 2008, forum at Columbia University on service, Obama was asked, "Should Columbia and elite universities that have excluded ROTC invite them back on campus?" Obama replied, "Yes. I think we've made a mistake on that." In reality, Columbia and other elite colleges never banned ROTC; they simply decreed that ROTC must follow the same rules for faculty control and open access as any other academic program. It was the military (following the rules imposed by Congress) that withdrew ROTC from Columbia and other colleges under these circumstances, not the reverse. And the Bush administration even tried to write new regulations that would force every college in the country to accept ROTC even if the process violated its campus rules.[12]

The main source of opposition today to ROTC programs is the military's discriminatory policy toward gay and lesbian soldiers. One of the first actions of President Obama should be to replace the terrible Clinton administration error of "don't ask, don't tell" with a "don't matter" approach. It's time to end the practice of homophobic bigotry as the explicit policy of the U.S. military, a policy that endangers our soldiers by removing key personnel (such as Arabic translators) and creating an atmosphere of witch-hunts rather than trust within the military.

However, even a commitment to equality will not solve all of the problems of having ROTC programs on campus, because it was the military's demand for control over the curriculum and faculty hiring, not homophobia, that caused the military to withdraw ROTC from many campuses.

What we need is a president who will turn ROTC into an independent, truly academic program rather than the current system. Having independent military studies programs would expand academic offerings about the military, allow all students to take these classes, and provide more faculty doing research on the military. It would be a winner for everyone: ROTC programs would be restored to all campuses, academic freedom would be preserved, and the quality of intellectual work and research about the military would greatly improve.

The creation of military studies programs that meet ROTC standards would be an innovative way for Obama to fulfill his goal of bringing ROTC to more campuses and more students while respecting academic freedom.

The Economic Crisis and the Obama Administration

The economic crisis puts a serious burden on the Obama presidency. With a deficit already likely to reach the $1 trillion mark, Obama will be pressured by fiscal conservatives to cut back on his ambitious ideas for reforming health care, improving education, and improving the social safety net.

Ultimately, the deficit is a burden on future generations only if it is wasted, as it has been during George W. Bush's presidency. A deficit caused by unnecessary wars, military contractors, corporate welfare, and tax breaks for the rich will be a tremendous weight holding down the economy and impeding American growth in the future. But we should embrace a deficit based on rebuilding our country's infrastructure, investing in education at all levels, providing tax breaks for the poor and middle class, and fixing our broken health care system.

This kind of deficit spending is not wasteful. It is an investment made in a sound resource. When our health care system fails to insure tens of millions of Americans, the result is the equivalent of a daily national disaster with huge numbers of casualties and billions of dollars spent in emergency medical care and lost productivity.

The severe recession provides Obama a unique opportunity to pursue his goals when there is widespread agreement among economists that deficit spending is necessary to stimulate the American economy and prevent it from falling into a depression. Obama needs to seize this opportunity and expand, not contract, his ambitions.

During his speech at the Democratic National Convention, Obama tackled conservative ideology head-on. He explicitly attacked the right-wing ideology of the unregulated free market that led America into the current financial disaster. And he rejected the conservative notion of every person for him- or herself, an approach that has ultimately failed. Obama could have taken a safe, centrist approach of vague promises and lofty rhetoric. Instead, Obama identified a long list of policy changes he wants to implement.

The economic crisis makes it more important, not less, for Obama to fulfill these promises. At a time of economic turmoil, restoring the social safety net is more essential than ever. And the failure of conservative ideology in the real estate bubble that led to this recession has made most Americans realize that a new economic approach is needed.

Obama as President

One key question is whether Obama will be able to build a larger political movement beyond his election. A huge part of the Obama landslide came from younger voters, who often skip midyear elections. Will Obama be able to mobilize voters when he's not on the ballot? Although the election of 2010 will be the first true political test of Obama's movement, long before that he will have to build a movement to support his legislative plans.

Obama has the benefit of a "honeymoon" period when voters will accurately blame Bush for the ongoing recession. However, unless Obama can get his proposals enacted and begin to have a positive effect on the economy, the widespread support for him will not last.

Barack Obama began his campaign with a vision of hope and change. He surmounted historic odds to win the presidency, and now he confronts a country that has lost faith in its government and faces what may be the worst recession in more than a half century. No one can underestimate the daunting task of guiding America through difficult times. But no one should doubt Obama's ability to accomplish this goal.

Conclusion

Obama's Hopes and Dreams

*The true test of the American ideal is whether we're able to recognize our
failings and then rise together to meet the challenges of our time; ... whether
we allow ourselves to be shaped by events and history, or whether we act
to shape them.*

—Barack Obama

Barack Obama's political journey has followed an unusual course. From
Hawaii to Indonesia, from Chicago to Harvard and back again, from obscure state senator to national celebrity, from underdog to president of the
United States. Along the way, Obama overcame the barriers of his race and
his unusual name, and he did so without the benefit of personal wealth or
a prominent family or a political machine behind him.

Today, Obama is a political rock star on a scale not seen since the popularity of JFK, if ever. Obama has disappointed some progressives who hoped
he would be a more aggressive critic of the Republicans. However, Obama
has always been someone who sought bipartisan consensus. It's precisely
that trait that makes him so popular and so effective. As Al Gore noted,
"Obama is rising because he is talking about politics in a way that feels
fresh to people."[1]

Obama's biggest flaw may be that he's not audacious enough, that he
holds his tongue to spare the feelings of his opponents, that he is too cynical even as he warns us against the dangers of cynicism. Obama thinks
we need to restore faith in government and hope in the better nature of

our fellow citizens. But sometimes he seems unwilling to trust the people enough to tell them what he really thinks and lead them to a better approach. Or perhaps he just doesn't trust the media and political pundits to let him engage in excessive honesty without destroying him. Instead, Obama's first instinct too often is to compromise and blur differences in order to reach common ground.

There is something satisfying about hearing an uncompromising voice for what you think is true and right. A noisemaker can draw attention to a problem, but it takes a leader to solve it. So the progressive movement needs both its noisemakers and its leaders. We must avoid the assumptions that the noisemakers are the true progressives and the leaders mere compromised sellouts. Noisemakers are far easier to find; it's the progressive leaders who are most essential. The genius of Obama is his ability to pursue a progressive agenda in a bipartisan manner, to merge liberalism with practical politics.

For a long time, progressives have been forced in the Democratic primary to choose between pragmatism and idealism, between electability and values. In 2004, many Democrats made the unfortunate choice of John Kerry over Howard Dean precisely because they thought Dean couldn't be elected. Progressives have been disappointed so often by so many deceitful politicians that they have formed a protective mask of cynicism and condescension. Putting one's hopes in any candidate can seem naive, or impossible, or stupid, in the face of a corrupt political system designed to support the rich and powerful. But Obama made a lot of people believe in the audacious decision to hope.

As Ralph Nader observed about Obama, "The question is whether he's going to mobilize the people, or he's going to parade in front of the people."[2] Obama understands the danger of becoming a leader based only on charisma. He witnessed firsthand what happened when Harold Washington, the first African American mayor of Chicago, was elected in the early 1980s and then died in office. Obama noted, "He was a classic charismatic leader, and when he died all of that dissipated. This potentially powerful collective spirit that went into supporting him was never translated into clear principles or into an articulable agenda for community change."[3]

Can Obama—now or in the future—create a political movement rather than a mere political campaign? Announcing his campaign for president, Obama declared that he was running "not just to hold an office, but to gather with you to transform a nation." With his new group Organizing for America, Obama is building a political movement outside of government made up of his supporters and volunteers. Obama understands that he needs to build a movement beyond the Internet, just as he used traditional community organizing to reinforce his online efforts in the presidential campaign.

The Obama Revolution

Much like the Reagan revolution that defined the American political landscape for a generation, even during the Clinton years, the Obama presidency has the potential to be a revolution. During the 2008 primary, Obama sparked controversy and attacks from the left because he acknowledged Reagan's influential changes in an interview with the *Reno Gazette* editorial board:

"I think Ronald Reagan changed the trajectory of America in a way that Richard Nixon did not and in a way that Bill Clinton did not. He put us on a fundamentally different path.... He just tapped into what people were already feeling, which was: We want clarity, we want optimism, we want a return to that sense of dynamism and entrepreneurship that had been missing."[4]

U.S. Rep. Barney Frank (D-MA) criticized Obama sharply: "Ronald Reagan was a dedicated right winger.... It's baffling to me that Sen. Obama would speak so favorably of him."[5] But Obama wasn't praising Reagan's ideology, he was praising Reagan's political skills. Reagan moved the government, but he also moved the country. When Bill Clinton proclaimed that "the era of Big Government is over," it reflected the success of the Reagan revolution. Reagan was also the last president before Obama who had a dramatic impact on youth voting.

Obama's campaign was based upon the repudiation of the Reagan revolution and its conservative ideology that government is always evil and regulation is always bad. In his acceptance speech to the Democratic National Convention in Denver, Obama explicitly denounced "that old, discredited Republican philosophy—give more and more to those with the most and hope that prosperity trickles down to everyone else." Obama argued, "Government cannot solve all our problems, but what it should do is that which we cannot do for ourselves—protect us from harm and provide every child a decent education; keep our water clean and our toys safe; invest in new schools and new roads and new science and technology. Our government should work for us, not against us. It should help us, not hurt us. It should ensure opportunity not just for those with the most money and influence, but for every American who's willing to work."

This is Obama's ideal for making America a more perfect union. Our union—our government—represents a strength that can help serve the common interest. Whereas conservatives sought to strangle government and make it ineffective with disastrous results, Obama seeks a progressive vision of government as a source of strength that helps everyone.

The economic crisis brought the failure of conservative ideology to the forefront. During his inaugural address, Obama noted that "this crisis has reminded us that without a watchful eye, the market can spin out of control—a nation cannot prosper long when it favors only the prosperous." Obama could have pursued a more explicitly ideological, left-wing agenda at the start of his presidency. But part of Obama's message of change is based on the idea of unity. Obama noted in his address that day that "we come to proclaim an end to the petty grievances and false promises, the recriminations and worn-out dogmas that for far too long have strangled our politics."

The Reagan revolution was much more than just a charismatic president shifting the political landscape in his direction. Reagan had the infrastructure of a conservative movement built to support him—think tanks, churches, and media outlets from magazines to talk radio—all organized on behalf not just of a politician but also an ideological movement. Progressive organizations need to move aggressively to develop the same kinds of institutions that conservatives created during the Reagan revolution.

No one can predict a political revolution with any certainty. Many conservatives imagined that George W. Bush was their political savior when he was named president in 2000. But Bush turned out to be a terrible failure and discredited the entire conservative movement along the way, leaving office in 2009 with an approval rating of 22 percent, the lowest in history.[6]

Obama has set the stage for a political revolution, albeit far from one as radical as some progressives might want. Still, Obama's economic stimulus plan is far more radical than anyone could have imagined being politically feasible a few months earlier. Whether he creates an Obama revolution depends not only upon him but also on the rest of us.

Throughout his life, Obama has become uniquely skilled at walking in two very different worlds simultaneously. He has lived the experience of a black man growing up with a white family, the privileged Harvard Law School graduate working among the poorest people on the South Side of Chicago, the law professor teaching constitutional ideals even while serving in the corrupt system of Illinois politics, and the idealistic politician navigating the real world of passing legislation. Obama has mastered the delicate art of being a pragmatic idealist, a politician who doesn't forget the people he is supposed to serve, a man who long ago tossed away his rose-colored glasses, yet who refuses to become a cynic.

As a child, Barack Obama idolized his absent father, only to experience the inevitable disappointment when he encountered the truth about the man's flaws and foibles. However, Obama's disappointment only strengthened his determination. In the end, Obama became the man he imagined his father was, a brilliant, selfless public servant who cared for his family and his troubled country. The American people have also faced absent leaders who disappointed them. For more than a generation, we have watched president after president treat the Oval Office like a personal empire, compromise the principles they swore to uphold, and be uncompromising in pursuit of their personal desires and the interests of their friends and donors.

Obama will inevitably disappoint those who idolize him. But what he brings us is the hope of a country that will try to perfect itself and live up to its espoused ideals of equality and justice, and the dream of having a president we can admire and trust.

Notes

Notes for the Introduction

1. Jennifer Steinhauer, "Charisma and a Search for Self in Obama's Hawaii Childhood," *New York Times*, March 17, 2007.
2. Garrett M. Graff, "The Legend of Barack Obama," *Washingtonian*, November 2006, available at http://www.washingtonian.com/articles/mediapolitics/1836.html.
3. Fox News Sunday, December 17, 2006.
4. John Podhoretz, "Obama: Rorschach Candidate," *New York Post*, December 13, 2006.
5. Scott Fornek and Dave McKinney, "Obama Makes It Official," *Chicago Sun-Times*, February 11, 2007.
2007.

Notes for Chapter One

1. Kenneth T. Walsh, "Talkin' 'bout My New Generation," *U.S. News and World Report*, January 8, 2007.
2. Bernard Schoenburg, "Durbin, LaHood Say Good Things about Obama," Copley News Service, December 18, 2006, http://qconline.com/archives/qco/display.php?id=319503.
3. Jennifer Senior, "Dreaming of Obama," *New York Magazine*, October 2, 2006, available at http://www.nymag.com/news/politics/21681.
4. Rick Pearson, "Obama on Obama," *Chicago Tribune*, December 15, 2006.
5. Ibid.
6. Dan Balz, "Obama Takes First Steps in N.H.," *Washington Post*, December 11, 2006.
7. Ibid.
8. Barack Obama, "Why Organize? Problems and Promise in the Inner City," *Illinois Issues* (August–September 1988), available at http://civic.uis.edu/Alinsky/AlinskyObamaChapter1990.htm.
9. Ryan Lizza, "The Agitator," *New Republic*, March 19, 2007.
10. Obama, "Why Organize?"
11. Lizza, "The Agitator."

12. Ibid.

13. David Moberg, "Obama's Community Roots," *Nation,* April 16, 2007, available at http://www.thenation.com/doc/20070416/moberg.

14. Ibid.

15. Ibid.

16. Ibid.

17. Lizza, "The Agitator."

18. Joel Hood, "Barack Obama's 'Citizen's Briefing Book,'" *Chicago Tribune,* January 23, 2009, available at http://www.chicagotribune.com/news/nationworld/chi-talk-citizenjan23,0,1151303.story; see http://citizensbriefingbook.change.gov.

19. Jonathan Alter, "Is America Ready for Hillary or Obama?" *Newsweek,* December 25, 2006–January 1, 2007.

20. Barack Obama, *The Audacity of Hope* (New York: Crown Publishers, 2006), 29.

21. Ibid.

22. Ibid., 30.

23. Ibid.

24. Graff, "The Legend of Barack Obama."

25. Mary Mitchell, "Obama Might Be the Candidate Who Can Bridge the Racial Divide," *Chicago Sun-Times,* January 18, 2007.

26. John M. Broder, "Shushing the Baby Boomers," *New York Times,* January 21, 2007.

27. Obama, *The Audacity of Hope,* 25.

28. David Remnick, "Testing the Waters," *New Yorker,* October 30, 2006, available at http://www.newyorker.com/061030on_onlineonly04.

29. Ibid.

30. Broder, "Shushing the Baby Boomers."

31. John Heilemann, "The Chicago Cipher," *New York Magazine,* December 25, 2006, available at http://nymag.com/news/politics/powergrid/25641/index.html.

32. Obama, *The Audacity of Hope,* 36.

33. Bob Herbert, "Mud, Dust, Whatever," *New York Times,* February 26, 2007.

34. Tom Bevan, "Will Obama Positively Not Go Negative?" *Chicago Sun-Times,* February 16, 2007.

35. John Fund, "Not So Fast: Why Barack Obama May Not Run," Opinionjournal.com, December 18, 2006, available at http://www.opinionjournal.com/diary/?id=110009401.

36. Michael Barone, "Obama and the Experience Factor," *U.S. News and World Report,* December 25, 2006.

37. Ibid.

38. "Bill Moyers and the State of American Journalism," *Rolling Stone,* April 18, 2007, available at http://www.rollingstone.com/rockdaily/index.php/2007/04/18/bill-moyers-and-the-state-of-american-journalism and quoted at http://www.dailykos.com/story/2007/4/20/205821/936.

39. Harvard Institute of Politics, "Obama, Giuliani Lead Pack in Race for President among 18–24-Year-Olds, Harvard Poll Finds," press release, April 17, 2007, available at http://www.iop.harvard.edu/newsroom_release_survey_s2007.html.

40. Kevin Chappell and Clarence Waldron, "Barack Obama Outlines 'Urban Agenda' as He Takes First Step toward Presidency," *Jet*, February 5, 2007.

41. Lois Romano, "Effect of Obama's Candor Remains to Be Seen," *Washington Post*, January 3, 2007; Barack Obama, *Dreams from My Father: A Story of Race and Inheritance*, rev. ed. (New York: Three Rivers Press, 2004), 93.

42. Obama, *Dreams from My Father*, 93.

43. Lynn Sweet, "Past Drug Use May Test Obama," *Chicago Sun-Times*, January 4, 2007.

44. *Hannity and Colmes*, Fox News Channel, January 3, 2007.

45. Eric Boehlert, "Did Bush Drop Out of the National Guard to Avoid Drug Testing?" *Salon*, February 6, 2004, available at http://dir.salon.com/story/news/feature/2004/02/06/drugs/index.html. See also Kitty Kelley, *The Family*, for an unverified claim of cocaine use by Bush in the 1980s.

46. Susan Milligan, "Obama's Antiwar Message Receives Cheers in Nashua, Durham," *Boston Globe*, February 13, 2007.

47. Graff, "The Legend of Barack Obama."

48. *NBC Nightly News with Brian Williams*, NBC, February 27, 2007.

49. David Crary, "Self-Centered Generation," Associated Press, February 27, 2007, http://www.azcentral.com/12news/news/articles/0227narcissistic-CR.html.

50. Eric Hoover, "Here's You Looking at You, Kid: Study Says Many Students Are Narcissists," *Chronicle of Higher Education*, March 9, 2007.

51. Editorial, "All Me, All the Time!" *Chicago Tribune*, May 31, 2007.

52. Sally Kalson, "Collegians Too Special for Their Own Good," *Pittsburgh Post-Gazette*, March 2, 2007.

53. Higher Education Research Institute, *The American Freshman: National Norms for Fall 2008*, January 2009, available at http://www.gseis.ucla.edu/heri/PDFs/pubs/briefs/brief-pr012208-08FreshmanNorms.pdf.

54. Crary, "Self-Centered Generation."

55. Jerome Armstrong, "Obama Blows into MySpace," *MyDD*, May 2, 2007, available at http://mydd.com/story/2007/5/2/93621/10103.

56. Sam Graham-Felsen, "Obama's Impressive Youthroots," TheNation.com blog, February 15, 2007, available at http://www.thenation.com/doc/20070305/graham-felsen.

57. Jose Antonio Vargas, "Young Voters Find Voice on Facebook," *Washington Post*, February 17, 2007, available at http://www.washingtonpost.com/wp-dyn/content/article/2007/02/16/AR2007021602084.html.

58. Dennis Conrad, "Obama Draws Large Crowd at College Rally," Associated Press, February 2, 2007, available at http://abcnews.go.com/Politics/wireStory?id=2846399&CMP=OTC-RSSFeeds0312.

59. Gary Younge, "The Power of Hope," *Guardian*, February 10, 2007.

60. David Plouffe (Obama cambaign manager), e-mail message, March 1, 2007.

61. Peter Suderman, "Be My Friend, Obama?" *National Review*, April 11, 2007, available at http://article.nationalreview.com/?q=N2UwZDk5MGFlYjcwZjkyOWU4MTBjN2Y4YjYyOTVhZjE=.

62. Mark Hugo Lopez, Emily Kirby, and Jared Sagoff, "The Youth Vote 2004,"

Center for Information and Research on Civic Learning and Engagement, July 2005, available at http://civicyouth.org/PopUps/FactSheets/FS_Youth_Voting_72-04.pdf.

63. Emily Hoban Kirby and Karlo Barrios Marcelo, "Young Voters in the 2006 Elections," Center for Information and Research on Civic Learning and Engagement, December 12, 2006, available at http://www.civicyouth.org/PopUps/FactSheets/FS-Midterm06.pdf.

64. Moberg, "Obama's Community Roots."

65. Barack Obama, speech at Democratic National Committee (DNC) winter meeting, Washington, DC, February 22, 2007.

66. *Tucker,* MSNBC, February 2, 2007.

67. Obama, speech at DNC winter meeting.

68. Ibid.

69. Ibid.

70. Ibid.

71. Ibid.

72. Eric Tucker, "Obama's Wife Sheds Former Skepticism," Associated Press, March 1, 2007, available at http://www.cbsnews.com/stories/2007/03/01/politics/ap/main2529323.shtml.

73. Richard Morin, "Jon Stewart, Enemy of Democracy?" *Washington Post,* June 23, 2006, available at http://www.washingtonpost.com/wp-dyn/content/article/2006/06/22/AR2006062201474_pf.html.

74. Jody Baumgartner and Jonathan S. Morris, "The *Daily Show* Effect: Candidate Evaluations, Efficacy, and American Youth," *American Politics Research* 34, no. 3 (2006): 341–367.

75. National Annenberg Election Survey, "*Daily Show* Viewers Knowledgeable about Presidential Campaign," September 21, 2004, available at http://www.annenbergpublicpolicycenter.org/Downloads/Political_Communication/naes/2004_03_late-night-knowledge-2_9-21_pr.pdf.

76. Morin, "Jon Stewart, Enemy of Democracy?"

77. Richard Nixon tapes, White House, March 25, 1971, available at http://tapes.millercenter.virginia.edu/clips/nixon_students_1971_03_25.html.

78. Jonathan Tilove, "Barack Obama: Is This the Dream?" *Montreal Gazette,* February 11, 2007.

79. Walsh, "Talkin' 'bout My New Generation."

80. *News and Notes,* National Public Radio, February 12, 2007.

81. Barack Obama, speech at Selma Voting Rights March commemoration, Selma, AL, March 4, 2007.

82. Lizza, "The Agitator."

83. Ibid.

84. Thomas Friedman, "The Quiet Americans," *New York Times,* May 27, 2007.

85. Eugene Robinson, "The Moment for This Messenger?" *Washington Post,* March 13, 2007.

86. Friedman, "The Quiet Americans."

87. Libby Copeland, "The Dreamy Candidate with the Swoon Vote," *Washington Post*, December 14, 2006.

88. Ibid.

89. "Bill Moyers and the State of American Journalism."

90. Fund, "Not So Fast."

Notes for Chapter Two

1. *Meet the Press*, NBC, February 11, 2007; *Reliable Sources*, CNN, January 21, 2007.

2. Lynn Sweet, "Obama in Campaign Mode on a Theme of 'Hope,'" *Chicago Sun-Times*, February 4, 2007.

3. *Special Report with Brit Hume*, Fox News Channel, April 23, 2007.

4. Keen, "The Big Question about Barack Obama"; Dante Chinni, "Obama-mania May Backfire," *Christian Science Monitor*, January 23, 2007.

5. Brent Budowsky, "Obamamania," *Huffington Post*, October 23, 2006, available at http://www.huffingtonpost.com/brent-budowsky/obamamania_b_32321.html.

6. Jonathan Zimmerman, "Playbooks for the White House," *Chicago Tribune*, January 30, 2007.

7. Earl Ofari Hutchinson, "Can Obama Really Win? (Part 2)," Alternet.org, February 12, 2007, available at http://www.alternet.org/story/47961.

8. "Racing for the White House," *Wall Street Journal*, December 19, 2006, available at http://link.brightcove.com/services/link/bcpid86195573/bctid372152899.

9. Ian Bishop, "Barack's Bills Hint of Clinton Pinchin'," *New York Post*, April 16, 2007.

10. Kenneth Bazinet, Michael McAuliff, and Helen Kennedy, "It's a Hil of a Surprise, Barack," *New York Daily News*, January 17, 2007.

11. "Taking 'Obama-mania' in Stride," *Christian Science Monitor*, December 15, 2006, available at http://www.csmonitor.com/2006/1215/p08s02-comv.html.

12. *Nightline*, ABC, January 16, 2007.

13. Nedra Pickler, "Is Obama All Style and Little Substance?" *Boston Globe*, March 27, 2007, available at http://www.boston.com/news/nation/articles/2007/ 03/27/ is_obama_all_style_and_little_substance.

14. Ibid.

15. Ibid.

16. Sarah Baxter, "Obama Stakes His Claim to History," *Times* (London), February 11, 2007, available at http://www.timesonline.co.uk/tol/news/world/us_and_americas/ article1364773.ece.

17. *Meet the Press*, February 11, 2007.

18. MSNBC, April 24, 2007.

19. *All Things Considered*, National Public Radio, December 19, 2006.

20. Arianna Huffington, "'Where's the Beef?' II: The Conventional Wisdumb on Barack Obama," *Huffington Post*, February 12, 2007, available at http://

www.huffingtonpost.com/arianna-huffington/wheres-the-beef-ii-t_b_41054.
html.

21. David Brooks, "Run, Barack, Run," *New York Times,* October 19, 2006.

22. Dick Morris and Eileen McGann, "Barack the Baby," FrontPageMagazine.
com, December 11, 2006, available at http://www.frontpagemag.com/Articles/Read.
aspx?GUID=D5C8A762-0FB9-45E4-9675-AFDE58BE8E4B.

23. Ibid.

24. Beth Fouhy, "Obama Addresses Question of Experience," Associated Press,
April 21, 2007, available at http://www.boston.com/news/nation/articles/2007/04/21/
obama_addresses_question_of_experience.

25. Jay Newton-Small and Kristin Jensen, "Obama's Fundraising Offers a Respite
from Stumbles," *Bloomberg News,* April 5, 2007, available at http://www.bloomberg.
com/apps/news?pid=20601070&sid=aPTAtKUv0nNM&refer=homr.

26. *Fox News Sunday,* Fox News Channel, February 11, 2007.

27. *Meet the Press,* NBC, April 1, 2007.

28. *Hardball with Chris Matthews,* MSNBC, December 17, 2006.

29. *Tucker,* MSNBC, December 15, 2006.

30. Pickler, "Is Obama All Style and Little Substance?"

31. *Rush Limbaugh Show,* Premiere Radio Networks, March 27, 2007.

32. *Meet the Press,* NBC, December 17, 2006.

33. "Bill Moyers and the State of American Journalism."

34. Frank Rich, "Stop Him Before He Gets More Experience," *New York Times,*
February 11, 2007.

35. Maureen Dowd, "Haunted by the Past," *New York Times,* November 1, 2006.

36. Leonard Pitts Jr., "Stepping into the Batter's Box with a Two-Strike Count,"
Seattle Times, January 21, 2007, available at http://seattletimes.nwsource.com/html/
opinion/2003532632_pitts21.html?syndication=rss.

37. E. J. Dionne Jr., "The Democrats' Foreign Policy Primary," *Washington Post,* May
1, 2007.

38. George Alexander, "Barack Obama for President?" *Black Enterprise,* April
2007.

39. Jeffrey M. Jones, "Experience a Major Reason Clinton Has Edge over Obama,"
Gallup News Service, May 10, 2007, available at http://www.galluppoll.com/content/
?ci=27547&pg=1.

40. Timothy Noah, "The Obama Messiah Watch," Slate.com, January 29, 2007,
available at http://www.slate.com/id/2158578/?nav/navoa.

41. John Kass, "How Will Daleys Pronounce Obama?" *Chicago Tribune,* December
22, 2006.

42. *Hardball with Chris Matthews,* MSNBC, January 17, 2007.

43. *CBS Evening News with Katie Couric,* CBS, April 27, 2007.

44. *This Week with George Stephanopoulos,* ABC, May 13, 2007.

45. Tim Novak, "Obama and His Rezko Ties," *Chicago Sun-Times,* April 23, 2007.

46. John Kass, "Obama Fuzzy on Fence That Tony Built," *Chicago Tribune,* November
2, 2006.

47. *Special Report with Brit Hume,* Fox News Channel, April 24, 2007.

48. Chris Fusco and Dave McKinney, "Obama's Neighbor Causing a Stir," *Chicago Sun-Times*, February 24, 2007.

49. John Kass, "Creeped Out by More than Cicadas," *Chicago Tribune*, June 1, 2007.

50. *Human Events* magazine, *Barack Obama Exposed!* (Washington, DC: Eagle Publishing, 2007).

51. Ben Wallace-Wells, "Destiny's Child," *Rolling Stone*, February 7, 2007, available at http://www.rollingstone.com/politics/story/13390609/campaign_08_the_radical_roots_of_barack_obama.

52. *Fox News Watch*, Fox News Channel, January 20, 2007.

53. Lynn Sweet, "Bush Here to Raise $3.5 Million for Campaign," *Chicago Sun-Times*, September 30, 2003.

54. Greg Hinz, "Stuart Levine Pleads Guilty," *Crain's Chicago Business*, October 27, 2006, available at http://www.chicagobusiness.com/cgi-bin/news.pl?id=22634&seenIt=1.

55. Ibid. See also, "*U.S. v. Levine, et al.* Superseding Indictment," available at http://www.usdoj.gov/usao/iln/indict/2006/us_v_levin_et_al_super.pdf.

56. Jeff Coen, Rudolph Bush, and Matt O'Connor, "The Federal Government's Charges against Rezko," *Chicago Tribune*, October 12, 2006.

57. Ibid.

58. Pearson, "Obama on Obama."

59. Chris Fusco and Tim Novak, "Rezko Cash Triple What Obama Says," *Chicago Sun-Times*, June 18, 2007.

60. Tom Novak, "Obama's Letters for Rezko," *Chicago Sun-Times*, June 13, 2007.

61. John Kass, "A TV Image Destined for Cancellation," *Chicago Tribune*, June 14, 2007.

62. Novak, "Obama's Letters for Rezko."

63. Novak, "Obama and His Rezko Ties."

64. For a puff piece on Rezko, see David Roeder and Fran Spielman, "Up to 5,000 Residential Units in Plans for Near S. Side Development," *Chicago Sun-Times*, July 31, 2003.

65. David Jackson and Ray Gibson, "Obama Intern Had Ties to Rezko," *Chicago Tribune*, December 24, 2006.

66. Tom Bevan, "The *Trib* Plays Gotcha with Obama," December 23, 2006, available at http://time-blog.com/real_clear_politics/2006/12/the_trib_plays_gotcha_with_oba.html.

67. Conor Clarke, "Show Trial," *New Republic*, December 20, 2006, https://ssl.tnr.com/p/docsub.mhtml?i=w061218&s=clarke122006.

68. Mike McIntire and Christopher Drew, "In '05 Investing, Obama Took Same Path as Donors," *New York Times*, March 7, 2007.

69. Ibid.

70. Christi Parsons and Jill Zuckman, "Obama Says He Was Unaware of Stocks in Trust Fund," *Chicago Tribune*, March 8, 2007.

71. *Hannity and Colmes*, Fox News Channel, March 7, 2007.

72. Barack Obama, *Dreams from My Father: A Story of Race and Inheritance*, rev. ed. (New York: Three Rivers Press, 2004), 30, 51.

73. Bob Secter, "Colbert Funny but Likely Wrong on Obama Story," *Swamp* (*Chicago Tribune* blog), May 25, 2007, available at http://weblogs.chicagotribune.com/news/politics/blog/2007/05/colbert_funny_but_likely_wrong.html.

74. Richard Cohen, "Obama's Back Story." *Washington Post,* March 27, 2007.

75. *Colbert Report,* Comedy Central, May 22, 2007.

76. Mike Allen, "Undoing Obama: Inside the Coming Effort to Dismantle a Candidate," *Politico,* February 10, 2007, available athttp://dyn.politico.com/printstory.cfm?uuid=A7248F96-3048-5C12-007B35A127E27946.

77. *Colbert Report,* May 22, 2007.

78. *Tucker,* MSNBC, February 12, 2007.

79. *Beltway Boys,* Fox News Channel, February 17, 2007.

80. Glenn Greenwald, "Presidential Candidates and 'Substance,'" *Salon,* March 31, 2007, available at http://www.salon.com/opinion/greenwald/2007/03/31/substance/index.html.

81. Paul Morton, "An Interview with Hendrik Hertzberg," *Bookslut,* April 2007, available at http://www.bookslut.com/features/2007_04_010889.php.

82. Nicholas Kristof, "Obama: Man of the World," *New York Times,* March 6, 2007.

83. Ibid.

84. Ibid.

85. Eric Zorn, "Obama Critics Build Cases on Faulty Premises," *Chicago Tribune,* December 19, 2006.

86. *Tucker,* December 15, 2006.

87. Kristof, "Obama."

88. *Hardball with Chris Matthews,* MSNBC, December 17, 2006.

89. *This Week with George Stephanopolous,* ABC, December 17, 2006.

90. Kristof, "Obama."

91. Richard Stern, "Intellectual Metabolism," *Open University* (*New Republic* blog), March 20, 2007, available at http://www.tnr.com/blog/openuniversity?pid=90628%22.

92. Kristof, "Obama."

93. Mortimer Zuckerman, "Who's the Real Obama?" *U.S. News and World Report,* May 14, 2007.

94. Morton M. Kondracke, "Obama Shows Promise of 'New Politics,' but Is He 'The Real Deal'?" *Roll Call,* March 22, 2007.

95. *CBS Evening News with Katie Couric,* CBS, October 23, 2006.

96. "Where's the Beef?" *Economist,* April 12, 2007, available at http://economist.com/world/na/displaystory.cfm?story_id=9006641.

97. Barack Obama, speech at Federal Plaza, Chicago, IL, October 26, 2002, available at http://en.wikisource.org/wiki/Barack_Obama's_Iraq_Speech.

98. Margaret Carlson, "For Obama, It's Public Character That Counts," *Bloomberg News,* January 4, 2007, available at http://www.bloomberg.com/apps/news?pid=206010 39&refer=columnist_carlson&sid=aROtpC6GRn1U.

99. Kristof, "Obama."

100. Robert D. Novak, "Hillary Up, Obama Down," Townhall.com, May 12,

2007, available at http://www.townhall.com/columnists/RobertDNovak/2007/05/12/hillary_up,_obama_down.

101. Ibid.

102. Lynn Sweet, "'I Was a Little Nervous' at Debate: Obama." *Chicago Sun-Times*, April 29, 2007.

103. Jack Jacobs, "Does Barack Obama Have a View on Defense?" MSNBC.com, April 29, 2007, available at http://www.msnbc.msn.com/id/18387695.

104. Obama, speech at Federal Plaza.

105. Ibid.

106. Richard Benedetto, "Poll: Most Support War as a Last Resort," *USA Today*, November 25, 2002.

107. Humphrey Taylor, "Polls, Politicians, and the Gulf War," *National Review*, May 13, 1991.

108. *This Week with George Stephanopoulos*, May 13, 2007.

109. Associated Press, "Adviser Regrets Pushing Edwards on Iraq," *New York Times*, March 13, 2007.

110. *Daily Show with Jon Stewart*, Comedy Central, June 12, 2007.

111. Jeff Zeleny, "As Candidate, Obama Carves Antiwar Stance," *New York Times*, February 26, 2007.

112. Joe Klein, "The Democrats' New Face." *Time*, October 15, 2006, available at http://www.time.com/time/magazine/article/0,9171,1546302,00.html.

113. *NewsHour with Jim Lehrer*, PBS, January 12, 2007.

114. Craig Gilbert, "Feingold Rules Out 2008 Run for President," *Milwaukee Journal-Sentinel*, November 11, 2006.

115. Ibid.

116. Monica Davey, "The Speaker: A Surprise Senate Contender Reaches His Biggest Stage Yet," *New York Times*, July 26, 2004.

117. *Meet the Press*, July 25, 2004.

118. United Press International, "Durbin Says Public Was Lied to about Iraq," April 27, 2007, available at http://www.dickdurbin.com/news/?id=0064.

119. Obama speech at Federal Plaza.

120. Senate Offices of Dick Lugar and Barack Obama, "Lugar-Obama Bill to Keep Weapons Out of Terrorists' Hands Heads to Senate Floor," press release, May 23, 2006, available at http://obama.senate.gov/press/060523-lugar-obama_bill_to_keep_weapons_out_of_terrorists_hands_heads_to_senate_floor/index.html.

121. Interview with Barack Obama, "Reaction to the State of the Union Address," MSNBC, January 23, 2007.

122. Ibid.

123. Ibid.

124. Barack Obama campaign, e-mail message, January 31, 2007.

125. Lynn Sweet, "Obama Was against War Funding, Now He's Undecided," *Chicago Sun-Times*, January 15, 2007.

126. Remnick, "Testing the Waters."

127. Lynn Sweet, "Facing the Experience Question," *Chicago Sun-Times*, February 15, 2007.

128. Matt Taibbi, "Obama Is the Best BS Artist since Bill Clinton," *Alternet*, February 14, 2007, available at http://www.alternet.org/story/48051.

129. *ABC World News with Charles Gibson*, ABC, January 16, 2007.

130. David Greenberg, "Sitting Out the Tennessee Waltz," *New York Times* blog, May 8, 2007, available at http://campaigningforhistory.blogs.nytimes.com/2007/05/08/sitting-out-the-tennessee-waltz.

131. Pearson, "Obama on Obama."

Notes for Chapter Three

1. *60 Minutes*, CBS, February 11, 2007.

2. Ben Smith, "Obama's Introduction: 'Black Enough,'" *Politico*, June 19, 2007, http://www.politico.com/blogs/bensmith/0607/Obamas_introduction_Black_enough.html.

3. Salim Muwakkil, "Barack Obama Made Smashing National Debut," *Progressive*, July 28, 2004, http://progressive.org/media_677.

4. Ted Kleine, "Is Bobby Rush in Trouble?" *Chicago Reader*, March 17, 2000, http://www.chicagoreader.com/obama/000317.

5. Ibid.

6. *Morning Edition*, National Public Radio, February 28, 2007.

7. Ibid.

8. *Morning Edition*, National Public Radio, February 9, 2007.

9. Don Terry, "The Skin Game," *Chicago Tribune*, October 24, 2004.

10. Ibid.

11. Muwakkil, "Barack Obama Made Smashing National Debut."

12. *NBC Nightly News with Brian Williams*, NBC, February 9, 2007.

13. Dawn Turner Trice, "Obama Unfazed by Foes' Doubts on Race Question," *Chicago Tribune*, March 15, 2004.

14. Debra Dickerson, "Color-blind," *Salon*, January 22, 2007, available at http://www.salon.com/opinion/feature/2007/01/22/obama.

15. Ibid.

16. *Colbert Report*, Comedy Central, February 8, 2007, available at http://www.comedycentral.com/motherload/index.jhtml?ml_video=81955.

17. Gregory Rodriguez, "Is Obama the New 'Black'?" *Los Angeles Times*, December 17, 2006.

18. Rachel Swarns, "So Far, Obama Can't Take Black Vote for Granted," *New York Times*, February 2, 2007.

19. Ibid.

20. Stanley Crouch, "What Obama Isn't: Black Like Me," *New York Daily News*, November 2, 2006.

21. Ibid.

22. *Morning Edition*, February 9, 2007.

23. Robert McCarthy, "Obama Base Could Be Elusive," *Buffalo News*, February 20, 2007.

24. Obama, *The Audacity of Hope,* 233.

25. Ibid., 23.

26. Leslie Fulbright, "Obama's Candidacy Sparks Debates on Race," *San Francisco Chronicle,* February 19, 2007.

27. Eric Deggans, "Shades of Black," *St. Petersburg Times,* April 15, 2007.

28. Bruce Dixon, "Black America's Real Issue with Barack Obama," *Black Agenda Report,* February 14, 2007, http://www.blackagendareport.com/index.php?option=com_content&task=view&id=81&Itemid=34.

29. Ibid.

30. Ibid.

31. Fulbright, "Obama's Candidacy Sparks Debates on Race."

32. John Ridley, "The Hocus Pocus 'igger." *Huffington Post,* March 21, 2007, http://www.huffingtonpost.com/john-ridley/the-hocus-pocus-igger_b_43946. html.

33. *Chicago Tonight,* WTTW, February 19, 2007.

34. Ibid.

35. Glen Ford, "Barack Obama: The Mania and the Mirage," *CounterPunch,* January 19, 2007, http://counterpunch.org/ford01192007.html.

36. Jonathan Tilove, "Barack Obama: Is This the Dream?" Newhouse News Service, *New Orleans Times-Picayune,* February 8, 2007.

37. Peter Wallsten, "Would Obama Be 'Black President'?" *Los Angeles Times,* February 10, 2007.

38. Swarns, "So Far, Obama Can't Take Black Vote for Granted."

39. Ibid.

40. Mike Robinson, "Law Grad Obama Got His Start in Civil Rights Practice," *Chicago Sun-Times,* February 20, 2007.

41. Mary Mitchell, "Grasping Obama's Big Picture," *Chicago Sun-Times,* February 10, 2007.

42. Howard Lesser, "Defining What Sen. Obama Candidacy Means to African-American Voters," *Voice of America News,* February 19, 2007.

43. Ridley, "The Hocus Pocus 'igger."

44. *NBC Nightly News with Brian Williams,* February 9, 2007.

45. Eugene Robinson, "Authentic Obama," *Washington Post,* February 20, 2007.

46. Laura Washington, "If He Can Turn Out His Black Base and Build a Coalition," *Chicago Sun-Times,* September 8, 2003.

47. Salim Muwakkil, "Worthy of the Land of Lincoln," *In These Times,* November 10, 2003, available at http://www.inthesetimes.com/article/480.

48. Patricia Williams, "Obama's Identity: Where Do We Start?" *Nation,* February 16, 2007, http://www.alternet.org/story/48133.

49. *Morning Edition,* February 9, 2007.

50. *CNN Newsroom,* CNN, March 22, 2007.

51. Kimberly Jade Norwood, "The Blackness of Obama," *Black Commentator,* February 8, 2007, available at http://www.blackcommentator.com/216/216_blackness_of_obama_norwood_guest.html.

52. *Hardball with Chris Matthews,* MSNBC, February 20, 2007.

53. Fulbright, "Obama's Candidacy Sparks Debates on Race."

54. *Media Matters,* WILL-AM, May 20, 2007.

55. Melissa Harris-Lacewell, "Note to Black Political Leadership: It Is Time to Fall in Line," *Open University* (*New Republic* blog), March 6, 2007, available at http://www.tnr.com/blog/openuniversity?pid=86467.

56. Tilove, "Barack Obama: Is This the Dream?"

57. Christi Parsons, "Michelle Obama: Not Easily Impressed," *Swamp* (*Chicago Tribune* blog), April 26, 2007, available at http://weblogs.chicagotribune.com/news/politics/blog/2007/04/michelle_obama_not_easily_impr.html.

58. Jonathan Tilove, "At Princeton, Michelle Obama Worried about Being on the Periphery," *Newark Star-Ledger,* February 18, 2007.

59. Rosalind Rossi, "The Woman Behind Obama," *Chicago Sun-Times,* January 20, 2007.

60. Tilove, "At Princeton, Michelle Obama Worried about Being on the Periphery."

61. Rossi, "The Woman Behind Obama."

62. Tilove, "At Princeton, Michelle Obama Worried about Being on the Periphery."

63. Anne E. Kornblut, "Michelle Obama Resigns from University of Chicago," *Washington Post,* May 11, 2007.

64. Rossi, "The Woman Behind Obama."

65. Ibid.

66. Obama, *Dreams from My Father,* 100, 101.

67. Tilove, "At Princeton, Michelle Obama Worried about Being on the Periphery."

68. Ibid.

69. Parsons, "Michelle Obama: Not Easily Impressed."

70. *This Week with George Stephanopoulos,* May 13, 2007.

71. Jonathan Chait, "Obama Brings the Blue Collar," *New Republic* blog, May 14, 2007, http://www.tnr.com/blog/theplank?pid=107521.

72. *This Week with George Stephanopoulos,* May 13, 2007.

73. Ibid.

74. Terry, "The Skin Game."

75. Eugene Robinson, "A Question of Race versus Class: Affirmative Action for the Obama Girls?" *Washington Post,* May 15, 2007.

76. Wallace-Wells, "Destiny's Child."

77. Paul Watson, "As a Child, Obama Crossed a Cultural Divide in Indonesia," *Los Angeles Times,* March 15, 2007.

78. Edward McClelland, "How Obama Learned to Be a Natural," *Salon,* February 12, 2007, available at http://www.salon.com/news/feature/2007/02/12/obama_natural/print.html.

79. "Five Minutes with Sen. Barack Obama," CampusProgress.org, March 28, 2005, available at http://www.campusprogress.org/features/210/five-minutes-with-sen-barack-obama.

80. Christopher Drew and Mike McIntire, "After 2000 Loss, Obama Built Donor Network from Roots Up," *New York Times,* April 3, 2007.

81. *Good Morning America,* ABC, February 9, 2007.

82. Swarns, "So Far, Obama Can't Take Black Vote for Granted."

83. Sylvester Monroe, "Sen. Barack Obama: On the Outside Looking In, or Part of the Civil Rights Legacy?" *Ebony,* May 2007.

84. Swarns, "So Far, Obama Can't Take Black Vote for Granted."

85. Monroe, "Sen. Barack Obama."

86. *Media Matters,* May 20, 2007.

87. *Bill Moyers' Journal,* PBS, May 18, 2007, http://www.pbs.org/moyers/journal/05182007/transcript1.html.

88. *Meet the Press,* February 11, 2007.

89. Brent Staples, "Decoding the Debate over the Blackness of Barack Obama," *New York Times,* February 11, 2007.

90. *Tucker,* March 2, 2007.

91. *All Things Considered,* National Public Radio, December 18, 2006.

92. Michael Fauntroy, "What Obama's Candidacy Will Mean for Black America," *Huffington Post,* Febrary 14, 2007, http://www.huffingtonpost.com/ michael-fauntroy-phd/what-obamas-candidacy-wi_b_41239.html.

93. Laura Washington, "Black Pols See Obama as Threat to Their Clout," *Chicago Sun-Times,* January 29, 2007, http://www.suntimes.com/news/washington/233307,CST-EDT-LAURA29.article.

94. Harris-Lacewell, "Note to Black Political Leadership."

95. James L. Merriner, "Obama 2008?" *Chicago Magazine,* March 2006, http://www.chicagomag.com/ME2/dirmod.asp?sid=8642F5EFCEA14A939100AB7214F31861&nm=Archives&type=PubPagi&mod=Publications%3A%3AArticle+Title&mid=61BFC65300D24DB58350C761094153A1&tier=4&id=BA3B7586E0DF479EAE57A803384C92B2.

96. Steve Sailer, "White Guilt, Obamania, and the Reality of Race," Vdare.com blog, January 2, 2007, http://www.vdare.com/sailer/070102_obamania.htm.

97. Ibid.

98. Steve Sailer, "Obama's Identity Crisis," *American Conservative,* March 26, 2007, http://www.amconmag.com/2007/2007_03_12/feature.html.

99. Heidi Beirich and Bob Moser, "Queer Science," *Intelligence Report* (Winter 2003), http://www.splcenter.org/intel/intelreport/article.jsp?sid=96.

100. Sailer, "Obama's Identity Crisis."

101. Suzanne Fields, "The Bigotry of Worn-Out Stereotypes," *Washington Times,* November 16, 2006.

102. *The Big Story with John Gibson,* Fox News Channel, January 17, 2007.

103. Sailer, "Obama's Identity Crisis."

104. Edward Blum, "Obama's Race Problem," *National Review,* February 12, 2007.

105. Michael Scherer, "The Republican Candidates—and Ann Coulter—Try Out Their Acts," *Salon,* March 3, 2007, http://www.salon.com/news/feature/ 2007/03/03/cpac.

106. KSFO, December 4, 2006; *Rush Limbaugh Show,* Premiere Radio Networks, January 24, 2007.

107. *Rush Limbaugh Show,* Premiere Radio Networks, December, 11, 2006.

108. "Limbaugh: Obama Should 'Renounce' His Race and Just 'Become White.'" ThinkProgress.org, February 14, 2007, http://thinkprogress.org/2007/02/14/limbaugh-obama-white.

109. *Rush Limbaugh Show,* Premiere Radio Networks, March 20, 2007.

110. *CNN Headline News,* February 12, 2007, http://www.dailykos.com/story/2007/2/13/12549/4298.

111. *Onion,* March 14, 2007, http://www.theonion.com/content/cartoon/mar-14-2007.

112. Manya A. Brachear and Bob Secter, "Race Is Sensitive Subtext in Campaign," *Chicago Tribune,* February 6, 2007.

113. *Tucker,* MSNBC, February 7, 2007.

114. *Hannity and Colmes,* Fox News Channel, February 28, 2007.

115. "In Reviving Obama Smears, Morgan Guest/Coauthor Cited Reported Anti-Semite with 'Well-Documented Ideation with a Paranoid Flavor and a Grandiose Character,'" *Media Matters for America,* March 2, 2007, http://mediamatters.org/items/200703020006.

116. Brachear and Secter, "Race Is Sensitive Subtext in Campaign."

117. Ibid.

118. Susan Hogan, "Obama's Liberal Church under the Microscope," *Chicago Sun-Times,* June 21, 2007.

119. Wallace-Wells, "Destiny's Child."

120. Laura Washington, "National Media Can't Get Enough of Obama," *Chicago Sun-Times,* March 12, 2007.

121. Michael Tarm, "Activist Obama Church Enters Spotlight," Associated Press, March 20, 2007, available at http://www.usatoday.com/news/elections/2007-03-20-690594000_x.htm.

122. Swarns, "So Far, Obama Can't Take Black Vote for Granted."

123. *Hardball with Chris Matthews,* MSNBC, January 27, 2007.

124. Salim Muwakkil, "Barack's Black Dilemma," *In These Times,* February 1, 2007, http://www.inthesetimes.com/article/3010/baracks_black_dilemma.

125. Obama, *The Audacity of Hope,* 247.

126. Paul Street, "Obama's Audacious Deference to Power," *Black Agenda Report,* January 31, 2007, http://www.blackagendareport.com/index.php?option=com_content&task=view&id=61&Itemid=34.

127. *Morning Edition,* February 9, 2007.

128. Ibid.

129. Ford, "Barack Obama: The Mania and the Mirage."

130. Obama, *The Audacity of Hope,* 232.

131. Rodriguez, "Is Obama the New 'Black'?"

132. Josh Benson, "The Biden Tapes," *New York Observer* blog, January 31, 2007, available at http://www.observer.com/node/31325.

133. Curtis Lawrence, "I Want a Black President, If He Speaks His Mind," *Chicago Sun Times,* February 17, 2007.

134. *This Week with George Stephanopolous,* May 13, 2007.

135. Eric Deggans, "Shades of Black," *St. Petersburg Times,* April 15, 2007.

136. Tilove, "Barack Obama: Is This the Dream?"

137. Gary Younge, "The Power of Hope," *London Guardian,* February 10, 2007.

138. Leon Wieseltier, "Audacities," *New Republic,* March 19, 2007.

139. Obama, speech at Selma Voting Rights March commemoration.

140. Obama, *Dreams from My Father,* xv.

141. *Boston Legal,* ABC, April 24, 2007, available at http://www.politico.com/blogs/bensmith/0407/Fictional_Boston_lawyers_for_Obama.html.

142. *30 Rock,* NBC, November 14, 2006, quoted at http://featuresblogs.chicagotribune.com/entertainment_tv/2006/11/the_office_merg.html.

143. Clarence Page, "Race Remains the Focus as Obama Hits the Trail," *Chicago Tribune,* February 18, 2007.

144. Ibid.

145. CNN, "Is Black America Ready to Embrace Obama?" March 1, 2007, http://www.cnn.com/2007/POLITICS/02/28/obama.black.vote/index.html.

146. Scott Martelle, "Obama: Racial Ills Haven't Healed," *Chicago Tribune,* April 30, 2007.

147. Paul Butler, "Supporting Obama Because He's Black," Blackprof.com, March 20, 2007, http://www.blackprof.com/archives/2007/03/supporting_obama_because_hes_b.html.

148. *Hannity and Colmes,* Fox News Channel, February 27, 2007.

149. Ibid.

150. Ibid.

151. Toni Morrison, "Clinton as the First Black President," *New Yorker,* October 1998, available at http://ontology.buffalo.edu./smith/clinton/morrison.html.

152. Jessica Curry, "Barack Obama: Under the Lights," *Chicago Life,* 2004, http://www.chicagolife.net/content/politics/Barack_Obama.

153. *Saturday Night Live,* NBC, February 17, 2007, available at http://www.nbc.com/Saturday_Night_Live/video/#mea=61789.

154. *Chris Matthews Show,* NBC, December 17, 2006.

155. Debra Dickerson, "Color-blind."

156. *Media Matters,* May 20, 2007.

157. Earl Ofari Hutchinson, "Obama Will Follow Democrat's Flawed Script on Race," *Huffington Post,* February 13, 2007, http://www.huffingtonpost.com/earl-ofari-hutchinson/obama-will-follow-democra_b_41118.html.

158. CNN, "Is Black America Ready to Embrace Obama?"

159. Monroe, "Sen. Barack Obama."

160. Dahleen Glanton, "'Blacks Will Determine the Winner,'" *Chicago Tribune,* February 16, 2007.

161. Monroe, "Sen. Barack Obama."

162. Dawn Turner Trice, "Obama Unfazed by Foes' Doubts on Race Question," *Chicago Tribune,* March 15, 2004.

163. *Morning Edition,* February 28, 2007.

164. *Good Morning America,* ABC, February 16, 2007.

165. Mary Mitchell, "Black Man Can't Win? Think Again, Obama Says in S.C. Stop," *Chicago Sun-Times,* February 18, 2007.

166. Lynn Sweet, "S.C. Round Goes to Clinton," *Chicago Sun-Times,* February 16, 2007.

167. Tilove, "Barack Obama: Is This the Dream?"

168. Glanton, "'Blacks Will Determine the Winner.'"

169. *Good Morning America,* February 16, 2007.

170. Mary Mitchell, "Why Are Black Lawmakers Already Jumping on Clinton Bandwagon?" *Chicago Sun-Times,* February 15, 2007.

171. John Dickerson, "Obama's South Carolina Debut," Slate.com, February 17, 2007, http://www.slate.com/id/2159915.

172. Mickey Kaus, "The 'Excitable Embedder,'" Slate.com, January 29, 2007, available at http://www.slate.com/id/2158010/&#obamablackupdate.

173. Paul Steinhauser, "Poll: Obama Makes Big Gains among Black Voters," CNN.com, January 19, 2008, available at http://www.cnn.com/2008/POLITICS/01/18/poll.2008/index.html.

174. *Media Matters,* May 20, 2007.

175. Laura Washington, "Whites May Embrace Obama, but Do 'Regular Black Folks'?" *Chicago Sun-Times,* January 1, 2007.

176. *Paula Zahn Now,* CNN, February 28, 2007.

177. *News and Notes,* February 12, 2007.

178. Hutchinson, "Obama Will Follow Democrat's Flawed Script on Race."

179. *All Things Considered,* December 18, 2006.

180. Kayce T. Ataiyero, "Blacks Debate Impact of Obama's Race on Campaign," *Chicago Tribune,* May 24, 2007.

181. Ibid.

182. Andrew Greeley, "Three Reasons Barack Obama Should Not Run for President," *Daily Southtown* (Chicago), December 8, 2006.

183. Jeremy Levitt, "Is America Really Ready for Obama?" *Chicago Sun Times,* January 20, 2007.

184. *American Morning,* CNN, February 27, 2007, available at http://transcripts.cnn.com/TRANSCRIPTS/0702/27/ltm.03.html.

185. Jeff Jacoby, "We'd Elect a Black President? Old News," *Boston Globe,* December 27, 2006.

186. *Paula Zahn Now,* January 18, 2007.

187. Harris Poll, June 4, 2007, available at http://www.dvercity.com/political_barack_obama.html.

188. *News and Notes,* February 12, 2007.

189. Earl Ofari Hutchinson, "Obama: Not for President?" *Alternet,* September 29, 2006, available at http://alternet.org/story/42357.

190. Bruce Dixon, "In Search of the Real Barack Obama," *Black Commentator,* June 5, 2003, available at http://www.blackcommentator.com/45/45_dixon.html.

191. Mary Mitchell, "Obama Can't Take Blacks for Granted," *Chicago Sun-Times,* July 1, 2007.

192. *Newsroom,* CNN, March 22, 2007.

193. *Larry King Live,* CNN, March 19, 2007.

194. Scott Keeter and Nilanthi Samaranayake, "Can You Trust What Polls Say about

Obama's Electoral Prospects?" Pew Research Center for the People and the Press, February 7, 2007, http://pewresearch.org/pubs/408/can-you-trust-what-polls-say-about-obamas-electoral-prospects.

195. Ron Walters, "Is America Ready for a Black President?" *District Chronicles,* January 8, 2007, http://media.www.districtchronicles.com/media/storage/paper263/news/2007/01/08/Cover/Is.America.Ready.For.A.Black.President-2605609-page2.shtml.

196. Keeter and Samaranayake, "Can You Trust What Polls Say about Obama's Electoral Prospects?"

197. Steve Kornacki, "Obama Skeptics Should Look to Massachusetts," *New York Observer,* June 24, 2007.

198. Carol M. Swain, "For a Black President?" *Ebony,* January 2007.

199. Drew Westen, "Gut Instincts," *American Prospect,* November 19, 2006, available at http://www.prospect.org/cs/articles?article=gut_instincts.

200. Swain, "For a Black President?"

201. Tom Curry, "Obama Seeks to Settle Racial Doubts," MSNBC.com, December 13, 2006, available at http://www.msnbc.msn.com/id/16177866/.

202. Alter, "Is America Ready for Hillary or Obama?"

203. Swain, "For a Black President?"

204. Michael McAuliff, "Nation Is More Likely to Elect Black President over Woman, Poll Finds," *New York Daily News,* December 18, 2006.

205. "*USA Today*/Gallup: Watch Out, Old Divorcees," *Hotline* (*National Journal* blog), February 16, 2007, available at http://hotlineblog.nationaljournal.com/archives/2007/02/usa_todaygallup_1.html.

206. McAuliff, "Nation Is More Likely to Elect Black President over Woman, Poll Finds."

207. *Good Morning America,* February 16, 2007.

208. Richard H. Davis, "The Anatomy of a Smear Campaign," *Boston Globe,* March 21, 2004; Todd S. Purdum, "Prisoner of Conscience," *Vanity Fair,* February 2007.

209. Margaret Carlson, "Is Obama Guilty of Insufficient Blackness?" *Bloomberg News,* February 15, 2007, available at http://www.huffingtonpost.com/margaret-carlson/is-obama-guilty-of-insuff_b_41346.html.

210. *Daily Show with Jon Stewart,* Comedy Central, February 12, 2007.

Notes for Chapter Four

1. "Schlussel: Should Barack Hussein Obama Be President 'When We Are Fighting the War of Our Lives against Islam'?" *Media Matters for America,* December 20, 2006, available at http://mediamatters.org/items/200612200005.

2. *Imus in the Morning,* MSNBC, February 2, 2007.

3. Ibid.

4. *Rush Limbaugh Show,* Premiere Radio Networks, December 14, 2006.

5. *Anderson Cooper: 360°,* CNN, January 23, 2007.

6. *Rush Limbaugh Show,* Premiere Radio Networks, January 16, 2007.

7. *Hannity and Colmes,* Fox News Channel, December 14, 2006.

8. Podhoretz, "Obama: Rorschach Candidate."

9. *Hardball with Chris Matthews,* MSNBC, November 28, 2006.

10. Peggy Noonan, "The Man from Nowhere," *Wall Street Journal,* December 15, 2006, available at http://www.opinionjournal.com/columnists/pnoonan/?id=110009388.

11. *Tucker,* MSNBC, January 16, 2007.

12. *Hannity and Colmes,* Fox News Channel, January 16, 2007.

13. John Hood, "Obama's Nondifferential Distinction," *National Review,* April 23, 2007, available at http://corner.nationalreview.com/post/?q= MTJhY2YzNjIwOTY4MGZmNjY5ODViYWUwODUzMmZiNGQ=.

14. "Hillary's Team Has Questions about Obama's Muslim Background," *Insight,* January 17, 2007, available at http://www.worldtribune.com/worldtribune/flash_4.html.

15. "Last Word: What *Insight* Reported and What It Did Not," *Insight,* February 1, 2007, available at http://family-house.blogspot.com/2007/02/last-word-what-insight-reported-and.html.

16. Howard Kurtz, "Hillary, Obama, and Anonymous Sources," *Washington Post,* January 22, 2007, available at http://www.washingtonpost.com/wp=dyn/content/blog/2007/02/22/BL2007012200260_pdf.html.

17. "Last Word," *Insight.*

18. Ibid.

19. Editorial, "Sticks, Stones, and Mr. Obama," *Washington Post,* January 28, 2007.

20. Mark Steyn, "Media Are Gonna Barack around the Clock," *Chicago Sun-Times,* January 21, 2007.

21. Editorial, "Mudslinging against Obama Irresponsible, Inexcusable," *Springfield State Journal-Register,* January 26, 2007.

22. *Fox News Sunday,* Fox News Channel, January 21, 2007.

23. *The Big Story with John Gibson,* Fox News Channel, January 19, 2007.

24. *Colbert Report,* Comedy Central, January 24, 2007.

25. *Colbert Report,* Comedy Central, January 23, 2007.

26. Ibid.

27. "The Enemy Within," Snopes.com, 2006, available at http://www.snopes.com/politics/obama/muslim.asp.

28. Ibid. See also "Barack Obama Is a Muslim," About.com Urban Legends and Folklore, 2007, available at http://urbanlegends.about.com/library/bl_barack_obama_muslim.htm.

29. Debbie Schlussel, "Barack Hussein Obama: Once a Muslim, Always a Muslim," DebbieSchlussel.com, December 18, 2006, available at http://www.debbieschlussel.com/archives/2006/12/barack_hussein.html.

30. Ibid.

31. Obama, *The Audacity of Hope,* 202.

32. Ibid., 204.

33. Ibid.

34. Watson, "As a Child, Obama Crossed a Cultural Divide in Indonesia."

35. Ibid.

36. *Situation Room*, CNN, January 22, 2007; see also "CNN Debunks False Report about Obama," CNN.com, January 22, 2007, available at http://www.cnn.com.2007/politics/01/22/obama.madrassa.

37. *Nightline*, ABC, January 25, 2007.

38. Editorial, "Mudslinging against Obama Irresponsible, Inexcusable."

39. Andy Martin, "Andy Martin Is the Guy Who Seems to Have Gotten This [Anti-Obama Reporting] Started," *Contrarian Commentary*, January 23, 2007, available at http://contrariancommentary.wordpress.com/2007/01/23/andy-martin-is-the-guy-who-seems-to-have-gotten-this-anti-obama-reporting-started.

40. Andy Martin Worldwide Communications, "Columnist Says Barack Obama 'Lied to the American People;' Asks Publisher to Withdraw Obama's Book," press release published on PR Newswire (a service that anyone can pay to publish a press release), August 10, 2004, available at http://www.freerepublic.com/focus/f-news/1189687/posts.

41. Ibid.

42. Ibid.

43. Ibid.

44. Ibid.

45. Available at http://andymartin.com/bio.htm.

46. John Chase and Rick Pearson, "Perennial Candidate Back for Another Race," *Chicago Tribune*, February 10, 2006.

47. Ibid.

48. Ibid.

49. Ibid.

50. Ibid.

51. Ibid.

52. Ibid.

53. Andy Martin Worldwide Communications, "Columnist Says Barack Obama 'Lied to the American People."

54. Ibid.

55. PR Newswire, available at http://www.prnewswire.com.

56. "In Reviving Obama Smears, Morgan Guest/Coauthor Cited Reported Anti-Semite with 'Well-Documented Ideation with a Paranoid Flavor and a Grandiose Character."

57. Chase and Pearson, "Perennial Candidate Back for Another Race."

58. Ibid.

59. Andy Martin Worldwide Communications, "Senator Barack Obama Faces New Charges from Internet Editor/Columnist Andy Martin," press release published on PR Newswire, March 12, 2007, available at http://www.prnewswire.com/cgi-bin/stories.pl?ACCT=104&STORY=/www/story/03-12-2007/0004544604&EDATE=.

60. Andy Martin, "*Chicago Tribune* joins ContrarianCommentary.com in Questioning Barack Obama," *Contrarian Commentary*, March 23, 2007, available at http://www.contrariancommentary.com/community/Home/tabid/36/mid/363/newsid363/94/Default.aspx.

61. Andy Martin, "Free Barack Obama's White Grandmother," *Contrarian Commentary*, March 26, 2007, available at http://www.contrariancommentary.com/community/Home/tabid/36/mid/363/newsid363/97/Default.aspx.

62. Andy Martin, "'Madrassa Madness' KO's Barack Obama," *Contrarian Commentary*, January 21, 2007, available at http://www.contrariancommentary.com/community/Home/tabid/36/mid/363/newsid363/68/Default.aspx.

63. Martin, "Free Barack Obama's White Grandmother."

64. Andy Martin, "Chicago-based ContrarianCommentary.com Leads the Way in Exposing Barack Obama," *Contrarian Commentary*, January 23, 2007, available at http://www.contrariancommentary.com/community/Home/tabid/36/mid/366/newsid366/69/Default.aspx.

65. Martin, "*Chicago Tribune* Joins ContrarianCommentary.com in Questioning Barack Obama."

66. Martin, "Andy Martin Is the Guy Who Seems to Have Gotten This [Anti-Obama Reporting] Started."

67. David D. Kirkpatrick, "Feeding Frenzy for a Big Story, Even If It's False," *New York Times*, January 29, 2007.

68. "In Reviving Obama Smears, Morgan Guest/Coauthor Cited Reported Anti-Semite with 'Well-Documented Ideation with a Paranoid Flavor and a Grandiose Character.'"

69. Andy Martin, "Obama 'Swift Boats' the Truth to Hide His Religious History," *Contrarian Commentary*, January 25, 2007, available at http://contrariancommentary.blogspot.com/2007_01_01_archive.html.

70. Debbie Schlussel, "Liberal Juan Williams Agrees with Schlussel on Obama Muslim Background," DebbieSchlussel.com, January 29, 2007, available at http://www.debbieschlussel.com/archives/2007/01/liberal_juan_wi.html#comments.

71. Debbie Schlussel, "Obama's 'Debunking' of Islamic Background Raises More Questions," DebbieSchlussel.com, January 25, 2007, available at http://debbieschlussel.com/archives/2007/01/obama_debunking.html.

72. Ibid.

73. Editorial, "Hats Off to CNN, but …" *Insight*, January 23, 2007, available at http://www.insightmag.com/Media/MediaManager/CNNResponse2.htm.

74. "Australia PM Slams U.S. Candidate," *BBC News*, February 12, 2007, available at http://news.bbc.co.uk/1/hi/world/asia-pacific/6352785.stm.

75. "Savage 'Doubt[s]' Obama and Clinton 'Would Take Our Side' after Terrorist Attack," *Media Matters for America*, January 30, 2007, available at http://mediamatters.org/items/200701300008.

76. *Hannity and Colmes*, Fox News Channel, February 12, 2007.

77. Dick Morris, "Obama's First Blunder," Vote.com, January 17, 2007, available at http://www.vote.com/magazine/columns/dickmorris/column60460327.phtml.

78. "*Wash. Times* and Others Repeated Morris' Obama Falsehood Despite Morris' Acknowledgment of Error," *Media Matters for America*, January 18, 2007, available at http://mediamatters.org/items/printable/200701180007.

79. "Keyes Says Christ Would Not Vote For Obama," NBC5.com, September 7, 2004, available at http://www.nbc5.com/politics/3712293/detail.html.

80. *Anderson Cooper: 360°,* CNN, January 23, 2007.
81. Maggie Haberman, "Newt Rips 'Nasty' Hill," *New York Post,* March 1, 2007.
82. "2008 and the Political Landscape," paper presented at Conservative Political Action Conference, Washington, DC, March 2, 2007.
83. "PEJ Talk Show Index: March 4–9, 2007," available at http://www. journalism.org/node/4582/print.
84. Available at http://hillaryspot.nationalreview.com.
85. Matt Towery, "Hang It Up, Obama—It's Hillary's Nomination," *Human Events,* January 18, 2007, available at http://www.humanevents.com/article. php?print=yes&id=19011.
86. Fox News, *Hannity and Colmes,* March 5, 2007.
87. Dick Morris and Eileen McGann, "Obama's Gift to Hillary," *Front Page Magazine,* December 27, 2006, available at http://frontpagemag.com/Articles/ ReadArticle.asp?ID=26166.
88. Barton Gellman, "A Strategy's Cautious Evolution," *Washington Post,* January 20, 2002.
89. *Hannity and Colmes,* February 12, 2007.
90. Robert VerBruggen, "Obama in Maryland: Will the Real Barack Obama Please Stand Up?" *Weekly Standard,* November 6, 2006, available at http://weeklystandard. com/content/public/articles/000/000/012/914vxshs.asp.
91. Dateline D.C., "Barack Obama's Closet," *Pittsburgh Tribune,* January 14, 2007, available at http://www.pittsburghlive.com/x/pittsburghtrib/opinion/columnists/ datelinedc/s_488184.html.
92. David Bernstein, "Battle Lines: How the GOP Might Attack If Obama Ran for Higher Office," *Chicago Magazine,* March 2006.
93. "Racing for the White House," *Wall Street Journal* video, December 19, 2006, available at http://online.wsj.com/public/page/8_0004.html?bcpid= 86195573&bclid=212338097&bctid=372152899.
94. Bernstein, "Battle Lines."
95. Frank Rich, "Obama Is Not a Miracle Elixir," *New York Times,* October 22, 2006.
96. Bob Herbert, "The Obama Bandwagon," *New York Times,* October 23, 2006.
97. Ibid.
98. Ramesh Ponnuru, "Clinton vs. Obama," *National Review,* April 27, 2007, available at http://corner.nationalreview.com/post/?q= OWZlZDAxYmI5NDgwOWIwNDQ0MzJmMjQ4YjZiYTYyY2Q=.
99. Jim Rutenberg, "Ex-Aide Details a Loss of Faith in the President," *New York Times,* April 1, 2007.
100. Richard A. Serrano and David G. Savage, "Early on, Obama Showed Talent for Bridging Divisions," *Los Angeles Times,* January 27, 2007.
101. Carol Platt Liebau, "The Barack I Knew," Townhall.com, March 5, 2007, available at http://www.townhall.com/columnists/CarolPlattLiebau/2007/03/05/the_barack_i_ knew.
102. *Hardball with Chris Matthews,* December 17, 2006.
103. *Fox News Sunday,* Fox News Channel, February 25, 2007.

104. Schoenburg, "Durbin, LaHood Say Good Things about Obama."

105. Graff, "The Legend of Barack Obama."

106. Wallace-Wells, "Destiny's Child."

107. Jennifer Senior, "Dreaming of Obama," *New York Magazine,* October 2, 2006, available at http://www.nymag.com/news/politics/21681.

108. Jennifer Hunter, "'I Trust Him'—Standoffish Iowans Flocking to Obama," *Chicago Sun-Times,* February 23, 2007.

109. Mike Van Winkle and Greg Blankenship, "The Obama Myth," *American Spectator,* August 12, 2004, available at http://www.spectator.org/dsp_article.asp?art_id=6967.

110. Philip Klein, "Obama Rising," *American Spectator,* July/August 2007.

Notes for Chapter Five

1. Rich, "Obama Is Not a Miracle Elixir."

2. Paul Street, "Keynote Reflections," *Z Magazine,* July 29, 2004, available at http://www.zmag.org/content/showarticle.cfm?ItemID=5951.

3. Ibid.

4. David Remnick, "Testing the Waters," *New Yorker,* October 27, 2006, available at http://www.newyorker.com/online/content/articles/061030on_onlineonly04.

5. Alexander Cockburn, "Meet Senator Slither," *CounterPunch,* December 9, 2006, available at http://www.counterpunch.org/cockburn12092006.html.

6. Ibid.

7. Available at http://nedlamont.com/blog/1976/barack-obama-writes-emails.

8. David Sirota, "I Want to Believe," *Daily Kos,* February 10, 2007, available at http://www.dailykos.com/story/2007/2/10/1427/83134.

9. David Sirota, "Hostile Takeover '08: Democrats Gone Wild," *Huffington Post,* April 3, 2007, available at http://www.huffingtonpost.com/david-sirota/hostile-takeover-08-dem_b_44894.html.

10. *Media Matters,* WILL-AM, February 25, 2007, available at http://www.will.uiuc.edu/am/mediamatters/default.htm.

11. John McCormick and Mike Dorning, "Obama Fund-Raising Close to $1 Billion," *Los Angeles Times,* December 5, 2008.

12. "Floor Statement of Senator Barack Obama on the Federal Marriage Amendment," June 5, 2006, available at http://obama.senate.gov/speech/060605-floor_statement_5.

13. Lynn Sweet, "How Obama, Clinton Tripped on Gay Rights," *Chicago Sun-Times,* March 22, 2007.

14. Ibid.

15. Ibid.

16. *Larry King Live,* March 19, 2007.

17. Ibid.

18. Jason Zengerle, "What Is the Plank?" *New Republic,* March 15, 2007, available at http://www.tnr.com/blog/theplank?pid=89122.

19. Neil Steinberg, "'Don't Ask' and Answered," *Chicago Sun-Times*, March 16, 2007.

20. Christi Parsons and John McCormick, "Protesters Disrupt Obama Rally," *Chicago Tribune*, February 12, 2007.

21. Bill Fletcher, "Questions for Candidate Obama," *Black Commentator*, May 10, 2007, available at http://www.blackcommentator.com/229/229_cover_questions_for_obama_fletcher_ed_bd.html.

22. Ali Abunimah, "How Barack Obama Learned to Love Israel," *Electronic Intifada*, March 4, 2007, available at http://electronicintifada.net/v2/article6619.shtml.

23. MondoWeiss, "Barack Obama Disappoints Re Israel/Palestine," *New York Observer* online, December 20, 2006, available at http://www.observer.com/node/33615.

24. Barack Obama, speech at American Israel Public Affairs Committee (AIPAC) Policy Forum, Chicago, IL, March 2, 2007, available at http://www.barackobama.com/2007/03/02/aipac_policy_forum.php.

25. Eli Lake, "Obama Rebuffs Soros," *New York Sun*, March 21, 2007, available at http://www.nysun.com/article/50846.

26. Abunimah, "How Barack Obama Learned to Love Israel."

27. Healy, "Clinton and Obama Court Jewish Vote."

28. Glen Ford, "Putting Black Faces on Imperial Aggression," *CounterPunch*, February 16, 2007, available at http://www.counterpunch.org/ford02162007.html.

29. Anthony Arnove, speech at Jane Addams Hull-House Museum, University of Illinois at Chicago, Chicago, IL, January 19, 2007.

30. National Security Council, *National Security Strategy of the United States* (Washington, DC: White House, September 20, 2002), available at http://www.whitehouse.gov/nsc/nss.html.

31. Obama, speech at Federal Plaza.

32. Obama, speech at AIPAC Policy Forum.

33. Democratic debate, South Carolina, April 26, 2007, available at http://www.msnbc.msn.com/id/18352397.

34. William Blum, "Fear Factors," *CounterPunch*, October 26, 2004, available at http://www.counterpunch.org/blum10262004.html.

35. Barack Obama, "Tone, Truth, and the Democratic Party," *Daily Kos*, September 30, 2005, available at http://www.dailykos.com/storyonly/2005/9/30/102745/165.

36. Ibid.

37. Barack Obama, "The War We Need to Win," speech in Washington, DC, August 1, 2007, available at http://www.barackobama.com/2007/08/01/remarks_of_senator_obama_the_w_1.php.

38. Republican Debate, *This Week*, ABC, August 5, 2007.

39. Kathleen Hennessey, "Obama Rejects Clinton Criticism, Defends Foreign Policy Plan," Associated Press, August 11, 2007, available at http://www.nctimes.com/articles/2007/08/12/news/politics/12_89_178_11_07.txt.

40. Beth Fouhy, "Clinton Discussed Use of Nukes Last Year," Associated Press, August 9, 2007, available at http://talkingpointsmemo.com/news/2007/08/clinton_discussed_use_of_nukes.php.

41. Samantha Power, "Conventional Washington versus the Change We Need," August 3, 2007, available at: http://blog.washingtonpost.com/the-trail/2007/08/03/campaign_memo_barack_obama_was_1.html.

42. Nedra Pickler, "Fact Check: Obama on Afghanistan," Associated Press, August 14, 2007, available at http://www.forbes.com/feeds/ap/2007/08/14/ap4019021.html.

43. *CBS Evening News*, CBS, August 15, 2007.

44. Katharine Seelye, "Obama and Clinton Find Pluses in Poll," *New York Times*, August 16, 2007.

45. Jeff Zeleny, "Obama Takes Sharper Tone to the Trail," *New York Times*, August 17, 2007.

46. Power, "Conventional Washington versus the Change We Need."

47. Katharine Seelye and Michael Falcone, "Obama Says Clinton Is 'Bush-Cheney Lite,'" *New York Times,* July 27, 2007.

48. Anne E. Kornblut and Dan Balz, "For Clinton and Obama, A Debate Point Won't Die," *Washington Post,* July 27, 2007; David Brooks, "The Uphill Struggle," *New York Times,* July 27, 2007.

49. Robert Novak, *Evans-Novak Political Report*, May 2, 2007, available at http://www.humanevents.com/article.php?id=20527.

50. *Beyond the Beltway*, WLS-AM, April 29, 2007, available at http://www.beyondthebeltway.com/btbarchives2007.html.

51. Clarence Page, "Democrats Neither Sizzle nor Fizzle at Debate," *Chicago Tribune*, April 30, 2007.

52. Katharine Seelye and Michael Falcone, "Obama Says Clinton Is 'Bush-Cheney Lite,'" *New York Times*, July 27, 2007.

53. Kornblut and Balz, "For Clinton and Obama, a Debate Point Won't Die"; Brooks, "The Uphill Struggle."

54. *NewsHour with Jim Lehrer,* PBS, July 27, 2007.

55. Ibid.

56. See votes at http://www.senate.gov/legislative/LIS/roll_call_lists/roll_call_vote_cfm.cfm?congress=109&session=2&vote=00001 and http://www.senate.gov/legislative/LIS/roll_call_lists/roll_call_vote_cfm.cfm?congress=109&session=1&vote=00245.

57. Ezra Klein, "Where's the Beef?" *Tapped* blog, March 27, 2007, available at http://blog.prospect.org/cgi-bin/mt/mt-tb.cgi/13872.

58. See "Federal Funding Accountability and Transparency Act of 2006," avail-able at http://www.govtrack.us/congress/bill.xpd?bill=s109-2590; "Cooperative Proliferation Detection, Interdiction Assistance, and Conventional Threat Reduction Act of 2006," available at http://www.govtrack.us/congress/bill.xpd?bill=s109-2566

59. Pat Guinane, "Star Power," *Illinois Issues* (October 2004), available at http://illinoisissues.uis.edu/features/2004oct/senate.html.

60. Adam Howard, "In Defense of Obama," *Nation,* January 18, 2007, available at http://www.thenation.com/blogs/notion?bid=15&pid=158499.

61. Ibid.

62. Eric Alterman, "What Did You Dream? It's All Right, We Told You What to Dream for America," *Media Matters for America*, April 2, 2007, available at http://mediamatters.org/altercation/200704020005#1.

63. Wallace-Wells, "Destiny's Child."

64. Scott McLemee, "Party in the Streets," InsideHigherEd.com, March 21, 2007, available at http://www.insidehighered.com/views/2007/03/21/mclemee.

65. Barack Obama, "Tone, Truth, and the Democratic Party," *Daily Kos*, September 30, 2005, available at http://www.dailykos.com/storyonly/2005/ 9/30/102745/165.

66. Ibid.

67. Ibid.

68. Ibid.

69. Ezra Klein, "We Want a Divider, Not a Uniter," *Guardian*, February 9, 2007, available at http://commentisfree.guardian.co.uk/ezra_klein/2007/02/obamania_in_check.html.printer.friendly.

70. Wieseltier, "Audacities."

71. Obama, "Tone, Truth, and the Democratic Party."

72. Cockburn, "Meet Senator Slither."

73. Senior, "Dreaming of Obama."

74. Obama, "Tone, Truth, and the Democratic Party."

75. Ibid.

76. Ibid.

77. Ibid.

78. Barack Obama, "Thanks for the Feedback," *Daily Kos*, October 20, 2005, available at http://www.dailykos.com/story/2005/10/20/235350/39.

79. Ibid.

80. *This Week with George Stephanopolous*, May 13, 2007.

Notes for Chapter Six

1. Tim Grieve, "Left Turn at Saddleback Church," *Salon*, December 2, 2006, available at http://www.salon.com/news/feature/2006/12/02/obama/print.html.

2. Terry McDermott, "What Is It about Obama?" *Los Angeles Times*, December 24, 2006.

3. Kevin McCullough, "Why Is Obama's Evil in Rick Warren's Pulpit?" Townhall.com, November 19, 2006, available at http://www.townhall.com/columnists/KevinMcCullough/2006/11/19/why_is_obamas_evil_in_rick_warrens_pulpit.

4. Christian Newswire, "Rick Warren/Barack Obama AIDS Partnership Must End, Say Pro-Life Groups," press release, November 28, 2006, available at http://www.christiannewswire.com/news/791771591.html.

5. Christian Newswire, "Christian Defense Coalition Joins Call Asking Pastor Rick Warren to Drop Senator Barack Obama from Speaking at Saddleback Church," press release, November 28, 2006, available at http://www.christiannewswire.com/news/475191599.html.

6. "Church Leaders Distressed over Obama Visit," Christian Newswire press release, November 28, 2006, available at http://www.christiannewswire.com/news/935091597.html.

7. Brett Arends, "A Less Self-Righteous Right," *Boston Herald*, March 21, 2007.

8. *Hannity and Colmes*, Fox News Channel, June 25, 2007.

9. Jan Frel, "But What If I Think 'People of Faith' Are a Little Crazy?" Alternet.org, June 28, 2006, available at http://www.alternet.org/blogs/themix/38280.

10. Kym Platt, "Calling for a Barack Ban," *Ask This Black Woman*, November 30, 2006, http://askthisblackwoman.com/2006/11/30/calling-for-a-barack-ban.aspx.

11. David Sirota, "Obama & McCain: The Reactions Say a Lot," *Sirotablog*, December 1, 2006, available at http://davidsirota.com/index.php/2006/12/01/obama-mccain-the-reactions-say-a-lot.

12. Barack Obama, "Call to Renewal," speech at National City Christian Church of Washington, DC, June 28, 2006, available at http://obama.senate.gov/speech/060628-call_to_renewal_keynote_address/print.php.

13. Ibid.

14. Joe Garcia, "Barack Obama: The Guise of Change," *Daily Kos*, December 16, 2006, available at http://www.dailykos.com/story/2006/12/ 16/14220/960.

15. Obama, *The Audacity of Hope*, 201.

16. Ibid., 204.

17. Obama, *Dreams from My Father* (2004), 50.

18. Ibid.

19. Ibid.

20. Obama, *The Audacity of Hope*, 203.

21. Ibid., 204.

22. Ibid.

23. Falsani, "Evangelical?" 47.

24. Obama, *The Audacity of Hope*, 205.

25. Ibid., 206.

26. Obama, "Call to Renewal."

27. Falsani, "Evangelical?" 48.

28. Ibid.

29. Obama, *The Audacity of Hope*, 206.

30. Ibid., 207.

31. Falsani, "Evangelical?" 48.

32. Obama, *The Audacity of Hope*, 206.

33. Ibid., 207.

34. Ibid., 208.

35. Falsani, "Evangelical?" 45.

36. Ibid., 48.

37. Ellen Goodman, "The First Openly Godless Member of Congress," *Boston Globe*, March 24, 2007, available at http://www.alternet.org/story/49632.

38. "The Jesus Factor," *Frontline*, PBS, May 6, 2004, available at http://www.pbs.org/wgbh/pages/frontline/shows/jesus/etc/script.html.

39. Obama, "Call to Renewal."

40. Ibid.
41. Falsani, "Evangelical?" 49.
42. Ibid.
43. Remnick, "Testing the Waters."
44. Ibid.
45. Falsani, "Evangelical?"
46. Remnick, "Testing the Waters."
47. Falsani, "Evangelical?" 50.
48. Ibid., 51.
49. Ibid.
50. Ibid., 46.
51. Ibid., 47.
52. Remnick, "Testing the Waters."
53. Falsani, "Evangelical?" 49.
54. Ibid., 48.
55. Ibid., 47.
56. Ibid., 48.
57. Ibid., 47.

Notes for Chapter Seven

1. Barack Obama, "Announcement for President," Springfield, IL, February 10, 2007, available at http://www.barackobama.com/2007/02/10/remarks_of_senator_barack_obam_11.php.
2. Eric Zorn, "Obama Critics Build Cases on Faulty Premises." *Chicago Tribune*, December 19, 2006.
3. Remnick, "Testing the Waters."
4. Editorial, "Rusting Star," *Investor's Business Daily*, December 14, 2006, available at http://www.investors.com/editorial/editorialcontent.asp?secid=1501&status=article&id=250991739789975.
5. Remnick, "Testing the Waters."
6. John K. Wilson, "The Bigot Who Runs Illinois," *Chicago Ink*, August 1997, available at http://ink.uchicago.edu/page_olga_made/archives/pate897.html.
7. Steve Neal, " Philip Makes Name as Backward Bully," *Chicago Sun-Times*, July 13, 1992.
8. Ted Kleine, "Is Bobby Rush in Trouble?" *Chicago Reader*, March 17, 2000, available at http://www.chicagoreader.com/obama/000317.
9. John Conroy, "Police Torture in Chicago," *Chicago Reader*, available at http://www.chicagoreader.com/policetorture.
10. Peter Slevin, "Obama Forged Political Mettle in Illinois Capitol," *Washington Post*, February 9, 2007, available at http://www.barackobama.com/2007/02/09/20070209wp.php.
11. Ibid.
12. Sam Youngman and Aaron Blake, "Obama's Crime Votes Are Fodder for Rivals,"

Hill, March 14, 2007, available at http://thehill.com/leading-the-news/obamas-crime-votes-are-fodder-for-rivals-2007-03-13.html.

13. Ibid.

14. Ibid.

15. Ibid.

16. *Media Matters*, May 20, 2007.

17. Muwakkil, "Barack Obama Made Smashing National Debut."

18. Fund, "Not So Fast."

19. Slevin, "Obama Forged Political Mettle in Illinois Capitol."

20. *Human Events* magazine, *Barack Obama Exposed!*

21. Ibid.

22. Nathan L. Gonzales, "The Ever-'Present' Obama," *RealClearPolitics*, February 13, 2007, available at http://rothenbergpoliticalreport.blogspot.com/2007/02/ever-present-obama.html.

23. Slevin, "Obama Forged Political Mettle in Illinois Capitol."

24. Edward McClelland, "How Obama Learned to Be a Natural," *Salon*, February 12, 2007, available at http://www.salon.com/news/feature/2007/02/12/obama_natural/print.html.

25. Marlene Targ Brill, *Barack Obama: Working to Make a Difference* (Minneapolis: Millbrook Press, 2006), 37.

26. McClelland, "How Obama Learned to Be a Natural."

27. Ibid.

28. Wallace-Wells, "Destiny's Child."

29. Slevin, "Obama Forged Political Mettle in Illinois Capitol."

30. Ibid.

31. *Chicago Tonight*, WTTW, June 28, 2007.

32. Ibid.

33. Slevin, "Obama Forged Political Mettle in Illinois Capitol."

34. Nat Hentoff, "Obama: Who Is He Now?" *Village Voice*, March 5, 2007.

35. Zorn, "Obama Critics Build Cases on Faulty Premises."

36. Clarence Lusane, "Obama Run Would Speak to Issue of Race," *Progressive*, November 28, 2006, available at http://progressive.org/media_mplusane112806.

37. Wieseltier, "Audacities."

38. Editorial, "Rusting Star."

39. David Sirota, "Mr. Obama Goes to Washington," *Nation*, June 26, 2006.

40. Heilemann, "The Chicago Cipher."

41. Zorn, "Obama Critics Build Cases on Faulty Premises."

42. Heilemann, "The Chicago Cipher."

43. Dick Morris, "Barack Obama: The Mystique of the Vacuous," FrontPageMagazine.com, January 4, 2007, available at http://frontpagemag.com/Articles/ReadArticle.asp?ID=26271.

44. "Senate Composite Scores," *National Journal*, available at http://nationaljournal.com/voteratings/sen/lib_cons.htm?o1=lib_composite&o2=desc.

45. Kurt Erickson and Ed Tibbetts, "Obama's Records Reveal His Liberal Side," *Pantagraph*, January 21, 2007.

46. Editorial, "Rusting Star."

47. Erickson and Tibbetts, "Obama's Records Reveal His Liberal Side."

48. Steve Ivey, "Obama: White House Blind to Poverty in U.S.," *Chicago Tribune,* September 22, 2005.

49. Ralph Nader, "Cronies, Contracts, and the No-Fault President," *CounterPunch,* October 8, 2005, available at http://www.counterpunch.org/nader10082005. html.

50. John McCormick, "Obama Vows Union-Boosting Law Will Pass," *Chicago Tribune,* March 4, 2007.

51. Ken Silverstein, *Harper's Magazine,* November 2006.

52. Barack Obama, Knox College Commencement Address, Galesburg, IL, June 4, 2005, http://www.knox.edu/x9803.xml.

53. Barack Obama, "Hope. Action. Change." (webcast from Iowa), March 31, 2007, available at http://my.barackobama.com/page/content/hacwebcast.

54. Remnick, "Testing the Waters."

55. Obama, "Hope. Action. Change."

56. Barack Obama, "Cutting Costs and Covering America: A 21st Century Health Care System," speech at University of Iowa, Iowa City, IA, May 29, 2007, available at http://www.barackobama.com/2007/05/29/cutting_costs_and_covering_ame.php.

57. Hillary Rodham Clinton and Barack Obama, "Making Patient Safety the Centerpiece of Medical Liability Reform," *New England Journal of Medicine,* May 25, 2006, available at http://content.nejm.org/cgi/content/full/354/21/2205.

58. Jeff Camplin, "Initiatives Aimed at Reducing Lead Exposures," *EnviroMentor,* Fall 2005, 20, available at http://www.asse.org/practicespecialties/environmental/docs/prac_spec_environmentor_sample.pdf.

59. Editorial, "Where's the Beef?" *Economist,* April 14, 2007.

60. Evan Derkacz, "When the Obama Train Gains Steam, the Racists Gear Up," Alternet.org, January 24, 2007, available at http://alternet.org/blogs/peek/47168; Carol Marin, "Has 'Low Blow Joe' Gone Goo-Goo, or Is There More to Story?" *Chicago Sun-Times,* August 9, 2006.

61. Mike Dorning, "Obama: Health Care for All," *Chicago Tribune,* January 26, 2007, available at http://www.swamppolitics.com/news/politics/blog/2007/01/obama_health_care_for_all.html.

62. *NOW,* PBS, July 1, 2007.

63. Obama, "Cutting Costs and Covering America."

64. Amanda Griscom, "Barack Star: Illinois Senate Candidate Barack Obama's Got Green Cred," *Grist Magazine,* August 4, 2004, http://www.grist.org/cgi-bin/printthis.pl?uri=/news/muck/2004/08/04/griscom-obama/index.html.

65. Amanda Griscom, "Muckraker," *Salon,* August 6, 2004, available at http:// dir.salon.com/story/opinion/feature/2004/08/06/muck_obama/index.html.

66. Ibid.

67. Ibid.

68. Ibid.

69. H. Josef Hebert, "Climate Bill Sets Stage for Debate," Associated Press, January

12, 2007, available at http://www.heatison.org/index.php/content/news_item/climate_bill_sets_stage_for_debate.

70. Erickson and Tibbetts, "Obama's Records Reveal His Liberal Side."

71. Associated Press, "Obama Pushes Carbon Reductions," *USA Today*, April 20, 2007.

72. Justin Hyde, "Obama, Others Offer a Less-Tough Mileage Bill," *Free Press*, March 6, 2007, available at http://www.freep.com/apps/pbcs.dll/article?AID=/20070306/BUSINESS01/703060340&template=printart.

73. Seth Borenstein, "Obama Suggests Money for Fuel Economy Deal for Auto-makers," *Philadelphia Inquirer*, March 1, 2006.

74. Michael Hawthorne, "U.S. Won't Sell Huge Stockpile of Mercury," *Chicago Tribune*, January 3, 2007.

75. Barack Obama, "Energy Security Is National Security," speech to the Governor's Ethanol Coalition, Washington, DC, February 28, 2006, available at http://www.barackobama.com/2006/02/28/energy_security_is_national_se.php.

76. "Obama, Lugar, Harkin Introduce Legislation to Increase Availability and Use of Renewable Fuels, Decrease U.S. Dependence on Foreign Oil," press release, January 6, 2007, available at http://lugar.senate.gov/press/record.cfm?id=267220.

77. Remnick, "Testing the Waters."

78. Patrick Healy and Adam Nagourney, "In Meetings with Allies, Clinton Hones '08 Strategy," *New York Times*, January 3, 2007.

79. "Obama's Unwavering Fight for Top Seat," *Africa News*, February 18, 2007.

80. "Lugar-Obama Bill Passes Congress to Keep Weapons out of Terrorists Hands," press release, December 11, 2006, available at http://www.topix.net/forum/city/kankakee-il/TEJEHH26UIGBAPNF3.

81. Rosa Brooks, "Barack's Ready," *Los Angeles Times*, December 15, 2006.

82. Holly Ramer, "Obama Declines to Bite in N.H.," *Nashua Telegraph*, April 3, 2007.

83. Dan Morain, "An Asterisk to Obama's Policy on Donations," *Los Angeles Times*, April 22, 2007.

84. Lynn Sweet, "McCain Mocks Obama," *Chicago Sun-Times*, February 7, 2006.

85. Ibid.

86. Lynn Sweet, "Obama to Pay Full Fare on Private Jet," *Chicago Sun-Times*, January 21, 2006.

87. Alexander Bolton, "Sens. Obama, Coburn Make Unlikely Duo," *The Hill*, March 27, 2006.

88. Daniel C. Vock, "Obama: He Puts Ethics on the Agenda," *Illinois Issues* (February 2007), available at http://illinoisissues.uis.edu/features/2007feb/obama.html.

89. Barack Obama, "A Chance to Change the Game," *Washington Post*, January 4, 2007.

90. Ibid.

91. Dori Meinert, "Obama's Record Is Firmly Partisan," *Springfield State Journal-Register*, January 21, 2007.

Notes for Chapter Eight

1. "The Long Siege," *Newsweek* (November 17, 2008), http://www.newsweek.com/id/167755/output/print.

2. "2008 Votes Cast—132.15 Million; Obama—69.45 Million; Discrepancies Identified," Daily Kos, December 10, 2008, http://www.dailykos.com/story/2008/12/10/22817/907/693/669512.

3. Stephen Ansolabehere and Charles Stewart III, "Amazing Race: How Post-Racial Was Obama's Victory?" *Boston Review* (January–February 2009), http://www.bostonreview.net/BR34.1/ansolabehere_stewart.php.

4. Center for Information and Research on Civic Learning and Engagement, "Young Voters in the 2008 Presidential Election," November 24, 2008, http://www.civicyouth.org/PopUps/FactSheets/FS_08_exit_polls.pdf.

5. Center for Information and Research on Civic Learning and Engagement, "A Voter Turnout Time Series for 1972–2004," http://www.civicyouth.org/?page_id=241.

6. Center for Information and Research on Civic Learning and Engagement, "Young Voters in the 2008 Presidential Election."

7. Tom Curry, "Young Voters Not Essential to Obama Triumph," MSNBC.com, November 7, 2008, http://www.msnbc.msn.com/id/27582147.

8. http://firstread.msnbc.msn.com/archive/2008/11/07/1662499.aspx?p=1.

9. Center for Information and Research on Civic Learning and Engagement, "Young Voters in the 2008 Presidential Election."

10. http://www.nytimes.com/2008/11/07/opinion/07patterson.html.

11. Associated Press, "Election Spurs 'Hundreds' of Race Threats, Crimes," *Chicago Sun-Times,* November 16, 2008, http://www.suntimes.com/news/elections/1281749,election-racial-obama111608.article.

12. Ibid.

13. Richard Wolffe and Daren Briscoe, "Across the Divide," *Newsweek* (July 16, 2007): 25.

14. Stephen Lewis, "Ode to President Obama," *Murfreesboro Post,* November 9, 2008, http://www.murfreesboropost.com/news.php?viewStory=13866.

15. *Rush Limbaugh* show, October 15, 2008.

16. *Rush Limbaugh* show, May 28, 2008.

17. *Rush Limbaugh* show, September 22, 2008.

18. *Rush Limbaugh* show, October 24, 2008.

19. *Rush Limbaugh* show, March 21, 2008.

20. *Rush Limbaugh* show, September 29, 2008.

21. *Rush Limbaugh* show, January 24, 2007.

22. *Rush Limbaugh* show, January 16, 2007.

23. *Rush Limbaugh* show, August 20, 2008.

24. *Rush Limbaugh* show, September 18, 2008.

25. David Horowitz blog, http://frontpagemag.com/blog/Read.aspx?guid=95f6df4d-4547-4e6d-81fd-2db2579c7095.

26. http://abcnews.go.com/PollingUnit/Vote2008/story?id=6189129&page=1.

27. John K. Wilson, "How Race Mattered on Nov. 4, and Why the National

Exit Poll Is Wrong," DailyKos.com, November 9, 2008, http://www.dailykos.com/ story/2008/11/9/124432/199/944/658066. For the original exit poll, see http://www. msnbc.msn.com/id/26843704; for my state-by-state analysis and national calculations, see http://spreadsheets.google.com/ccc?key=prY2gP8lDlcrFy-hLJY1eDw.

28. http://www.dailykos.com/story/2008/5/14/85241/3477/284/515353.

29. Kate Phillips, "Clinton Touts White Support," *New York Times* blog, May 8, 2008, http://thecaucus.blogs.nytimes.com/2008/05/08/clinton-touts-white-support/ ?hp.

30. John K. Wilson, "Racism and Sexism on Super Tuesday," DailyKos.com, February 6, 2008, http://www.dailykos.com/story/2008/2/6/155024/3338/265/451293.

31. Wolffe and Briscoe, "Across the Divide," 25.

32. Frank Rich, "It Still Felt Good the Morning After," *New York Times*, November 9, 2008, http://www.nytimes.com/2008/11/09/opinion/09rich.html.

33. Ansolabehere and Stewart, "Amazing Race."

34. Barack Obama, speech in Philadelphia, March 18, 2008, http://www.npr.org/ templates/story/story.php?storyId=88478467.

35. "The Long Siege."

36. *Rush Limbaugh* show, July 22, 2008.

37. *Rush Limbaugh* show, July 21, 2008.

38. *Rush Limbaugh* show, November 7, 2008.

39. Joseph McQuaid, "Obama Orgy," *New Hampshire Union Leader*, July 21, 2008, http://www.unionleader.com/article.aspx?articleID=c59bf7fa-c458-40aa-819d-efd11aa13974.

40. Michael S. Malone, "Media's Presidential Bias and Decline," ABCNews.com, October 24, 2008, http://abcnews.go.com/Business/Story?id=6099188&page=1.

41. Newt Gingrich, "Annoy the Media: Go Vote and the 'Common Sense Effect,'" *Human Events*, November 4, 2008, http://www.humanevents.com/article. php?id=29338.

42. http://www.newsweek.com/id/168017/output/print.

43. Mark Leibovich, "Between Obama and the Press," *New York Times Magazine* (December 21, 2008), http://www.nytimes.com/2008/12/21/magazine/21Gibbs-t. html?_r=1&ref=politics&pagewanted=all.

44. Alexander Burns, "Halperin at Politico/USC Conf.: 'Extreme Pro-Obama' Press Bias," *Politico*, November 22, 2008, http://www.politico.com/news/stories/1108/15885. html.

45. Rasmussen Reports, July 21, 2008, http://www.rasmussenreports.com/public_ content/politics/election_20082/2008_presidential_election/belief_growing_that_ reporters_are_trying_to_help_obama_win.

46. Paul Farhi, "Rush Limbaugh Signs $400 Million Radio Deal," *Washington Post*, July 3, 2008, http://www.washingtonpost.com/wp-dyn/content/article/2008/07/02/ AR2008070202063.html.

47. Center for American Progress and Free Press, "The Structural Imbalance of Political Talk Radio," June 21, 2007, www.americanprogress.org/issues/2007/06/pdf/ talk_radio.pdf.

48. Kathleen Hall Jamieson and Brooks Jackson, "Our Disinformed Electorate," factcheck.org, December 13, 2008, http://www.newsweek.com/id/174299/page/2.

49. http://www.foxnews.com/projects/pdf/FoxPoll.pdf.

50. November 12, 2008, http://www.wnd.com/index.php?fa=PAGE.view&pageId=80831.

51. Project for Excellence in Journalism, "How the Press Reported the 2008 General Election," October 22, 2008, http://journalism.org/node/13307.

52. Ibid.

53. Center for Media and Public Affairs, "Media Bash Barack (Not a Typo)," July 28, 2008, http://www.cmpa.com/media_room_press_2.htm.

54. Rich Noyes, "Obama's Margin of Victory: The Media," Media Research Center, August 20, 2008, http://www.mrc.org/SpecialReports/2008/obama/obama.asp.

55. John K. Wilson, "Media Research Center Lies Exposed about Obama and the Press," DailyKos, August 20, 2008, http://www.dailykos.com/story/ 2008/8/20/171236/523/211/571337.

56. Howard Kurtz, "Conservative Group Finds Networks Positive on Obama," *Washington Post,* August 20, 2008, http://voices.washingtonpost.com/the-trail/2008/08/20/conservative_group_finds_netwo.html.

57. Dana Milbank, "For Obama and McCain, the Bitter and the Sweet," *Washington Post,* April 15, 2008, http://www.washingtonpost.com/wp-dyn/content/article/2008/04/14/AR2008041402633_pf.html.

58. Michael Calderone, "One of Fournier's Job Options: McCain," *Politico,* July 29, 2008, http://www.politico.com/news/stories/0708/12149.html.

59. MSNBC, February 12, 2008; Eric Alterman and George Zornick, "Loving John McCain," *Nation* (July 7, 2008), http://www.thenation.com/doc/20080707/alterman; MSNBC, June 13, 2007, www.salon.com/opinion/greenwald/2007/12/26/quotes.

60. Media Matters, "Media Continue to Uncritically Report McCain Campaign Attacks on Their Coverage, but Case Studies Still Show Disparate Coverage in McCain's Favor," November 5, 2008, http://mediamatters.org/items/200811050005?f=s_search.

61. Media Matters, *"Wash. Post* and *NY Times* Published More Than 12 Times as Many Articles Mentioning Obama and Wright as They Did Mentioning McCain and Hagee," April 30, 2008, http://mediamatters.org/items/200804300007.

62. Media Matters, "Media Continue to Uncritically Report McCain Attacks."

63. Michael Calderone, "Potter: Most 'Horrific' McCain Stories Never Ran," *Politico,* December 4, 2008, http://www.politico.com/blogs/michaelcalderone/1208/Potter_Most_horrific_McCain_stories_never_ran.html.

64. Evan Thomas, "Back from the Dead," *Newsweek* (November 17, 2008), http://www.newsweek.com/id/167639/output/print.

65. CNN, May 16, 2008.

66. John K. Wilson, "Barack Obama and the Myth of Inexperience," DailyKos, October 6, 2008, http://www.dailykos.com/story/2008/10/6/20593/5557/230/622176; see also http://spreadsheets.google.com/pub?key=prY2gP8lDlcrHI0f3zAUzYg.

67. "The Rankings," *Wall Street Journal*, September 12, 2005, http://www.opinionjournal.com/extra/?id=110007243.

68. Michael Luo and Jeff Zeleny, "Obama, in Shift, Says He'll Reject Public Financing," *New York Times*, June 20, 2008, http://www.nytimes.com/2008/06/20/us/politics/20obama.html?_r=1.

69. Don Gonyea, "Obama Rejects Public Financing," NPR, *All Things Considered*, June 19, 2008, http://www.npr.org/templates/story/story.php?storyId=91703936&ft=1&f=1001.

70. *Hardball*, MSNBC, June 19, 2008.

71. *New York Post*, June 20, 2008.

72. *Jim Lehrer News Hour*, PBS, June 20, 2008.

73. Jake Tapper, "Obama Takes Political Hit for Rejecting Spending Limits," *ABC News*, June 20, 2008, http://abcnews.go.com/GMA/Vote2008/story?id=5210799&page=1.

74. Ben Smith, "Obama Spokesman: Public Financing Just an 'Option,'" *Politico*, February 14, 2008, http://www.politico.com/blogs/bensmith/0208/Obama_spokesman_Public_financing_just_an_option.html.

75. Midwest Democracy Network questionnaire, http://media.washingtonpost.com/wp-srv/politics/content/Questionnaire_Midwest_Democracy_Network_Obama_02192008.pdf.

76. Barack Obama, "Opposing View: Both Sides Must Agree," *USA Today*, February 20, 2008, http://blogs.usatoday.com/oped/2008/02/opposing-view-3.html.

77. Ben Smith, "Obama Would Seek McCain Deal," *Politico*, February 15, 2008, http://www.politico.com/blogs/bensmith/0208/Obama_would_seek_McCain_deal.html.

78. Jim Kuhnhenn, "Obama Reverses Course, Will Privately Finance Campaign," Associated Press, June 19, 2008, http://www.nysun.com/national/obama-reverses-course-will-privately-finance/80329.

79. Media Matters for America, "*NY Times* and *Newsweek* Report on Public Funding in General Election, but Not That McCain May Be Breaking Federal Campaign Financing Laws," April 10, 2008, http://mediamatters.org/items/200804100004.

80. http://change.gov/open_government/yourseatatthetable.

Notes for Chapter Nine

1. *The O'Reilly Factor*, Fox News Channel, September 4, 2008, http://mediamatters.org/items/200809060004.

2. Steve Luxenberg, "U.S. Spied on Iraqi Leaders, Book Says," *Washington Post*, September 5, 2008, http://www.washingtonpost.com/wp-dyn/content/article/2008/09/04/AR2008090403160.html.

3. Juan Cole, "A Social History of the Surge," *Informed Comment*, July 24, 2008, http://www.juancole.com/2008/07/social-history-of-surge.html; Nir Rosen, "The Myth of the Surge," *Rolling Stone* (March 6, 2008), http://www.rollingstone.com/politics/story/18722376/the_myth_of_the_surge.

4. Marc Ambinder, "Obama on the Surge," *Atlantic Monthly* blog, August 21, 2007, http://marcambinder.theatlantic.com/archives/2007/08/obama_on_the_surge.php.

5. Paul Krugman, "Bigger Than Bush," *New York Times*, January 1, 2009, http://www.nytimes.com/2009/01/02/opinion/02krugman.html?ref=opinion.

6. Eric Rauchway, "Learning from the New Deal's Mistakes," *American Prospect*, December 22, 2008, http://www.prospect.org/cs/articles?article=learning_from_the_new_deals_mistakes.

7. Reginald Wilson, "The G.I. Bill and the Transformation of America," *National Forum* (Fall 1995), http://findarticles.com/p/articles/mi_qa3651/is_199510/ai_n8720508.

8. "'Shovel-Ready' on Campus" (editorial), *Wall Street Journal*, December 17, 2008, http://online.wsj.com/article/SB122956325068716801.html.

9. Jack Stripling, "So Goes the Nation," InsideHigherEd.com, November 13, 2008, http://www.insidehighered.com/news/2008/11/13/cuts.

10. Larry Gordon, "Ivory Towers Are Feeling the Economic Pinch," *Los Angeles Times*, January 1, 2009, http://www.latimes.com/news/education/la-me-language1-2009jan01,0,4104726.story.

11. Charles Murray, "Should the Obama Generation Drop Out?" *New York Times*, December 28, 2008, http://www.nytimes.com/2008/12/28/opinion/28murray.html.

12. John K. Wilson, "The Defense Department vs. Free Speech on Campus," InsideHigherEd.com, June 25, 2007, http://insidehighered.com/views/2007/06/25/wilson.

Notes for the Conclusion

1. Eric Pooley, "The Last Temptation of Al Gore," *Time* (May 28, 2007): 39.

2. Remarks at "Taming the Giant Corporation" conference, Washington, D.C., June 10, 2007.

3. Hank De Zutter, "What Makes Obama Run?" *Chicago Reader*, December 8, 1995, available at http://www.chicagoreader.com/features/stories/archive/barackobama.

4. Matt Stoller, "Obama's Admiration of Ronald Reagan," OpenLeft, January 16, 2008, available at http://www.openleft.com/showDiary.do?diaryId=3263.

5. Amy Chozick, "Obama, Clinton Battle over Reagan," *Wall Street Journal* online, January 18, 2008, available at http://blogs.wsj.com/washwire/2008/01/18/obama-clinton-battle-over-reagan.

6. Megan Thee-Brenan, "Poll Finds Disapproval of Bush Unwavering," *New York Times*, January 16, 2009, available at http://www.nytimes.com/2009/01/17/us/politics/17poll.html.

Index

abortion issue, 132, 148
Abunimah, Ali, 116–117
Adi, Zulfin, 98
affirmative action, 65–66
Afghanistan, 119
Africa, 40, 160
African American Leadership Institute
  (University of Maryland), 68, 89
African Americans, 16, 53–54; black
  critics of Obama, 57–58; blackness
  police, 55–57; Clintons, support for,
  80–84; Illinois legislation and, 145–
  147; leftist, 83; pessimistic, 84–88;
  stereotypes of, 77–78; supporters of
  Obama, 61–63. *See also* race issue
African American Studies and Research
  Program (University of Illinois), 147
African Union peacekeeping mission, 160
agitation, 4
AIDS, 40, 148
Alexander, Peter, 27
Alinsky, Saul, 4
Alito filibuster, 120
Allen, Mike, 36
Allen, Rob, 55
Alter, Jonathan, 7
Alterman, Eric, 121–123
alternet.org, 87
American Enterprise Institute, 28, 72
American ideals, 112, 117
American Israel Public Affairs
  Committee (AIPAC), 116–117
American nationalism, 61
Americans for Tax Reform, 107
American Spectator, 105, 110

AmeriCorps, 5, 64
anger, as stereotype, 77–78
anti-Semitism, 100
ArchPundit, 101
Arctic National Wildlife Refuge, 159
Armey, Dick, 95
Arnove, Anthony, 117
articulate, as stereotypical term, 77–78
Ask This Black Woman (Platt), 132
Associated Press, 27, 28, 29
Association of Community Organizations
  for Reform Now (ACORN), 60, 107
Audacity of Hope, The (Obama), 9, 18, 73,
  76, 77, 98, 160
Augustine-Herron, Loretta, 3
automobile emissions, 159
Axelrod, David, 9, 22–23, 87

baby boomers, 2, 6–9
Barack Obama Exposed!, 147
Barone, Michael, 11, 105
Bauer, Michael, 115
Baumgartner, Jody, 19
Beck, Glenn, 73
Belafonte, Harry, 59
Berenson, Brad, 108–109
Bernstein, Carl, 20
Bevan, Tom, 35
Biden, Joseph, 30, 77, 118
Bill of Rights, 49
Bin Laden, Osama, 118
Bipartisan Health Care Reform
  Commission (Illinois), 150
Black Agenda Report, 58
Black Commentator, 87, 116

Black Independent Political Organization, 59

black nationalism, 61

Blagojevich, Rod, 33, 145

blank slate metaphor, v

Bleifuss, Joel, 121–123

Blum, Edward, 72

Blum, William, 118

Boortz, Neal, 36

Bositis, David, 76, 84–85

Bossie, David, 104

Boston Legal, 80

Boxer, Barbara, 58

Boyle, Mary, 163

Bradley, Tom, 88

Bradley effect, 88–90

Braun, Carol Moseley, 16, 89

Brazile, Donna, 70

Brooks, David, 28, 29, 120

Brooks, Rosa, 37–38

Brownback, Sam, 131, 160

Budowsky, Brent, 26

Bush, George H. W., 5, 44

Bush, George W., iv, 9–10, 11; censure of, 120–121; 2004 election results, 58–59; lack of experience, 30, 106; legacy preference in college, 66, 67; lying, 13, 128; Obama's challenge to, 42–43; racist campaign, 92; religion of, 137

Bush Doctrine, 117–120

Butler, Paul, 81

Calumet Community Religious Conference, 3

campaign financing, iv, 34, 49–50, 149, 155; ethics, 161; by health care industry, 157

Canary, Cynthia, 150

Carlson, Margaret, 39

Carlson, Tucker, 17, 29, 69–70, 74

Carter, Jimmy, 30, 106, 125, 137

Catholic Church, 139

Central American Free Trade Act, 155

centrist Democrats, 125–126

Chait, Jonathan, 66

Cha-Jua, Sundiata, 62, 68, 83, 86, 147

charisma, 128–129, 166

Chateauvert, Melinda, 62

Chávez, Hugo, 120

Cheney, Dick, 30, 106

Chicago Defender, 62–63

Chicago Reader, 54

Chicago Sun-Times, 25, 34, 41, 96, 110

Chicago Tribune, 26, 31, 32, 34–35, 84, 99–100

Chomsky, Noam, 27

Christian Science Monitor, 26

Christiel, Carolyn, 86

Citizens United, 104

civil rights movement, 23, 69–71

civil unions, 114–115

Clarke, Conor, 35

Class Action Fairness Act of 2005, 155

class-action suits, 155

Clean Air Act, 158

Clinton, Bill, 5, 9–10, 11; black voters and, 80–84; defense of Hillary, 45; impeachment, 81–82; lack of experience, 30; lying, 12, 128

Clinton, Hillary, 104; black support for, 80–81, 83; campaign financing, 161; conservative attacks and, 104–106; Iraq war, support for, 44, 45; lack of experience, 29, 31; liberal rating, 153; madrassa myth and, 101; media coverage of, 28–31; 1984 parody ad, 16; on Obama's foreign policy experience, 118, 119, 160; on Obama's YouTube debate, 120

Clinton/Bush generation, 9–10

CNN, 97

Coburn, Tom, 110, 155, 164

Cockburn, Alexander, 113, 120, 124

Cohen, Richard, 36

Colbert, Stephen, 36, 56–57, 79, 97

Colbert Report, 56

colleges, affirmative action and, 65–66

college students, 2, 10, 12; Narcissistic Personality Inventory (NPI), 13–14

Colmes, Alan, 36, 81
Comedy Central, 79, 92, 97
Common Cause, 163
Common (rapper), v
community organizing, 2–6, 15, 37, 49, 50, 70, 125
community politics, 4–5
community service, 4, 14
Community Service Center (University of Chicago), 64
Congo, 160
Congress: ethics reform in, 162–164
Congressional Black Caucus, 58
consensus, 21–22, 113–114
Conservative Political Action Conference, 104
conservatives, 93–95; Clintons and, 104–106; Illinois legislation, critiques of, 147–148; lack of basis for attacks, 94–95; Muslim allegations, 93, 95–98; race issues and, 71–73, 78–79, 104–105; terrorism issue, 102–104. *See also* Republicans
Contrarian Commentary, 101
Conway, Kellyanne, 105
coolness stereotype, 79
Corriveau, Garth, 13
Coulter, Ann, 72, 104–105
CounterPunch, 76–77, 118
Couric, Katie, 31
credibility, 44
Crouch, Stanley, 57
cultural conservatives, 127
culture wars, 10–11, 148
cynicism, 3, 17–19; political culture and, 19–21

Daily Kos, 123–124, 133
Daily Show, 19–20, 92
Daley, Richard, 64, 151
Darin, Jack, 158
Daschle, Tom, v
Dean, Howard, 37, 50, 91
death penalty reform, Illinois, 146
debates, 118–120

Debating Race (Dyson), 61–62
debt, 67–68
Deceptive Practices and Voter Intimidation Prevention Act of 2007, 154
Defense of Marriage Act, 147
DeLay, Tom, 105, 144
Democratic Leadership Council (DLC), 87, 124
Democratic National Convention (2004), iv, 21–23, 77, 112, 117
Democrats: centrists, 125–126; faults of, 21, 22; racist wing, 91; Reagan Democrats, 128–129
de Vellis, Phil, 15
Developing Communities Project (Chicago), 3
Dickerson, Debra, 56–57, 83
Dillard, Kirk, 109–110, 146, 150
Dinkins, David, 89
distractions, 50
Dixon, Bruce, 58–59, 87
Dodd, Chris, 30
Dole, Bob, 30, 107
Doocy, Steve, 96
Do the Right Thing, 65
Dowd, Matthew, 108
Dreams from My Father (Obama), 12, 36, 63, 64, 79, 100
drug issue, 12–13
DuMont, Bruce, 119
Durbin, Dick, 1, 45–46
Dyson, Michael Eric, 61–62, 65

Ebony, 83–84
Economist, 39, 156
Edwards, John, 29, 30, 59, 104; Iraq war, support for, 44, 45
Elders, Jocelyn, 81, 83
Electronic Intifada, 116
Ellis, Steve, 154
Emerging Black GOP Majority, The (Hutchinson), 87
Employee Free Choice Act, 154–155
employment legislation, 154–155

End of Blackness, The (Dickerson), 56
environmental issues, 158–160
Environmental Protection Agency, 156
ethics, 161–164
expectations, 60–61, 151–152
experience issue, 25–30, 37–38, 106;
  comparison with other candidates,
  29–31; D.C. considered more valuable,
  48–50; foreign policy, 38–40, 160

Facebook, 14–15
Fauntroy, Michael, 60, 70
Federal Election Commission (FEC),
  114
Federal Emergency Management Agency
  (FEMA), 155
Federal Funding Accountability and
  Transparency Act, 164
Federal Marriage Amendment, 114–115
Feingold, Russell, 45, 120
Fey, Tina, 80
Fields, Suzanne, 72
Fineman, Howard, 82
Fitton, Tom, 32
Fletcher, Bill, 116
Ford, Gerald, 30
Ford, Glen, 76–77, 117
Ford, Harold, 90
Ford, Robert, 83, 85
foreign policy, 38–40, 160; Bush
  Doctrine, 117–119
Fortier, John, 28
Fox and Friends, 96
Fox News, 28, 32, 33, 36, 37, 95, 96–97,
  102
framing, 127
Frank, Thomas, 127
Fraternal Order of Police, Illinois, 146
Friedman, Thomas, 23–24
Fund, John, 11, 26, 107, 147

G. W. on the Hill, 86
Gallup News Service, 31
Gantt, Harvey, 89
Garcia, Joe, 133

gay marriage, 114–115
generational change, 1–2, 76; baby
  boomers, 6–9; civil rights movement
  and, 69–71; cynicism and, 17–19;
  new political generation, 11– 12;
  transformation, 23–24; voting, 16, 19
Generation Me, 13–16
Generation X, 2, 13
Gerson, Michael, 132
Gibson, John, 97
Gift Ban Act, 145
Gingrich, Newt, 29, 105
Giuliani, Rudy, 29, 89
"Global Summit on AIDS and the
  Church," 131
Goldhaber, Gerald, 58
Goldwater, Barry, 125
Gonzales, Nathan, 149
Good Morning America, 85
Gore, Al, 26, 30, 45, 102, 127, 165
Gravel, Mike, 118
Greeley, Andrew, 86–87
Greenberg, David, 51
Greenfield, Jeff, 93
Greenwald, Glenn, 37
guilt, 75–77; whiteness of, 78–80
Guinier, Lani, 82–83
gun control, Illinois, 148

Haldeman, H. R., 20
Hamas, 116
Hammond, Peter, 68
Hannity, Sean, 81, 104, 106
Hardball, 75–76, 94
Harper's Magazine, 155
Harris-Lacewell, Melissa, 62, 68–69, 71,
  75
Harvard Institute of Politics survey, 12
Harvard Law Review, 49, 54, 67, 108–109
Hawkinson, Carl, 151
Haywood, George, 35
health care, 15, 114, 124, 149, 156–157
Health Care for Hybrids, 159
Health Care Justice Act (Illinois), 150
Heilemann, John, 8–9, 152, 153

Herbert, Bob, 9, 87–88, 108
Hertzberg, Hendrik, 37
Higher Education Research Institute, 14
Hill, The, 102
Hood, John, 95
Howard, Adam, 121
Howard, John, 102
Huffington, Ariana, 27
Huffington Post, 26, 27, 86
Hughes, Cathy, 88
Human Biodiversity Institute, 71
Human Events, 106, 147
Hussein, Saddam, 46–47
Hutchinson, Earl Ofari, 26, 83, 86, 87
Hyde Park mafia, 54–55

identity politics, 55
Ifill, Gwen, 69
Illinois Association of Chiefs of Police,
    146
Illinois legislation, 144; conservative
    critiques, 147–148; earned income
    tax credit, 144, 145; Obama in
    Democratic minority, 145–147; police
    abuse, 144, 145; "present" vote, 147,
    148–149; progressive critiques, 148–
    151; racial profiling, 145–146
immigration, 68–69
Imus, Don, 94
individual rights, 146
Insight, 95–96, 101–102
Internet, 5; blogs, 31, 56, 104;
    "draft Obama" movements, 12;
    My.BarackObama.com, 15; 1984
    parody ad, 15–16; social networking
    sites, 14–15
In These Times, 61, 76, 113, 121–122, 133
Investor's Business Daily, 152
Iran, 118
Iraq war: ending, 47–48; left's view of
    Obama, 115–117; New Hampshire
    petition, 5; Obama's opposition to,
    39, 41–48, 120; 2002 antiwar speech,
    43, 116; weapons of mass destruction,
    46–47

Iraq War Deescalation Act of 2007, 48
Israel, 116–117
Jackson, Darrell, 84
Jackson, Jesse, 12, 83
Jacobs, Denny, 151
Jacobs, Jack, 41–42
Jensen, Robert, 114
John Locke Foundation, 95
Johnson, Lyndon B., 125
Joint Center for Political and Economic
    Studies, 84–85
Jones, Alondra, 86
Jones, Emil, Jr., 60, 150
judgment, 39
Judicial Watch, 32

kakistocracy, 49
Kasinitz, Philip, 75
Kass, John, 31, 32, 34
Katrina disaster, 22, 154
Kelly, Cliff, 61
Kennedy, Edward, 94
Kennedy, John F., 4, 24, 30
Kerry, John, 26, 30, 94, 102, 127; Iraq
    war, support for, 45, 46
Keyes, Alan, 55, 102, 132
Kid Care and Family Care, 149
King, Larry, 115
King Jr., Martin Luther, 88
Klein, Ezra, 124
Kondracke, Morton, 37, 39
Kristof, Nicholas, 37, 38, 40
Kroft, Steve, 53
KSFO, 72, 101
Kucinich, Dennis, 30, 59, 153
Kurtz, Howard, 25

LaHood, Ray, 109
Lamont, Ned, 113
Lasch-Quinn, Elisabeth, 78
Lawrence, Curtis, 77
leadership, 166
League of Conservation Voters, 154, 159
Lebanon, 116
Lee, Spike, 65

left, 111–112; Bush Doctrine and, 117–
120; centrists and, 125–126; *Daily
Kos*, 122–123; disagreements with
Obama, 113–114; divisiveness desired,
122–124; gay marriage and civil
unions, 114–115; Illinois legislation,
critiques of, 148–151; Middle East,
views of, 115–117; progressives, 120–
122, 148–151; reasons for failures of,
127–129; religion, view of, 132–133
legacy preference, 66, 67
legislation, national, 151–153, 154; poor,
concern for, 154–156. *See also* Illinois
legislation
Lehane, Chris, 8
Leno, Jay, 12, 19
Letterman, David, 19, 20
Levine, Stuart, 33
Levitt, Jeremy, 87
Lewinsky, Monica, 9
Lewis, John, 87
Liebau, Carol Platt, 109
Lieberman, Joe, 113, 158
Limbaugh, Rush, 29, 72–73, 94, 102
Lincoln, Abraham, 29–30
Liu, Eric, 7
lobbying, 161, 162–164
Love, Alvin, 4
Lugar, Richard, 110, 160
Lugar-Obama Act, 47, 160

madrassa myth, 97–99, 101
Mahoney, Patrick J., 132
Manhattan Institute, 72
Martin, Andy, 99–101
Martin, Roland, 62–63
Marty, Martin, 74
Matalin, Marie, 94
Matthews, Chris, 38, 75–76, 93
McCain, John, 29, 44–45, 92, 109, 151,
154, 158; letter to Obama, 162
McGovern, George, 30, 125
McGuirk, Bernard, 94
McKinnon, Mark, 24
McWhorter, John, 72

media, v; Clinton, coverage of, 28–31;
corruption allegations, 31–35; D.
C. experience considered more
valuable, 48–50; deceptiveness of,
36–37; defense of Obama, 37–38; on
democratic debate, 2007, 40–42; on
foreign policy experience,
38–40; inexperience, allegations of,
25–30, 37–38; madrassa myth and,
97–99, 101; on Obama's investments,
35–36; rise of right-wing, 102;
substance and style questions, 27–28;
war, view of, 118–119
Medicaid, 149
Meet the Press, 27
Middle East: left views of, 115–117
Midwest Academy, 107
Miller, Rich, 150
Miner, Barnhill, and Galland, 60
minimum wage, 155
60 Minutes, 53
Mitchell, Mary, 60, 88
Mondale, Walter, 30
Moore, Michael, 157
Moos, Jeanne, 93
Morris, Dick, 28, 95, 102, 104, 106, 153
Morris, Jonathan, 19
Morrison, Toni, 81–82
Movement for a Democratic Society, 7
Moy, Catherine, 74, 101
Moyers, Bill, 11, 29–30
Muslim allegations, 93, 95–98
Muwakkil, Salim, 54, 55, 61, 76, 147
MySpace, 14–15

Nader, Ralph, 206
Narcissistic Personality Inventory (NPI),
13–14
Nargelenas, Laimutis, 146
Nation, 113, 121, 133
National Association for the
Advancement of Colored People
(NAACP), 131
National Journal, 153
National Review, 105–106, 108

national town meetings, 5
NBC Nightly News, 55
negative advertising, 125, 127–128
neighborhood meetings, 5
neighborhood walk day, 5
New Democratic Network, 1
New Republic, 35, 78, 115, 124, 152
Newsweek, v
New York Daily News, 26
New York Magazine, 152
New York Post, 26
New York Times, 28, 29, 30–31, 51, 108, 109
Nightline, 26
Nixon, Richard, 20, 125
No Excuses: Concessions of a Serial Campaigner (Shrum), 44
Noonan, Peggy, 95
Norquist, Grover, 107
Norwood, Kimberly Jade, 62
Novak, Joe, 157
Novak, Robert, 13, 41, 106, 119
nuclear nonproliferation treaty, 47

Obama, Barack: African American view of, 53–54; African trip, 39–40; as community organizer, 2–6, 15, 37, 49, 50, 70, 125; conservative attitudes, 6–7; consistency of, 44–45; on cynicism, 17–19; diplomatic skills, 39; drug use, 12–13; education in Indonesia, 58, 98–103; on foreign policy experience, 38–40; at George Mason University, 20; *Harvard Law Review* editorship, 49, 54, 67, 108–109; idealism of, 20–21, 24; intellectual abilities, 108–109; investments, 35–36; judgment of, 39, 45, 48; liberal rating, 153; on magazine covers, v; middle name, 93, 94, 96, 105; on new generation, 23; as outsider, 51; pragmatism of, 123–125, 128, 147; presidential campaign announcement, 165; realism of, 20–21; Republican support for, 107–110; on sixties generation, 6, 7–8; in state

senate, 25; as teacher of constitutional law, 49, 50; 2002 antiwar speech, 43, 47; U.S. legislation, 151–153, 154; whiteness attributed to, 54–55. *See also specific topics*
Obama, Barack, speeches: December 10, 2006, 1; 2004 Democratic National Convention, iv, 21–23, 77, 112, 117
Obama, Michelle, 4, 18–19, 50, 63–65, 68
"Obama Messiah Watch," 31
"Obama Project," 55

Page, Clarence, 80, 119
Palestine, 30–31, 116–117
Palmer, Lu, 54
Parker, Star, 102
Patrick, Deval, 89–90
patriotism, 112
Peace Corps, 4
Pell Grants, 154
Perle, Richard, 43
pessimism, 84–88
petitions, 5
Philip, Pate, 144, 145
Pinkerton, Jim, 33
Pittsburgh Tribune, 107
Platt, Kym, 132
Podhoretz, John, 94
police abuse, Illinois, 144, 145
policy: conservative critiques, 147–148; Illinois legislation, 144–151; liberal politics, 153; progressive critiques, 148–151; U.S. legislation, 151–153, 154
Polling Company, 105
polls, 80–81, 84, 85; bigotry expressed, 91–92; Bradley effect, 88–90
Ponnuru, Ramesh, 108
poverty, 59–61; affirmative action and, 65–66
Power, Samantha, 120, 160
pragmatism, 123–125, 128
"Princeton Educated Blacks and the Black Community" (Robinson), 63–64
PR Newswire, 99

Progressive, 54, 152
propaganda, 46–47
Public Allies, 64
public financing system, 114
Purpose Driven Life, The (Warren), 131

race issue, 53–54; affirmative action,
    65–66; bigotry expressed in polls,
    91–92; Bradley effect, 88–90; civil
    rights movement, 69–71; conservative
    views, 71–73, 78–79, 104–105; guilt
    and, 75–77; as imaginary concept, 56;
    immigration, 68–69; Michelle Obama
    and, 63–65; poverty and debt, 67–68;
    religion and, 73–75; slavery issue, 56–
    58, 62, 76; whiteness of guilt, 78–80.
    See also African Americans
racial profiling, 145–146
racism, 50–51; Bradley effect, 88–90;
    color-blindness as, 71; of conservatives,
    93–94, 104–105; environmental,
    157–158
Radio One, 88
Rangel, Charles, 28–29
Read, Eddie, 59
Reagan, Ronald, 16, 126; lack of
    experience, 30, 106
Reagan Democrats, 128–129
Reed, Scott, 107
religion, 73–75; church and state, 140–
    141; commonality of, 139–140; doubt
    and, 137, 138–139; historic black
    church, 73–75, 135; leftist attacks on,
    132–133; politics of faith, 137–138;
    prayer, 138; right-wing evangelists,
    131–133
religious imagery, 11, 23
Remnick, David, 8, 113
Republican National Committee, 90
Republicans, 87–88, 91–92;
    discouragement of voting, 126; racism
    and, 72; support for Obama, 107–110.
    see also conservatives
Republicans and the Black Vote (Fauntroy),
    60, 70

revenge, 119
Rezko, Tony, 31–35
Rice, Condoleezza, 87, 109
Rice, Susan, 161
Rich, Frank, 111–112
Ridley, John, 61
Roberts, John, 120
Robinson, Eugene, 61, 62
Robinson, Michelle LaVaughn. *See*
    Obama, Michelle
Rodriguez, Gregory, 77
Rogers, Ed, 93, 94
Roll Call, 39
Rolling Stone, 32, 50, 75
Romney, Mitt, 29, 53, 118, 119
Rooney, J. Patrick, 157
Roosevelt, Franklin Delano, 122
Rosenberg, Simon, 1
Rove, Karl, 43
Rules for Radicals (Alinsky), 4
Rumsfeld, Donald, 30, 106
Rush, Bobby, 54, 55, 150
Rush, Erik, 74
Russert, Tim, 27

Sabato, Larry, 25
Saddleback Church, 131
Said, Edward, 116
Sailer, Steve, 71–72
Salon, 37, 56
Saturday Night Live, 82
Saudi Arabia, 119
Savage, Michael, 102
Sawyer, Diane, 85
Schenck, Rob, 132
Schilling, Nicole, v
Schlafly, Phyllis, 132
Schlussel, Debbie, 97–98, 101
Schumer, Chuck, 154
Secure America and Orderly Immigration
    Act, 154
Selma Voting Rights March
    commemoration, 23
Senate Foreign Relations Committee, 39,
    45, 46, 109

Senate Intelligence Committee, 45, 46
Senior Citizen Prescription Drug
    Discount Program Act (Illinois), 149
September 11, 2001, terrorist attacks, 41
sex offenders, Illinois, 147, 148
Sharpton, Al, 58, 73
Shatner, William, 80
Shrum, Robert, 44
Sierra Club, 158
Silverstein, Ken, 155
Sirota, David, 113, 114, 133, 152
Sittenfeld, Tiernan, 158
Slate.com, 31
slavery issue, 56–58, 62, 76
Smiley, Tavis, 59
Soetoro, Lolo, 97
Soetoro-Ng, Maya, iv
Soros, George, 116
Souljah, Sister, 83
Standing with Minimum Wage Earners
    Act of 2006, 155
Staples, Brent, 69
State of the Black Union conference, 59
state politics, 48–49
Steele, Michael, 81, 89
Steinberg, Stephen, 78
Stengel, Richard, v
Stephanopoulos, George, 31, 42, 77–78
Stern, Richard, 38
Stewart, Jon, 19
StopHerNow.com, 104
Street, Paul, 76, 112
Street, Ted, 146
Students for a Democratic Society, 7
Students for Barack Obama, 15
Suderman, Peter, 15
suggestion boxes, 5
Swain, Carol, 60, 61, 90
Sweet, Lynn, 25, 41
swiftblogging, 134
swiftboating, 125, 134
Swift Boat Veterans for Truth, 134

Taibbi, Matt, 50
Tapper, Jack, 26, 51, 91

taxes, 155–156
terrorism issue, 102–104
30 Rock, 80
This Week with George Stephanopoulos,
    31–32, 77–78
Thompson, Fred, 29
thousand points of light program, 5
TIME, v
Tonight Show, 12
Trachtenberg, Stephen, 24
triangulation, 124
Trinity United Church of Christ, 73–75,
    135
Trippi, Joe, 15
Tutu, Desmond, v
Twenge, Jean, 13
two-party system, 127

University of Chicago, 64
University of Chicago Hospitals, 64
U.S. News & World Report, 39, 105

values, 112, 117
Vause, John, 98
Vietnam War, 9
voting: generational differences, 16,
    19; legislation, 154; Republican
    discouragement of, 126

Wallace-Wells, Ben, 32, 75
Wall Street Journal, 26, 95, 107, 147
Walters, Ronald, 68, 89
Warren, Jim, 31
Warren, Rick, 131
Washington, Harold, 88–89, 206
Washington, Laura, 61, 70, 75, 86
Washington Post, 12, 19, 25
Washington Times, 95–96
Washington Week in Review, 69
Watts, J. C., 31
weapons, 46–47, 160
Weekly Standard, 107
West, Cornel, 59
"What Obama Isn't: Black Like Me"
    (Crouch), 57

What's the Matter with Kansas? (Frank), 127

whiteness of guilt, 78–80

Wieseltier, Leon, 78, 124, 152

wigger, 71

Wilder, Douglas, 87, 89

Wilkins, Roger, 54

Will, George, 38

Williams, Brian, 13, 31, 40, 118

Williams, Juan, 57–58, 76, 96–97

Williams, Patricia, 61

Wilmore, Larry, 92

Wilson, George, 86

Wolfowitz, Paul, 43

Woodward, Bob, 20

Wright, Jeremiah, 73, 74

YouTube, 15–16

Zengerle, Jason, 115

Zimmerman, Jonathan, 26

Z Magazine, 76, 112

Zorn, Eric, 37, 143, 151, 153

Zuckerman, Mortimer, 39

About the Author

John K. Wilson is the author of *Patriotic Correctness: Academic Freedom and Its Enemies* (Paradigm Publishers 2008); *Newt Gingrich: Capitol Crimes and Misdemeanors* (Common Courage Press 1996); and *The Myth of Political Correctness: The Conservative Attack on Higher Education* (Duke University Press 1995), among several other titles. A former student of Barack Obama at the University of Chicago, Wilson is an Illinois native who currently lives in Chicago and has watched Obama rise from state senator to U.S. senator to president of the United States.

Wilson has discussed his work in major media forums including C-SPAN, the *O'Reilly Factor*, and the *Huffington Post*. Visit his website and blog at www.obamapolitics.com.